AF863253

Translational Systems Sciences

Volume 32

Editors-in-Chief

Kyoichi Kijima, School of Business Management, Bandung Institute of Technology, Tokyo, Japan

Hiroshi Deguchi, Faculty of Commerce and Economics, Chiba University of Commerce, Tokyo, Japan

Eri Yokota
Editor

Frontiers of Japanese Management Control Systems

Theoretical Ideas and Empirical Evidence

Springer

Editor
Eri Yokota
Faculty of Business and Commerce
Keio University
Tokyo, Japan

ISSN 2197-8832 ISSN 2197-8840 (electronic)
Translational Systems Sciences
ISBN 978-981-19-9777-8 ISBN 978-981-19-9778-5 (eBook)
https://doi.org/10.1007/978-981-19-9778-5

© Springer Nature Singapore Pte Ltd. 2023
This work is subject to copyright. All rights are reserved by the Publisher, whether the whole or part of the material is concerned, specifically the rights of translation, reprinting, reuse of illustrations, recitation, broadcasting, reproduction on microfilms or in any other physical way, and transmission or information storage and retrieval, electronic adaptation, computer software, or by similar or dissimilar methodology now known or hereafter developed.
The use of general descriptive names, registered names, trademarks, service marks, etc. in this publication does not imply, even in the absence of a specific statement, that such names are exempt from the relevant protective laws and regulations and therefore free for general use.
The publisher, the authors, and the editors are safe to assume that the advice and information in this book are believed to be true and accurate at the date of publication. Neither the publisher nor the authors or the editors give a warranty, expressed or implied, with respect to the material contained herein or for any errors or omissions that may have been made. The publisher remains neutral with regard to jurisdictional claims in published maps and institutional affiliations.

This Springer imprint is published by the registered company Springer Nature Singapore Pte Ltd.
The registered company address is: 152 Beach Road, #21-01/04 Gateway East, Singapore 189721, Singapore

Preface

This book is a compilation of studies in Japanese prepared with my research colleagues, the core members of which have been conducting joint research on management control in Japan since 2014. The authors belong to various universities in Japan and are researchers in the field of management accounting. This book is the fruit of their wisdom. The studies discuss a wide range of issues of management control in Japan.

In 1965, Robert Anthony presented a framework of management control; however, this framework has now diversified, and various perspectives have been added. In recent years, ample management control research has been conducted in Europe, the United States, and Japan. This book describes these research trends in Japan and offers quantitative evidence using survey methods and qualitative case studies.

Specifically, after the introduction, a bibliometric analysis of management control research in Japan is presented. Next, four studies that quantitatively grasp the characteristics of management control practices in Japanese firms are provided. Furthermore, four qualitative research studies that examined the manufacturing and service industries among Japanese firms are displayed.

This book was made possible by the efforts of Professor Emeritus Kyoichi Kijima of the Tokyo Institute of Technology, who was formerly president of the Japan Society of Management Information Science. We express our gratitude to him. This book was supported by JSPS (Japan Society for the Promotion of Science) KAKENHI grant numbers 19H01551 and 22H00898.

We believe this book will give readers rich insights into the management control research and practices in Japan and will contribute to future research.

Tokyo, Japan — Eri Yokota

Contents

About the Editor

Eri Yokota has been a professor of Business and Commerce since 2005 and is the Dean of the Graduate School of Business and Commerce (2021–2023) at Keio University in Japan. Prior to that, she was at Musashi University from 1995 to 2004. She received a doctoral degree from the Graduate School of Business Administration at Keio University. Her research interests include management control systems, management accounting, and organizational behavior. Her books include *Management and Psychology of Flattened Organizations* (in Japanese, Keio University Press, 1998) and *Management control of Japanese Companies* (in Japanese, Chuo-Keizaisha, 2022).

Chapter 1
Introduction

Eri Yokota

Anthony (1965) considered management control as a process in which middle managers use several accounting systems, including budgets and performance evaluations, to effectively use resources within the authority given to them to achieve organizational goals and execute strategies. Since Anthony (1965), there has been an increasing number of studies in the management accounting field, leading to diversification in management control research concerning both research subjects and regions.

The scope of research has expanded from financial controls to non-financial controls. In Japan, management control research has been conducted based on the corporate practice unique to Japan, as well as research accumulated in North America and Europe. Management control has been a major research theme in the field of management accounting worldwide (Chapman et al., 2007a, 2007b).

Ample research and knowledge have accumulated since Anthony's first management control topic publication over 50 years ago. However, the recent diverse management control research has not provided sufficient clarity on the overall characteristics of management control. Therefore, reviewing the current research and practice of management control in Japan will prove useful for the future development of management control research in Japan.

In this volume, in response to the recent dramatic changes in the management infrastructure, our aim is to present to academic and business communities the management control systems of Japanese firms, based on previous studies and empirical findings on management control.

E. Yokota (✉)
Faculty of Business and Commerce, Keio University, Tokyo, Japan
e-mail: yokota@fbc.keio.ac.jp

© Springer Nature Singapore Pte Ltd. 2023

E. Yokota (ed.), *Frontiers of Japanese Management Control Systems*, Translational Systems Sciences 32, https://doi.org/10.1007/978-981-19-9778-5_1

1.1 Diversity of Management Control Research

Management control is a fundamental concept to understand planning and control activities within an organization (Anthony, 1965). According to Anthony (1965), management control is "the process by which managers assume that resources are obtained and used effectively and efficiently in the accomplishment of the organization's objectives" (p. 17). Since this concept was proposed, management control (in management accounting) has become a core research theme in Europe, the United States, and Japan (Itami, 1986; Tani et al., 2010).

However, the corporate environment has changed since Anthony presented the concept of management control; therefore, studies in Europe and the United States have reexamined the concept of management control. For example, Simons (1995) proposed "interactive" control systems for top management to control managers through discussion. Additionally, Malmi and Brown (2008) expanded the management control framework by considering various control systems, including accounting as interrelated "control packages." Some earlier studies on management accounting in Japan have also applied the newly proposed theoretical framework of management control to understand corporate practices in the face of environmental changes (Yokota et al., 2016).

Furthermore, in recent years, there has been a shift to management that emphasizes intangible assets (intangibles) over tangible assets. This shift drove the globalization of research and development; production and sales; the diversification of human resources and employment patterns (changes in the human infrastructure); sophistication of information processing, including artificial intelligence (AI) and cloud computing (changes in the information infrastructure); network organization of strategic collaboration; supply chain management; and the development of group management such as pure holding companies (change in the organizational infrastructure). The management infrastructure of firms is changing substantially in Japan and globally (Kaplan & Norton, 2001; Lev, 2001; Sakurai, 2012). These changes in the management infrastructure also affect management control: the process of planning and controlling firms' activities (Brooke, 2012; Kolbjørnsrud et al., 2016). Therefore, to address how management control in companies responds to dramatic changes in the management infrastructure, there is a need to clarify recent trends and characteristics related to management control in Japanese firms using empirical methods such as interviews and questionnaire surveys. We believe this is a crucial academic issue in management accounting research in Japan and worldwide.

Most of the earlier studies in Japan, except for some pioneering attempts, relied on Anthony's traditional framework consisting of phrases such as "goal setting," "planning and budgeting," "performance evaluation," and "incentives" (Yokota & Kaneko, 2014; Yokota et al., 2016). Moreover, the linkage between subsystems such as "goal setting" and "planning and budgeting," "planning and budgeting" and "performance evaluation," "performance evaluation" and "incentives," and "incentives" and "goal setting," which many studies have implicitly assumed, are not necessarily self-evident. There are concerns that they have not been linked owing to recent changes in the management infrastructure. Therefore, to respond to how management control is implemented in Japanese firms, we comprehensively examined the previous studies on management control in Japanese firms based on Anthony's traditional management process and comprehended the main arguments and limitations that are discussed. It is essential to construct a new theoretical framework more suitable for the current situation to strengthen the linkage between research and practice and increase the probability that the research will contribute to practice.

Based on this academic background, the present volume focuses on current trends in management control in Japanese firms facing dramatic changes in management infrastructure and summarizes empirical findings related to practice. The findings from the review of management control literature contrast with earlier studies. In this volume, we provide valuable information to the academic and business communities. We aim to answer the question, "How does corporate management control respond to dramatic changes in the management infrastructure in Japan?"

This volume also provides a wealth of knowledge on the trends and characteristics of management control considering the current fundamental changes in management infrastructure (human, information, and organizational infrastructure). These studies are unique for Japanese researchers as well as non-Japanese researchers. Additionally, this volume provides a concrete and usable theoretical framework to answer the question, "How is management control implemented in Japanese firms?" Therefore, we believe that it will strongly contribute to the academic and business communities.

1.2 Issues in This Volume

Management control, a concept related to the processes of corporate planning and control, is a central research theme in Europe, the United States, and the field of management accounting in Japan. Yokota—the editor of this volume and the principal investigator of this study—has focused on management control for over 20 years and has published many studies on Japanese companies. Specifically, Yokota has conducted case studies of Japanese firms and has examined the trends and characteristics of their practices (Yokota, 1998, 2015, 2016; Yokota & Kaneko, 2014). Additionally, Yokota has highlighted the general trend of management control in Japanese firms by analyzing the results of questionnaire surveys on budget and performance evaluation (Yokota & Senoo, 2012; Yokota et al., 2012, 2013).

From these research activities, it is believed that the management control framework by Anthony (1965) is limited in explaining the management process of Japanese companies because it assumes the traditional pyramidal organization found mainly in Western companies as the norm (Yokota, 1998). Additionally, as over 50 years have passed since Anthony's management control was proposed, its inadequacies have been identified through our investigation of Japanese companies.

It does not account for previous changes in corporate planning and control activities (Yokota et al., 2016).

In particular, as mentioned previously, the current diversification of human resources; globalization; the sophistication of information processing owing to the rapid development of AI and cloud computing; and the fundamental changes in management infrastructure, including the development of strategic alliances and group management, have dramatically affected corporate planning and control activities (Bartlett & Ghoshal, 1989; Brooke, 2012; Kolbjørnsrud et al., 2016). Additionally, these effects are believed to be true for Western and Japanese firms (Sakurai, 2012). Therefore, we should organize a team consisting of multiple researchers with a common awareness of the problem and employ empirical methods such as interview surveys and questionnaire surveys from various perspectives to clarify the trends and characteristics of management control in Japanese firms that are facing the change. In addition to compiling a body of such empirical findings, through comparisons with previous studies, in this volume, we investigate management control in Japanese firms and contribute to their practice.

The problems and limitations of the concept of management control proposed by Anthony (1965) have been identified in management accounting in Europe and the United States (Chenhall, 2006; Otley, 1980, 1994). Moreover, some earlier studies in Europe and the United States have presented new theoretical frameworks for management control. The three representative examples are (1) the framework by Simons (1995), which focused on the methods of control (levers) and presenting "diagnostic," "interactive," "belief," and "boundary" control systems; (2) the framework by Merchant (Merchant & Van der Stede, 2007), which focuses on the object of control (objects) and presenting "results," "behavior," "personnel," and "culture" systems; and (3) the concept of "control packages" (Malmi & Brown, 2008), which considers management control as the interaction of multiple controls. However, these theoretical frameworks do not directly reflect changes in the human resource infrastructure, such as diversification of human resources and employment forms; changes in the information infrastructure, such as increasing sophistication of information processing; and changes in the organizational infrastructure, such as network organization and development of group management. Therefore, they do not adequately explain the actual planning and control processes in today's companies.

Several earlier studies have provided empirical findings on management control practices in management accounting in Japan (Takahashi et al., 2003; Yoshida et al., 2012, 2017). However, the previous studies were mainly intended to conduct a comprehensive survey of Japanese management accounting practices at a specific point in time, and cannot be said to have empirically examined the impact of the fundamental changes in today's management infrastructure.

To resolve the above limitations, the studies in this volume focus on management control in Japanese companies, which faced drastic changes in the management infrastructure, and compare their empirical findings with those of earlier studies. Our aim is to contribute to the theory of management accounting and its practice. From the perspective of domestic and international research trends, it is unique and will contribute greatly to the study of management control.

1.3 Structure of This Book

The following is a broad outline of the structure of this volume. First, we analyze the current Japanese and global trends in management control research to grasp the characteristics of management control research in Japan.

Next, we conduct survey research on various Japanese firms. In addition to the management control survey, we examine the results of a survey on the actual status of performance management systems (PMS), a survey on PMS in foreign subsidiaries in Japan, and a study on capital budgeting. In addition, we present the results of a quantitative analysis of investment decisions in Japan.

Then, we present four case studies of management control in Japanese companies. We analyze a case study of "balanced scorecard" (BSC) in Kirin Brewery Holdings, which is a Japanese traditional food company; a case study of BSC in Company X, a long-established snack food manufacturer; a case study of the selection of environmental performance measures in Misawa Home, a prefabricated housing manufacturer; and a case study of management control at Hoshino Resort, Co. Ltd.

From these studies, we can acquire knowledge about Japanese management control and understand how management control systems are used in Japan.

Some studies in this book were originally published in Japanese academic journals and bulletins and have been translated with corrections. The first publication of each study is indicated in the notes at the beginning of each chapter.

References

Anthony, R. N. (1965). *Planning and control systems: A framework for analysis*. Harvard University. Division of Research.

Bartlett, C. A., & Ghoshal, S. (1989). *Managing across borders: The transnational solution*. Harvard Business School Press.

Brooke, B. (2012). The art of developing truly global leaders. *Harvard Business Review, 90*(11), 34.

Chapman, C. S., Hopwood, A. G., & Shields, M. D. (Eds.). (2007a). *Handbook of management accounting research* (Vol. 2). Elsevier.

Chapman, C. S., Hopwood, A. G., & Shields, M. D. (Eds.). (2007b). *Handbook of management accounting research* (Vol. 3). Elsevier.

Chenhall, R. H. (2006). Theorizing contingencies in management control systems research. In C. S. Chapman, A. G. Hopwood, & M. D. Shields (Eds.), *Handbook of management accounting research* (Vol. 1, pp. 163–205).

Itami, H. (1986). *Theory of management control (Manejimento Kontororu no Riron)*. Iwarnami-Shoten. (in Japanese).

Kaplan, R. S., & Norton, D. P. (2001). *The strategy-focused organization: How balanced scorecard companies thrive in the new business environment*. Harvard Business Review Press.

Kolbjørnsrud, V., Amico, R., & Thomas, R. J. (2016). How artificial intelligence will redefine management. *Harvard Business Review Digital Articles*, 2–6. (https://hbr.org/2016/11/how-artificial-intelligence-will-redefine-management)

Lev, B. (2001). *Intangibles management, measurement, and reporting*. Brookings Institution Press.

Malmi, T., & Brown, D. A. (2008). Management control systems as a package: Opportunities, challenges and research directions. *Management Accounting Research, 19*(4), 287–300.

Merchant, K. A., & Van der Stede, W. A. (2007). *Management control systems: Performance measurement, evaluation and incentives* (2nd ed.). Prentice Hall.

Otley, D. (1980). The contingency theory of management accounting: Achievement and prognosis. In C. Emmanuel, D. Otley, & K. Merchant (Eds.), *Readings in accounting for management control* (pp. 83–106). Springer.

Otley, D. (1994). Management control in contemporary organizations: Towards a wider framework. *Management Accounting Research, 5*(3–4), 289–299.

Sakurai, M. (2012). *Management accounting for intangible (Intanjiburu no Kanri Kaikei)*. Chuo Keizaisya. (in Japanese).

Simons, R. L. (1995). *Levers of control: How managers use innovative control systems to drive strategic renewal*. Harvard Business School Press.

Takahashi, F., Arae, T., & Chin, T. (2003). Establishment of a comprehensive database of cost accounting and management accounting practices. *The Study of Accounting, 16*, 1–158. (in Japanese).

Tani, T., Noboru, N., & Kobayashi, Y. (2010). *Performance management accounting (Gyoseki Kanri Kaikei)*. Chuo Keizaisya. (in Japanese).

Yokota, E. (1998). *Management and psychology of horizontal organizations: Management control in era of change (Furattoka Soshiki no Shinri to Kanri: Henaka no Jidai no Manejiment Kontorol)*. Keio University Press. (in Japanese).

Yokota, E. (2015). An examination of the characteristics of management control in Japanese firms: Through interviews with Japanese firms in Finland. *Financial and Cost Accounting, 75*(2), 43–56. (in Japanese).

Yokota, E. (2016). A study on management control influencing innovation activities. *Aoyama Journal of Business, 51*(3), 137–150. (in Japanese).

Yokota, E., & Kaneko, S. (2014). *Management control: Considering the direction of people corporation through eight cases (Manejimento Kontorol: 8tu no ke-su kara kangaeru hito to kigyoukeiei no houkousei)*. Yuhikaku. (in Japanese).

Yokota, E., & Senoo, T. (2012). Examining the balanced scorecard as an interactive control system: A case study of a food company. *Melco Journal of Management Accounting Research, 5*, 3–14. (in Japanese).

Yokota, E., Otomasa, S., Sakaguchi, J., Kawai, T., Onishi, Y., & Senoo, T. (2016). Management control frameworks and management accounting tools: A bibliographic study of contemporary research in Japan. *Japan Cost Accounting Research, 40*(2), 125–138. (in Japanese).

Yokota, E., Senoo, T., Takahashi, S., & Goto, Y. (2013). Survey of performance management systems in Japanese Companies. *Mita Business Review, 55*(6), 67–87. (in Japanese).

Yokota, E., Takada, A., Senoo, T., & Kaneko, S. (2012). A survey of management control systems and behavior of managers in Japanese companies. *Mita Business Review, 55*(4), 93–117. (in Japanese).

Yoshida, E., Fukushima, K., & Senoo, T. (2012). *The investigation of Japanese management accounting (Nihon teki Kanri Kaikei no Tankyu)*. Chuo Keizaisya. (in Japanese).

Yoshida, E., Fukushima, K., Senoo, T., & Xu, Z. (2017). *The exploration of Japanese management accounting (Nihon teki Kanri Kaikei no Shinso)*. Chuo Keizaisya. (in Japanese).

Chapter 2
Contemporary Management Control Research in Japan

Eri Yokota, Sakichi Otomasa, Junya Sakaguchi, Takaharu Kawai, Yasushi Onishi, Takeyoshi Senoo, and Yudai Onitsuka

2.1 Introduction

Management control is a concept proposed by Anthony (1965) for understanding practices related to planning and control activities in companies. Anthony (1965, p. 17) defines management control as follows:

> Management Control is the process by which managers assure that resources are obtained and used effectively and efficiently in the accomplishment of the organization's objectives.

E. Yokota (✉)
Faculty of Business and Commerce, Keio University, Tokyo, Japan
e-mail: yokota@fbc.keio.ac.jp

S. Otomasa
Faculty of Commerce, Otaru University of Commerce, Hokkaido, Japan
e-mail: otomasa@res.otaru-uc.ac.jp

J. Sakaguchi
Graduate School of Economics, Nagoya University, Nagoya, Japan
e-mail: ju_sakaguc@soec.nagoya-u.ac.jp

T. Kawai
Faculty of Commerce, Doshisha University, Kyoto, Japan
e-mail: tkawai@mail.doshisha.ac.jp

Y. Onishi
School of Accountancy, Kansai University, Osaka, Japan
e-mail: yonishi@kansai-u.ac.jp

T. Senoo
Faculty of Commerce, Chuo University, Tokyo, Japan
e-mail: senoo81@tamacc.chuo-u.ac.jp

Y. Onitsuka
School of Business Administration, Tokai University, Kanagawa, Japan
e-mail: oy320225@tsc.u-tokai.ac.jp

© Springer Nature Singapore Pte Ltd. 2023

E. Yokota (ed.), *Frontiers of Japanese Management Control Systems*, Translational Systems Sciences 32, https://doi.org/10.1007/978-981-19-9778-5_2

Since its advocacy by Anthony (1965), management control has become a core research topic in the field of management accounting internationally (Merchant & Otley, 2007; Shirinashihama, 2011).

Anthony's traditional concept of management control focused on budgets. Owing to changes in the business environment, dimensions, and contexts of management control have changed (Chenhall, 2007). For example, interactive control is presented by Simons (1995) as a new control mechanism that utilizes dialogue between top management and managers to direct managers' attention toward changes in the intentions of top management. Simons (1995) refers to Anthony's (1965) traditional management control as a diagnostic control system. Further, Malmi and Brown (2008) proposed an extended management control framework that includes several management control systems such as non-accounting controls as a package.

Various management control studies have been conducted by Japanese management accounting researchers since Anthony's seminal work was published. Yoshida et al. (2009), who surveyed trends in management accounting research in Japan, reported that management control research trends have increased: 49, 71, and 121 studies in the periods 1980–1989, 1990–1999, and 2000–2007, respectively.

Not only traditional concepts but also new concepts and frameworks related to management control have been actively adopted in Japan. In particular, a series of studies by Simons (1987, 1990, 1995) has been widely adopted in management accounting research in Japan today (Arae, 2008; Kobayashi, 1988; Tani, 1992, 1994; Yokota, 2007; Yokota & Senoo, 2012). The idea of management control as a package is also attracting attention (Arae & Ito, 2010; Fukushima, 2012; Tani, 2013; Tani & Kubota, 2012).

Management control studies in Japan are influenced by international research trends. Japanese scholars on management control have paid attention not only to traditional budgets but also to new management accounting tools such as balanced scorecard (BSC) and amoeba management system (Tani, 2013; Tani & Kubota, 2012; Yokota & Senoo, 2012). Their research subjects and content around management control are expanding, such as expansion from a single domestic organization to overseas organizations or across multiple organizations (Kimura, 2011; Matsugi et al., 2014; Sakaguchi et al., 2015).

However, as the concept of management control has diversified and the subject and content of research have expanded, the whole picture of management control research in Japan currently lacks clarity. Therefore, to explore the prospects of management accounting research in Japan, it is necessary to understand "what is the research objective" and "how is the research objective approached" for management control research in Japan. Consequently, the objective of this study is to show the current state of management control research in Japan through a literature analysis.

The rest of this study is organized as follows: Sect. 2.2 outlines the literature analysis method; Sect. 2.3 presents the results of the bibliographic study in relation to the research objective (Japanese-specific practices, regions, industries, organizational scope, and management accounting tools) and the approach (research method

Table 2.1 Number of management control studies published in journals

GEN	KAN	KPR	MEL	KAI	KIG	SAN	Total
44 31.2%	22 15.6%	3 2.1%	12 8.5%	22 15.6%	20 14.2%	18 12.8%	141 100.0%

Number of studies, and row percentages in parentheses
The seven journals considered are *Genka Keisan Kenkyu* (*The Journal of Cost Accounting Research:* GEN), *Kanri Kaikei Gaku* (*The Journal of Management Accounting, JAPAN:* KAN), *Kaikei Progress* (*Accounting Progress:* KPR), *Melco Kanri Kaikei Kenkyu* (*Melco Journal of Management Accounting Research:* MEL), *Kaikei* (*Accounting:* KAI), *Kigyou Kaikei* (KIG), *and Sangyou Keiri* (SAN)

and source disciplines) for management control research in Japan; finally, the characteristics of recent management control research in Japan are discussed.

2.2 Literature Analysis Method

A bibliographic study was conducted with reference to previous literature on bibliometric studies (Hesford et al., 2007; Kato et al., 2010; Kawai & Otomasa, 2012, 2013; Shields, 1997; Yoshida et al., 2009).

First, studies on management accounting were selected among all the studies published in seven major Japanese accounting journals[1] between 2011 and 2013. Thereafter, studies containing the terms "planning" or "control," which are key terms in management control, in either (1) the title, (2) keywords, (3) the abstract, (4) the first section of the text, or (5) the last section of the text, were extracted as "management control research" studies.[2] To explore the diversified frameworks of management control and to understand the current situation in Japanese practice, we collected the studies published from 2011 to 2013.

The overview of the collected studies is presented in Table 2.1. Seventy-seven studies were collected.[3] The results indicated that many studies were collected from academic journals specializing in management accounting, such as *The Journal of Cost Accounting Research* (29.9%) and *The Journal of Management Accounting, Japan* (20.8%).

Second, to understand the current state of management control research in Japan, the following questions were examined: (1) region (which region, domestic or

[1]The seven journals considered are *Genka Keisan Kenkyu* (*The Journal of Cost Accounting Research*: GEN), *Kanri Kaikei Gaku* (*The Journal of Management Accounting, JAPAN*: KAN), *Kaikei Progress* (*Accounting Progress*: KPR), *Melco Kanri Kaikei Kenkyu* (*Melco Journal of Management Accounting Research*: MEL), *Kaikei* (*Accounting*: KAI), *Kigyou Kaikei* (KIG), and *Sangyou Keiri* (SAN).

[2]However, in cases where the term "control" is used in the main text, it was excluded from the scope in the manipulation of a measurement scale.

[3]Studies published in parts under the same title were considered as a single study.

international, is the focal point?), (2) research site (which industry is the subject?), (3) industry (what is the perceived scope of organization?), (4) management accounting tool (which management accounting tool is the main focus?), (5) research method (what method is used?), and (6) source discipline (what discipline does it rely on?). Codes were established for each of the six items through discussions with all the authors. In addition, to deepen the analysis, a code was established with reference to (7) Japanese-specific practices (whether it describes the characteristics of management control practices in Japanese companies).[4]

Third, multiple pre-tests were performed before the code classification was conducted. In the pre-tests, the validity of the codes and the uniformity of the code classification were confirmed among the authors by cross-checking against the results of each author's individual code classification.

Finally, the authors were divided into three groups of two each, and the selected studies were also divided into three parts. After assigning the studies to the three groups, each group conducted code classification on the assigned studies. In addition, the final code classification for all selected studies was determined through consultation with the six authors.

In the following section, the results of the code classification are presented for subjects of management control research in Japan (descriptions to Japanese-specific practices, regions, organizational scope, and techniques assumed by researchers to the research subject) and the approach (research method and theoretical base).

2.3 Bibliographic Study of Management Control Research in Japan

2.3.1 Research Objectives

2.3.1.1 Descriptions to Japanese-Specific Practice

To clarify the current state of management control research in Japan, the primary focus is placed on "descriptions to Japanese-specific practice" as an analytical perspective. For "descriptions to Japanese-specific practice," we confirmed whether the author describes the characteristics of management control practices in Japanese companies.

Table 2.2 presents the results of the tabulation regarding the presence or absence of "descriptions to Japanese-specific practice." The upper rows indicate the tabulated

[4]In addition to the seven items discussed in this study, a code classification method was applied for six other items, including "relationship to strategy," "relationship to operations," "relevant parties," "information," "relationship to Simons' series of studies," and "relationship to Merchant's series of studies." For details, please refer to the tabulated code table (Supplementary Material 1) at the end of this study. The items other than the seven items discussed in this study will be examined in a separate study.

Table 2.2 Descriptions to Japanese-specific practice

Described	Not described	Total
Panel A: In the title		
10 (13.0%)	67 (87.0%)	77 (100.0%)
Panel B: In the text		
38 (49.4%)	39 (50.6%)	77 (100.0%)

Number of studies and row percentages in parentheses

Table 2.3 Region

	n (%)
Domestic	51 (66.2%)
Overseas	4 (5.2%)
Domestic and overseas	2 (2.6%)
Other/unknown	20 (20.6%)
Total	77 (100.0%)

results according to whether the title of the study contains the word "Japan" or "our country." The lower rows summarize the results of the judgment on whether descriptions to Japanese-specific practice exist based on the full text of the studies.

Table 2.2 reveals that the proportion of studies with words similar to "Japan" in the title is limited to 13.0% (10/77). However, when determined based on the full text, about half (38/77) of Japanese management control research mentioned Japanese-specific practice. Thus, the remaining half (39/77) examined management control without reference to Japanese-specific practice.

2.3.1.2 Region

Table 2.3 indicates the regions covered by management control research conducted in Japan. The regions are assigned four codes: "domestic," "overseas," "domestic/overseas," and "other/unknown."

Table 2.3 further reveals that more than 60% (51/77) of the management control research in Japan is "domestic" in nature. Research with an "overseas" focus accounted for 5.2% (4/77). Although there are calls for globalization for progress in Japanese companies, arguably, the interest of most of the research is within Japan.

2.3.1.3 Research Site (Industry)

Table 2.4 displays the types of industries that were selected as research sites for management control research. The research sites were categorized into "manufacturing" (e.g., processing and assembly industries, process industries), "non-manufacturing" (e.g., distributors, restaurants, banks), "for-profit organizations overall" (covering both manufacturing and non-manufacturing industries), "non-profit organizations" (e.g., hospitals, government, municipalities), "no research site," and "unknown" (no company information specified).

Table 2.4 Industry

	n (%)
Manufacturing	24 (31.2%)
Non-manufacturing	9 (11.7%)
Cover whole for-profit	7 (9.1%)
Government, not-for-profit, hospitals	10 (13.0%)
All types	1 (1.3%)
No setting	26 (33.8%)
Total	77 (100.0%)

Table 2.5 Organizational scope

	n (%)
Single organization	56 (72.7%)
Intra-group	9 (11.7%)
Inter-organizational	4 (5.2%)
Other	8 (10.4%)
Total	77 (100.0%)

Table 2.4 indicates that the largest number of studies (33.8%) in management control research in Japan have "no research site." However, we observe that there are around as many studies (31.2%) that consider "manufacturing" as a research site as "no research site." Management accounting research in Japan has developed with the manufacturing industry as the main research subject (Kawai & Otomasa, 2012; Yoshida et al., 2009), and it can be further observed that the manufacturing industry continues to be the main research site.

In Table 2.4, the second highest percentage after "manufacturing" is "Government, not-for-profit organizations, hospitals." This reflects the fact that non-profit organizations such as hospitals and local governments (Kinugasa, 2013; Matsuo, 2009) have been attracting attention as research sites for management accounting in recent years.

2.3.1.4 Organizational Scope

Table 2.5 displays the range of organizations covered by management control research in Japan. Organizational scope is categorized into "single organization," "intra-group" (e.g., consolidated management, group management), "inter-organizational" (e.g., supply chain management, strategic alliances), and "other."

Table 2.5 indicates that "single organization" accounts for nearly 70% (56/77) of the total. "Intra-group" which consisted of consolidated and group management accounted for 11.7% (9/77), while "inter-organizational" which comprised multiple organizations dealing with supply chain management and strategic alliances accounted for 5.2% (4/77). It indicates that there are only a few studies on management control that focus on "intra-group" and "inter-organizational" research.

Table 2.6 Management accounting tools

	n
Budgeting	22
Target costing	2
Amoeba management	3
Balanced scorecard	5
Management planning	6
Others	10
Unspecified	33
Total	81

Number of studies

2.3.1.5 Management Accounting Tools

Table 2.6 shows the tabulation results of the management accounting tools covered in Japanese management control research. We classified them into the following categories: "Budgeting," "Target costing," "Amoeba management" (hereafter abbreviated as "Amoeba"), "BSC," "Management planning," "Unspecified," and "Others."

Our data shows that "Unspecified" is dominant (40.7%; 33/81).[5] In Japanese management control studies, most research do not focus on specific tools.

Except for "Unspecified," "Budgeting," which has traditionally been discussed, has the highest ratio of 27.2% (22/81). "BSC," a relatively new management accounting tool, is only 6.2% (5/81). In addition, the number of studies on "Target costing" and "Amoeba," which are representative tools of Japanese management accounting, is limited to 2.5% (2/81) and 3.7% (3/81), respectively.[6]

2.3.1.6 Cross-Tabulation with Descriptions to Japanese-Specific Practice

To further understand the above results, cross-tabulations are used to examine the relationship between descriptions to Japanese-specific practice and other factors.

First, Table 2.7 cross-tabulates "region" with "descriptions to Japanese-specific practice."

Table 2.7 reveals that studies that focus on "Domestic" tend to discuss Japanese-specific practice. Our data shows that a total of 58.8% (30/51) of "domestic" studies focus on "descriptions to Japanese-specific practice." In describing management

[5] "The management accounting tools" are counted more than once if more than one management accounting tool is discussed in a study; therefore, the total number is 81.

[6] "Tools" classified as "Others" include "Life cycle costing," "Activity-based costing)," "Quality costing," "Transfer pricing," "Revenue management," "Intellectual asset management," and "Control charts."

Table 2.7 "Region" and "descriptions to Japanese-specific practice"

Region	Descriptions to Japanese-specific practice		
	Described	Not described	Total
Domestic	30 (78.9%)	21 (53.8%)	51 (66.2%)
Overseas	0 (0.0%)	4 (10.3%)	4 (5.2%)
Domestic and overseas	1 (2.6%)	1 (2.6%)	2 (2.6%)
Other/unknown	7 (18.4%)	13 (33.3%)	20 (26.0%)
Total	38 (100.0%)	39 (100.0%)	77 (100.0%)

Number of studies and column percentages in parentheses

Table 2.8 "Organizational scope" and "descriptions to Japanese-specific practice"

Organizational scope	Descriptions to Japanese-specific practice		
	Described	Not described	Total
Single organization	26 (68.4%)	30 (76.9%)	56 (72.7%)
Intra-group	7 (18.4%)	2 (5.1%)	9 (11.7%)
Inter-organizational	2 (5.3%)	2 (5.1%)	4 (5.2%)
Other	3 (7.9%)	5 (12.8%)	8 (10.4%)
Total	38 (100.0%)	39 (100.0%)	77 (100.0%)

Number of studies, and column percentages in parentheses

control practices in Japan, it is suggested that studies focus on understanding the features of practices in Japanese companies.

Second, Table 2.8 cross-tabulates the organizational scope with descriptions to Japanese-specific practices. It shows that nearly half (46.4%, 26/56) of the studies made "descriptions to Japanese-specific practices" related to a "single organization." Half of the "inter-organizational" studies were also described to them. A total of 77.8% (7/9) of the "intra-group" studies were described to them. In the current situation, many of the "intra-group" management controls, including management systems in holding companies, are discussed with reference to Japanese-specific practices.

Finally, Table 2.9 cross-tabulates the management accounting tools with the descriptions to Japanese-specific practices. Table 2.9 indicates that all the studies

Table 2.9 "Management accounting tools" and "descriptions to Japanese-specific practice"

Management accounting tools	Descriptions to Japanese-specific practice		
	Described	Not described	Total
Budgeting	8	14	22
Target costing	2	0	2
Amoeba management	3	0	3
Balanced scorecard	1	4	5
Management planning	6	0	6
Others	6	4	10
Unspecified	15	18	33
Total	41	40	81

Number of studies

discussing the Japanese management accounting tools such as "Target costing" and "Amoeba" are described along with the specific practices of Japanese companies (2/2 and 3/3). Descriptions to Japanese-specific practices are also described in all the "Management planning" studies.

Regarding other tools, the cross-tabulations of "Budgeting" and "BSC" with descriptions to Japanese-specific practices are 36.4% (8/22) and 20.0% (1/5), respectively. The arguments in the "Budgeting" and "BSC" studies are not limited to the Japanese-specific practices.

2.3.2 Approach

2.3.2.1 Research Methods

Table 2.10 presents the tabulation of the research methods of Japanese management control research. We classify research methods into the following categories: "Normative" research (research that mainly considers author's logical development), "Case/field" (research that mainly conducts interviews with research objects), "Survey: Empirical" (research that mainly examines the relationship between constructs), "Survey: Descriptive" (research that mainly examines the current practices), "Archival" (research that mainly uses quantitative data on research objects), "Review (research that derives research questions while reviewing prior literatures), "Analytical" (research that mainly uses mathematical models), "Experiment" (research that conducts experiments on subjects under experimental designs), "Historical" (research that mainly considers historical backgrounds of phenomena or management tools), and "Others."

As exhibited in Table 2.10, the research method adopted in Japanese management control research is "Normative" with the highest ratio of 24.7% (19/77).

Although not indicated in Table 2.10, if "Empirical" and "Descriptive" are combined in the "Survey," the ratio is 28.6% (22/77). The "Case/field" method was also used in 22.1% (17/77) of studies. Therefore, our data shows that almost half the studies used empirical methods.

This result contrasts prior research (Kawai & Otomasa, 2012; Yoshida et al., 2009) that indicated that "Normative" was dominant in Japan. Most research selected in this study are published in journals specializing in management accounting that adopt referee systems, such as *Genka Keisan Kenkyu (The Journal of Cost Accounting Research)* and *Kanri Kaikei Gaku (The Journal of Management Accounting, Japan)*. Hence, these studies tend to conduct empirical methods in the expectation of being accepted by above refereed journals.

Table 2.10 Research methods

	n (%)
Archival	2 (2.6%)
Analytical	1 (1.3%)
Case/field	17 (22.1%)
Experiment	1 (1.3%)
Historical	2 (2.6%)
Normative	19 (24.7%)
Survey	
Empirical	17 (22.1%)
Descriptive	5 (6.5%)
Review	10 (13.0%)
Multi-methods	3 (3.9%)
Others	0 (0.0%)
Total	77 (100.0%)

2.3.2.2 Source Discipline

Table 2.11 summarizes the source discipline (Yoshida et al., 2009) on which management control research in Japan relies. The source disciplines are broadly divided into "economics" (e.g., agency theory); "sociology" (e.g., contingency theory, new institutionalism in sociology); "psychology/behavioral science" (e.g., attribution theory); "combination" (two or more combinations of economics, sociology, and psychology/behavioral science); and "those other than economics, sociology, and psychology."

Table 2.11 shows that less than 20% (13/77) of the total research is based on theories such as "economics," "sociology," "psychology/behavioral science," and "multiple." Further, 83.1% (64/77) fall under "those other than economics, sociology, and psychology." The tendency for most studies to be based on theories "other than economics, sociology, and psychology" is similar to the results of existing surveys of BSC research and management accounting research in Japan (Kawai & Otomasa, 2012; Yoshida et al., 2009).

This demonstrates that the management control research in Japan, not based on theories such as "economics," analyzes phenomena related to management accounting based on the management control concept. Conversely, it can be assumed that it will be possible to analyze phenomena related to management accounting with a view to re-examine the concept of management control if theoretical bases such as "economics" are applied.

The finding that most studies do not have a theoretical base in areas such as "economics" or "sociology" suggests that there is further scope for research progress. In the future, management accounting researchers in Japan should explore the phenomena related to management accounting with a view to re-examine the concept of management control.

Table 2.11 Source discipline

	n (%)
Economics	6 (7.8%)
Psychology	2 (2.6%)
Sociology	3 (3.9%)
Multiple	2 (2.6%)
Other	64 (83.1%)
Total	77 (100.0%)

Table 2.12 Type of journals published (peer-reviewed or not)

Reviewed	Non-reviewed	Total
46 (59.7%)	31 (40.3%)	77 (100.0%)

Number of studies and row percentages in parentheses

2.3.2.3 Cross-Tabulation with Existence of Peer Review

This section examines the relationship between the research methods and theoretical base and the existence of peer review in the published journals.

Table 2.12 indicates the results of a classification of the studies covered in this study according to the existence of peer review[7] based on the journal in which they were published. As shown in Table 2.12, 59.7% (46/77) of the studies covered in this study have been published in the journals after peer review.

Further, Tables 2.13 and 2.14 respectively present the cross-tabulation table between the existence of peer review and the research method employed, and the cross-tabulation table between the existence of peer review and the theoretical base employed.

Table 2.14 shows that research published in "peer-reviewed" journals tends to be based on disciplines such as "economics," "sociology," and "psychology." In the "non- reviewed" category, all but one of the studies using "economics" are counted as "those other than economics, sociology, and psychology."

From the above, the operation of the peer review system in Japan has contributed to the accumulation of rigorous empirical evidence in management control research during the period covered by this study.

Finally, we examine the relationship between the "references to Japanese-specific practice" and the "existence of peer review" as discussed in the previous section. Table 2.15 demonstrates the relationship between the existence of peer review based on the journal in which the study was published and references to Japanese-specific practice. In Table 2.15, 61.3% (19/31) of the studies published in the "non-reviewed" journals made "references to Japanese-specific practice," while 41.3% (19/46) of the studies published in the "peer-reviewed" journals made "references to

[7] Studies published in *Melco Journal of Management Accounting Research*, *Accounting Progress*, *The Journal of Management Accounting in Japan*, and *The Journal of Cost Accounting Research in Japan* are counted as "peer-reviewed;" and studies published in *Kaikei (Accounting)*, *Accounting*, and *Industrial Accounting* are counted as "non-reviewed."

Table 2.13 "Research methods" and "type of journals published"

Region	Peer-reviewed or not		
	Reviewed	Non-reviewed	Total
Archival	2 (4.3%)	0 (0.0%)	2 (2.6%)
Analytical	1 (2.2%)	0 (0.0%)	1 (1.3%)
Case/field	12 (26.1%)	5 (16.1%)	17 (22.1%)
Experiment	1 (2.2%)	0 (0.0%)	1 (1.3%)
Historical	1 (2.2%)	1 (3.2%)	2 (2.6%)
Normative	7 (15.2%)	12 (38.7%)	19 (24.7%)
Survey			
Empirical	13 (28.3%)	4 (12.9%)	17 (22.1%)
Descriptive	1 (2.2%)	4 (12.9%)	5 (6.5%)
Review	6 (13.0%)	4 (12.9%)	10 (2.6%)
Multi-methods	2 (4.3%)	1 (3.2%)	3 (13.0%)
Others	0 (0.0%)	0 (0.0%)	0 (0.0%)
Total	46 (100.0)	31 (100.0)	77 (100.0)

Number of studies, and column percentages in parentheses

Table 2.14 "Source disciplines" and "type of journals published"

Region	Peer-reviewed or not		
	Reviewed	Non-reviewed	Total
Economics	5 (10.9%)	1 (3.2%)	6 (7.8%)
Psychology	2 (4.3%)	0 (0.0%)	2 (2.6%)
Sociology	3 (6.5%)	0 (0.0%)	3 (3.9%)
Multiple	2 (4.3%)	0 (0.0%)	2 (2.6%)
Other	34 (73.9%)	30 (96.8%)	64 (83.1%)
Total	46 (100.0)	31 (100.0)	77 (100.0)

Number of studies, and column percentages in parentheses

Table 2.15 "Descriptions to Japanese-specific practice" and "type of journals published"

	Reviewed	Non-reviewed	Total
Described	19 (41.3%)	19 (61.3%)	38 (49.4%)
Not described	27 (58.7%)	12 (38.7%)	39 (50.6%)
Total	46 (100.0%)	31 (100.0%)	77 (100.0%)

Number of studies and column percentages in parentheses

Japanese-specific practice." This implies that studies published in journals that adopt a peer review system aim to acquire more general evidence, rather than Japanese-specific practices, in management control research.

2.4 Conclusion

In this study, the current state of diversified management control research in Japan was examined through a literature analysis. The studies to be examined were selected from those published in seven major accounting journals in Japan from 2011 to 2013. The analysis was conducted from two aspects: the research object (Japanese-specific practice, region, industry, organizational scope, and management accounting tool) and the approach (research method and source discipline).

About half of the management control studies in Japan refer to Japanese-specific practices. For "region," more than 60% of the research focused on "Japan." For industry, research targeting the "manufacturing industry" was as common as that found in the "no research site." As for the "organizational scope," about 70% of all the studies were conducted for a "single organization." Cross-tabulation between "references to Japanese-specific practice" and other research objects revealed that studies that focused on "Japan" and "intra-group" tended to discuss Japanese-specific practice, while discussions on "budgeting" and "BSC" were not limited to Japanese-specific practice.

Concerning source discipline, most of the research was classified as "those other than economics, sociology, and psychology." Conversely, empirical methods such as "case" and "survey" have been adopted in more studies compared to results of existing studies. Cross-tabulation with "peer-reviewed" based on the journal in which the study was published revealed that source discipline such as "economics," "sociology," and "psychology" and empirical methods such as "case" and "survey" tended to be adopted more frequently in studies published in "peer-reviewed" journals than "non-reviewed journals." The operation of the peer review system in Japan has contributed to the accumulation of rigorous empirical evidence in management control research.

These results provide useful insights for understanding the current state of management control research in Japan. However, this study had several limitations. First, the literature analysis, which was conducted based on previous studies, is only suitable for presenting general trends and cannot reflect the detailed content of each study. Second, there are potential risks in selecting management control studies. Even if "planning" and "control"—which were used as key terms in this study to identify the research objects, are not described in a study—it may still have been a study that discusses management control. Finally, even though the coding process was rigorously conducted by six researchers, potential errors cannot be eliminated.

To further explore the current findings, it is desirable to understand the long-term research trends of management control research in Japan and compare them with the current state and trends of management control research in Europe and the United States. It will also be necessary to clarify the characteristics of management control research in Japan from perspectives other than the "research object" and "approach" analyzed in this study.

References

Anthony, R. N. (1965). *Planning and control systems: A framework for analysis*. Harvard University. Division of Research.

Arae, T. (2008). Using the balanced scorecard as an interactive control system: Importance of process research. *Keiri Kenkyu, 51*, 218–230. (in Japanese).

Arae, T., & Ito, K. (2010). A fundamental reconsideration of management control concepts: Studies of diversification of control devices. *The Journal of Cost Accounting Research in Japan, 34*(1), 150–160. (in Japanese).

Chenhall, R. H. (2007). Theorizing contingencies in management control research. In C. S. Chapman, A. G. Hopwood, & M. D. Shields (Eds.), *Handbook of management accounting research* (Vol. 1, pp. 163–205). Elsevier.

Fukushima, M. (2012). Examining the concept of control package. *The Journal of Management Accounting in Japan., 20*(2), 79–96. (in Japanese).

Hesford, J. M., Lee, S. H., Van der Stede, W. A., & Young, S. M. (2007). Management accounting: A bibliographic study. In C. S. Chapman, A. G. Hopwood, & M. D. Shields (Eds.), *Handbook of management accounting research* (Vol. 1, pp. 3–26). Elsevier.

Kato, Y., Matsuo, T., & Kajiwara, T. (2010). *Frontiers in management accounting research*. Chuokeizai-Sha. (in Japanese).

Kawai, T., & Otomasa, S. (2012). Literature analysis of balanced scorecard studies in Japan: Through comparison with major European and U.S. accounting research and practice journals. *Accounting Progress, 13*, 112–124. (in Japanese).

Kawai, T., & Otomasa, S. (2013). Trends in balanced scorecard research in Japan: Based on accumulated research in Europe and the U.S. *The Doshisha Business Review, 65*(1), 1–62. (in Japanese).

Kimura, S. (2011). Inter-organization management accounting. In T. Asada & Y. Ito (Eds.), *Taikei Gendai Kaikeigaku Vol. 11: Strategic management accounting* (pp. 33–61). Chuokeizai-Sha. (in Japanese).

Kinugasa, Y. (2013). *Management accounting in the medical field: Aiming to build a management accounting system that enhances the quality of health care*. Chuokeizai-Sha. (in Japanese).

Kobayashi, T. (1988). Interactive control systems and the role of accounting information. *Industrial Accounting in Japan, 48*(2), 10–18. (in Japanese).

Malmi, T., & Brown, D. A. (2008). Management control systems as a package: Opportunities, challenges and research directions. *Management Accounting Research, 19*(4), 287–300.

Matsugi, S., Nakagawa, M., Shima, Y., & Yasukata, K. (2014). Nationality of subsidiary top management and management control style: A case study of Japanese global firms. *The Journal of Cost Accounting Research in Japan, 38*(2), 27–38. (in Japanese).

Matsuo, T. (2009). *Management accounting systems in municipality*. Chuokeizai-Sha. (in Japanese).

Merchant, K. A., & Otley, D. T. (2007). A review of the literature on control and accountability. In C. S. Chapman, A. G. Hopwood, & M. D. Shields (Eds.), *Handbook of management accounting research* (Vol. 2, pp. 785–802). Elsevier.

Sakaguchi, J., Kawai, T., & Kazusa, Y. (2015). Issues in Japanese inter-firm management control research. *Melco Journal of Management Accounting Research, 7*(2), 3–13. (in Japanese).

Shields, M. D. (1997). Research in management accounting by North Americans in the 1990s. *Journal of Management Accounting Research, 9*, 3–61.

Shirinashihama, Y. (2011). A study on the influence of Anthony's planning and control theory on management control literatures. *Hitotsubashi Review of Commerce and Management, 6*(1), 63–76. (in Japanese).

Simons, R. (1987). Accounting control systems and business strategy: An empirical analysis. *Accounting, Organizations and Society, 12*(4), 357–374.

Simons, R. (1990). The role of management control systems in creating competitive advantage: New perspectives. *Accounting, Organizations and Society, 15*(1/2), 127–143.

Simons, R. L. (1995). *Levers of control: How managers use innovative control systems to drive strategic renewal*. Harvard Business School Press.

Tani, T. (1992). Empirical study on interactive control. *Journal of Economics & Business Administration (in Kobe University in Japan), 165*(6), 27–40. (in Japanese).

Tani, T. (1994). Reengineering and management accounting: Interactive control as a point of contact. *Accounting (in Japan), 46*(5), 602–607. (in Japanese).

Tani, T. (2013). Conceptual model of amoeba management: Revitalization of the organization through the philosophy and control package. *Accounting (in Japan), 65*(2), 161–171. (in Japanese).

Tani, T., & Kubota, Y. (2012). Successful integration of an acquired firm and implementation of strategies through management control systems. *The Journal of Cost Accounting Research in Japan, 36*(1), 107–118. (in Japanese).

Yokota, E. (2007). A note on the importance of interactive control systems: Based on a field study. *Mita Business Review, 50*(1), 47–60. (in Japanese).

Yokota, E., & Senoo, T. (2012). Examining the balanced scorecard as an interactive control system: A case study of a food company. *Melco Journal of Management Accounting Research, 5*, 3–14. (in Japanese).

Yoshida, E., Kondo, T., Fukushima, K., & Senoo, T. (2009). A bibliometric study of Japanese management accounting: 1980-2007. *Industrial Accounting in Japan, 69*(3), 70–81. (in Japanese).

Chapter 3
A Survey of Management Control Systems and Managerial Behavior in Japanese Companies

Eri Yokota, Asako Takada, Takeyoshi Senoo, and Shinya Kaneko

3.1 Introduction

The developments in theoretical research on management control systems (MCS) that took place in the early 2000s (Ferreira & Otley, 2009; Malmi & Brown, 2008; Merchant & Otley, 2007) motivated Yokota and Senoo (2011) to conduct a mail-based questionnaire survey during February and March 2010 to clarify the status of and changes in MCS in Japanese companies. However, the Great East Japan Earthquake that occurred in March 2011 impacted Japanese companies such that their MCS may have further changed. Therefore, to clarify the status of MCS in Japanese companies, we conducted a mail-based questionnaire survey from February through March 2012. Specifically, the survey gathered information about budgeting, business environments, organizational characteristics, and managerial leadership and behaviors.

Reprinted with permission of The Society of Business and Commerce, Keio University. Originally published in *Mita Business Review* 55(4): 93–117, 2012 (in Japanese).

E. Yokota (✉)
Faculty of Business and Commerce, Keio University, Tokyo, Japan
e-mail: yokota@fbc.keio.ac.jp

A. Takada
Hosei Business School of Innovation Management, Hosei University, Tokyo, Japan
e-mail: atakada@hosei.ac.jp

T. Senoo
Faculty of Commerce, Chuo University, Tokyo, Japan
e-mail: senoo81@tamacc.chuo-u.ac.jp

S. Kaneko
Certified Public Accountant, Tokyo, Japan
e-mail: shinya.kaneko@ms02.jicpa.or.jp

© Springer Nature Singapore Pte Ltd. 2023
E. Yokota (ed.), *Frontiers of Japanese Management Control Systems*, Translational Systems Sciences 32, https://doi.org/10.1007/978-981-19-9778-5_3

This study reports the simple tabulation results of the survey. The term "manager" was broadly defined in the questionnaire as management; the term is used in this study to describe only high-ranking managers such as organizational unit managers (e.g., business division managers, company system managers, department managers) who head an organizational unit (e.g., business division, company system, department). The tables in the study reflect the questions as written in the questionnaire; thus, "manager" in the tables refers to all managers—a meaning different from the term "manager" as used in this study.

3.2 Survey Method and Sample Characteristics

The survey was administered as follows. On February 27, 2012, a mail-based questionnaire survey titled "2012 Factual Investigation on MCS in Japanese Companies" was sent to those responsible for management control at 1674 companies listed on the First Section of the Tokyo Stock Exchange, with a reply deadline of March 14, 2012. The postal addresses were extracted from Diamond's "D-VISION" series, "Employee/Manager Information File." Specifically, the highest priority was to select the person who functioned as the division/department manager of the corporate planning department; the division/department manager of the accounting and finance department was selected for companies without such a position. When companies reported no data for either, the person in charge of management control was independently identified from the company website.[1]

A total of 263 companies responded, including responses from 40 companies that were received after the response deadline, resulting in a response rate of 15.7%. Using a 5% significance level, test for non-response bias was performed as follows.[2] We first compared the industry-type distribution of the responding and non-responding companies; the responses by industry are shown in Table 3.1.[3] As a result of the goodness-of-fit test (χ^2-test), it was confirmed that the industry distribution of the responding companies conformed to the industry distribution of the companies listed on the First Section of the Tokyo Stock Exchange. Second, the sizes of responding and non-responding companies were compared. Table 3.2 reports the differences between the mean values of the size measures (sales, number of employees) of responding and non-responding companies.[4] The mean for responding companies is higher for both sales and number of employees, and a

[1] If the person in charge of management control could not be identified after going through this process, a questionnaire was sent to the "person in charge of management control."

[2] The data for the test were obtained from recent surveys by Nikkei NEEDS. However, when the necessary data for a company was not available from Nikkei NEEDS, the data were obtained from the company's securities report.

[3] We used TOPIX Sector Indices to identify industries.

[4] Since the surveyed companies included pure holding companies, consolidated data were used. If there was no consolidated company, non-consolidated data were used instead. In addition, instead

Table 3.1 Response by industry

Industry	Number of responding companies	Number of companies survey was sent to	Industry	Number of responding companies	Number of companies survey was sent to
Fisheries, agriculture, and forestry	1 (.4%)	5 (.3%)	Precision equipment	2 (.8%)	26 (1.6%)
Mining	1 (.4%)	7 (.4%)	Other products	7 (2.7%)	46 (2.7%)
Construction	16 (6.1%)	95 (5.7%)	Electric, power, and gas	2 (.8%)	17 (1.0%)
Food	13 (4.9%)	65 (3.9%)	Land transportation	10 (3.8%)	34 (2.0%)
Textiles and apparels	3 (1.1%)	39 (2.3%)	Marine transportation	1 (.4%)	9 (.5%)
Pulp and paper	0 (.0%)	11 (.7%)	Air transportation	1 (.4%)	3 (.2%)
Chemicals	14 (5.3%)	120 (7.2%)	Warehouse and harbor transportation	2 (.8%)	19 (1.1%)
Pharmaceutical	4 (1.5%)	36 (2.2%)	Information and communications	18 (6.8%)	100 (6.0%)
Oil and coal products	3 (1.1%)	10 (.6%)	Wholesale trade	30 (11.4%)	144 (8.6%)
Rubber products	3 (1.1%)	11 (.7%)	Retail trade	29 (11.0%)	148 (8.8%)
Glass and ceramics products	4 (1.5%)	29 (1.7%)	Banks	11 (4.2%)	84 (5.0%)
Iron and steel	5 (1.9%)	35 (2.1%)	Securities and commodities futures	4 (1.5%)	21 (1.3%)
Nonferrous metals	2 (.8%)	24 (1.4%)	Insurance	1 (.4%)	6 (.4%)
Metal products	5 (1.9%)	36 (2.2%)	Other financial business	1 (.4%)	20 (1.2%)
Machinery	17 (6.5%)	118 (7.0%)	Real estate	8 (3.0%)	45 (2.7%)
Electrical appliances	23 (8.7%)	154 (9.2%)	Services	9 (3.4%)	95 (5.7%)
Transport equipment	13 (4.9%)	62 (3.7%)	Total	263 (100.0%)	1674 (100.0%)

Note 1: The numbers in parentheses indicate the composition ratio
Note 2: Goodness-of-fit test: $\chi^2 = 25.452$, degrees of freedom $= 32$, $p = .787$

---

of sales, ordinary income is used in the banking industry, and operating revenue is used in securities and commodities futures industries.

Table 3.2 Difference in mean values of size of responding and non-responding companies

	Mean value of responding companies (n = 263)	Standard deviation	Mean value of non-responding companies (n = 1411)	Standard deviation	*t*	*p*
Sales: million dollars ($1 = ¥80)	6977.45	22289.70	4176.45	12,498.90	1.981	.049
Number of employees	9982.14	30,561.30	7266.69	21,504.78	1.379	.169

t-test of the differences between the means of the two independent groups showed only the difference in sales was significant. Third, when the response results for those received before and after the deadline were compared, there were no significant differences in mean values or ratios. Therefore, the results of this survey appear to reflect the actual status of relatively large companies, and there is no significant non-response bias.

To improve comparability with previous research, whenever possible, the questions in this survey were prepared by referring to previous research. However, as many of the references used in previous studies come from countries other than Japan, revisions were made to be consistent with the actual situation faced by Japanese companies. In addition, some new concepts were established, and scales were developed in regard to concepts and measurements that were not necessarily clarified in previous studies. During the questionnaire design, the questions were confirmed by two management accounting researchers and one businessperson who did not participate in the survey.

The descriptive statistics of the survey results are shown in tables in this study, which also describe the previous studies referenced. The abbreviations in the table are as follows: "*n*" is the number of valid responses, "Mean" is the mean value, "SD" is the standard deviation, "Median" is the median value, "Min" is the minimum value, and "Max" is the maximum value. Most question items were measured using a seven-point scale. In addition, when measurement scales of previous studies were referenced, Cronbach's alphas were calculated to examine internal consistency. In the table, "α" indicates Cronbach's alpha coefficient. The questions in the table are not presented in the order in which they were presented in the questionnaire; rather, they are sorted from high to low using the ratio of the number of responses to the total number of valid answers or the mean value. However, the number preceding the question in the table reflects the order of the items in the questionnaire.

First, to clarify the characteristics of the responding companies, Question 1 enquired about the organizational structure. Table 3.3 shows the survey findings regarding the sample firms' basic organizational structures. These results indicate that many of the responding companies have either a functional or divisional organizational structure.

Table 3.3 Basic organizational structure (n = 262) (Q1)

	n	%
1. Functional organization (e.g., manufacturing department (business division), sales department (business division))	114	43.5
2. Product/business divisional organization	83	31.7
3. Regional divisional organization	25	9.5
5. (Pure) holding company system	21	8.0
4. Company system	13	5.0
6. Other	6	2.3

Note: The percentages displayed in the table indicate the ratio of that response to the total number of valid responses

3.3 Budgeting (Question 2)

Budgeting has been central to management control (Hansen et al., 2003, p. 95); however, Hope and Fraser (2003) advocated that firms go "beyond budgeting" and claimed that budgets should be abolished. In recent years, increasingly more studies have been conducted outside Japan to examine the validity of their claims (e.g., Libby & Lindsay, 2010).

In Question 2, to clarify the actual state of company-wide budgeting in Japanese companies, budgeting was defined as, "formulation of a budget for a certain period (within one year) in the future from a comprehensive perspective of the company, and the use of this as a means to guide and coordinate daily activities of each department, in addition to a variance analysis between the budget and the actual results; it is a comprehensive management control method based on numbers to take appropriate improvement measures based on the analysis, and is a specific means of corporate profit management."[5] The survey was conducted primarily using Miki et al. (2003)[6] and Libby and Lindsay (2010) as references.

Table 3.4 shows the survey results regarding whether the sample companies use budgeting across the company. The questions were created with reference to Miki et al. (2003 p. 130) and Libby and Lindsay (2010 p. 69).

Table 3.5 presents the results of survey questions regarding how budgets affect purposes. In recent years, an increasing number of studies have analyzed the effect of budgets on purposes (e.g., Hansen & Van der Stede, 2004); however, the questions in this survey were created with reference to Ekholm and Wallin (2011, p. 158). Each item was measured on a seven-point scale, from "1: no effect at all" to "4: neutral" and "7: extremely effective." However, since the measurement scale has not

[5] The questionnaire describes it as a "budget system." This definition was created with reference to Miki et al. (2003, p. 130).

[6] Miki et al. (2003) summarized the methods and results of the "Fact-finding Survey of Japan's Corporate Budgeting System" conducted in November 2002 by the Japanese Association of Management Accounting, Corporate Research Project; and the Budget System Committee, which comprehensively clarified the actual budget management practices in Japanese companies.

Table 3.4 Implementation of company-wide budgeting ($n = 262$) [Q2 (A)]

	n	%
1. Is implemented	259	98.9
2. Is not implemented	3	1.1
3. Is implemented, but abolishment is being considered	0	.0

Note: The percentages displayed in the table indicate the ratio of that response to the total number of valid responses

Table 3.5 Effects of budgeting on purposes [Q2 (B)]

	n	Mean	SD	Median	Min	Max
(9) Operationalization of objectives	257	5.87	.87	6	2	7
(7) Communication of goals and policies	256	5.78	.91	6	2	7
(8) Creating awareness of what is important to achieve	256	5.66	.99	6	2	7
(1) Planning linked to the company's strategies	257	5.59	1.00	6	2	7
(5) Allocation of responsibility	257	5.41	1.18	6	1	7
(3) Allocation of resources to the units	256	5.28	1.05	5	1	7
(10) Motivation of managers and employees	257	5.25	1.09	5	1	7
(2) Coordination of the company's units organizational units	255	5.09	1.12	5	1	7
(6) Follow-up to facilitate rapid corrections	256	4.90	1.23	5	1	7
(11) Functioning as a basis for compensation and bonus systems	257	4.74	1.31	5	1	7
(4) Determination of operational volumes	255	4.48	1.27	5	1	7

Note: Since there are instances where certain questions were not answered, the number of valid answers (n) differs for each question

been established in previous studies, Table 3.5 does not include Cronbach's alpha coefficients.

Table 3.6 shows the results of survey questions about whether budgeted financial statements are prepared (multiple answers were allowed). The questions were created with reference to the "Questionnaire Survey on Understanding the Actual Conditions of Management Accounting in Japanese Companies" (FY2011), by the Global Center of Excellence (COE) Program (Management, Accounting, and Commercial Group), a collaboration between Keio University's Graduate School of Economics and Graduate School of Business and Commerce and Kyoto University's Institute of Economic Research.

Table 3.7 shows the results of survey questions about the degree of linkage between budget and strategy. The questions were created with reference to Libby and Lindsay (2010, p. 72). Each item was measured on a seven-point scale from "1: not at all" to "4: neutral" to "7: absolutely agree." Table 3.8 shows the budget period and Table 3.9 shows the budget preparation time.

Table 3.6 Whether budgeted financial statements are prepared ($n = 254$) [Q2 (C)]

	n	%
2. Non-consolidated budgeted income statement	226	89.0
5. Consolidated budgeted income statement	208	81.9
4. Consolidated budgeted balance sheet	127	50.0
1. Non-consolidated budgeted balance sheet	124	48.8
6. Consolidated budgeted cash flow statement	114	44.9
3. Non-consolidated budgeted cash flow statement	113	44.5
7. None of the budgeted financial statements listed in 1–6 are prepared	8	3.1
8. Other	4	1.6

Note: Since there are instances where certain questions were not answered, the number of valid answers (n) differs for each question

Table 3.7 Link between budget and strategy [Q2 (D)]

	n	Mean	SD	Median	Min	Max
$n = 255$, $\alpha = .822$ (4) Within the budgeting process, managers are expected to identify tactical initiatives to close the gap between current performance and the desired level of performance	256	5.64	1.13	6	1	7
(1) The budget system is explicitly linked to strategic objectives	257	5.63	1.14	6	2	7
(2) Setting the budget causes us to talk about and reflect upon our strategy	256	5.48	1.12	6	1	7
(3) We sometimes change our strategy/tactics based on the feedback derived from going through the budgeting process	255	5.18	1.26	5	1	7

Table 3.8 Budget period ($n = 255$) [Q2 (E)]

	n	%
1 year	164	64.3
6 months	63	24.7
3 months	14	5.5
1 month	14	5.5
2 months	0	.0

Table 3.10 presents the responses to questions about whether the initial budget was revised and the revision method (multiple answers were allowed). Number 3 in Table 3.10 (Question 2 (G)) is a question regarding "rolling budgets." The questions

Table 3.9 Budget preparation time ($n = 258$) [Q2 (F)]

	n	%
3 months	78	30.2
2 months	45	17.4
4 months	33	12.8
2.5 months	30	11.6
3.5 months	22	8.5
Over 4 months	17	6.6
1.5 months	17	6.6
1 month	15	5.8
Less than 1 month	1	.4

Table 3.10 Whether revisions are made to the initial budget and revision method ($n = 256$) [Q2 (G)]

	n (%)	*n* (%)
Whether the initial budget is revised 4. The initial budget is fixed and there are no revisions during the period	41 (16.0)	
There are revisions	215 (84.0)	
Method of revising initial budget (n = 215) 2. The initial budget is reviewed periodically (e.g., monthly, quarterly, etc.) and revisions are made as needed		167 (77.7)
3. The budget is periodically (e.g., monthly, quarterly, etc.) updated		37 (17.2)
1. The initial budget is reviewed irregularly, and revisions are made as needed		27 (12.6)

were created with reference to Miki et al. (2003, p. 131, p. 133) and Libby and Lindsay (2010, p. 70, p. 72).[7]

Table 3.11 reports the results of questions on the company-wide performance measures that are most important for budgeting. The question items were created with reference to Miki et al. (2003, p. 132) and Yokota and Senoo (2011, p. 70).

Table 3.12 shows the results of questions about the properties of the company-wide performance measures that are most important for budgeting. In these questions, the focus was placed on the precision and sensitivity of the performance measures. Precision is the degree that performance measures are affected by factors outside the manager's control, and sensitivity is the degree that performance measures are influenced by manager behavior (Moers, 2006, p. 899). The questions were created with reference to Moers (2006, pp. 920–921). Each item in Table 3.12 was measured on a seven-point scale from "1: not at all" to "4: neutral" to "7: absolutely

[7] Libby and Lindsay (2010, p. 70) do not ask for a response regarding the budgeting period when a rolling budget has been implemented. In contrast, since the initial budget preparation time is examined in this chapter, a response is requested even if a rolling budget is implemented.

Table 3.11 Most important company-wide performance measures in budgeting ($n = 247$) [Q2 (H)]

	n	%
2. Operating income	103	41.7
3. Ordinary income	76	30.8
4. Net income	25	10.1
1. Sales	22	8.9
6. Return on sales	10	4.0
9. Other	7	2.8
7. Return on equity	2	.8
8. Residual income (EVA, etc.)	2	.8
5. Comprehensive income	0	.0

Note: EVA: Economic Value Added, developed by Stern Stewart & Co.

Table 3.12 Properties of company-wide performance measures most important for budgeting [Q2 (I)]

	n	Mean	SD	Median	Min	Max
Precision of performance measures ($n = 247$, $\alpha = .706$) (3) The actual value of this performance measure is strongly affected by changes in the behavior or strategies of business partners and suppliers (R)	247	2.99	1.36	3	1	7
(1) The actual value of this performance measure is strongly affected by changes in the economic situation (R)	247	2.28	1.05	2	1	7
(2) The actual value of this performance measure is strongly affected by changes in customer behavior (R)	247	2.26	.97	2	1	6
Sensitivity of performance measures ($n = 247$, $\alpha = .918$) (6) If the manager of the organizational unit performs management tasks well, then the value of the performance measure will immediately and significantly improve	247	4.74	1.28	5	1	7
(5) If the manager properly fulfills their role, then the value of the performance measure will immediately and significantly improve	247	4.38	1.37	5	1	7
(4) If employees are enthusiastic about their work, then the value of the performance measure will immediately and significantly improve	247	4.06	1.40	4	1	7

Note: (R) indicates a reverse-scored item

agree." All questions related to the precision of performance measures are reverse scored; thus, the numbers in the table have been reversed.

Table 3.13 shows the results of questions about performance evaluation methods and the existence of budget-based performance evaluation for organizational unit

Table 3.13 Performance evaluation methods and existence of budget-based performance evaluations for organizational unit managers ($n = 250$) [Q2 (J)]

	n (%)	*n* (%)
Existence of budget-based performance evaluations 5. The budget is not used for the performance evaluation of the organizational unit manager	37 (14.8)	
It is used	213 (85.2)	
Budget-based performance evaluation methods (n = 213) 4. Performance evaluation is performed by comparing actual results with budget targets. However, the evaluator makes a subjective judgment based on the organizational unit manager's explanation, who is the person being evaluated, as well as changes in situation.		116 (54.5)
1. Performance evaluation is performed by comparing performance rigidly with the pre-established budget target		41 (19.2)
3. Performance evaluation is performed by comparing actual results with budget targets. However, budget targets may be adjusted using pre-set formulas to consider the effects of unexpected and important factors.		37 (17.4)
2. Organizational unit managers are evaluated based solely on variances between the budget and actual results within their control and are not evaluated on variances beyond their control		19 (8.9)

Table 3.14 Degree of link between results of budget-based performance evaluations for organizational unit managers and reward [Q2 (K)]

	n	Mean	SD	Median	Min	Max
(2) Bonus	220	5.76	1.10	6	1	7
(3) Promotion and advancement	219	4.99	1.04	5	1	7
(1) Basic salary	218	3.87	1.53	4	1	7

managers. Note that Number 1 in Table 3.13 (Question 2 (J)) is a question regarding evaluation based on a "fixed performance contract" (Hope & Fraser, 2003). The questions were created with reference to Libby and Lindsay (2010, p. 73).

Table 3.14 presents the results of questions on the degree of linkage between the results of budget-based performance evaluations for organizational unit managers and reward.[8] The questions were created with reference to Yokota and Senoo (2011, p. 72) and Bouwens and van Lent (2007, pp. 691–692). The items in Table 3.14 were measured on a seven-point scale, from "1: no influence at all" to "4: neutral" to "7: extremely influential."

Table 3.15 shows the results of questions about budget culture. Budget culture is a concept developed by Anderson and Lillis (2011) based on Marginson and Ogden (2005) and Van der Stede (2000). It is categorized into four sub-concepts: budget firmness, management attention, target difficulty, and reward link. The questions

[8] In addition to money, incentives include non-monetary items such as promotions and awards; in this chapter, the term 'reward' is used as a broad concept that includes these items.

Table 3.15 Budget culture [Q2 (L)]

	n	Mean	SD	Median	Min	Max
Budget firmness ($n = 254$, $\alpha = .452$) (2) Managers are always expected to take corrective action to reduce budget variances	255	5.87	.85	6	2	7
(1) Managers are always expected to meet short-term budgets even if budget variances are caused by events outside their control	254	4.64	1.27	5	1	7
(3) Budget targets are firm commitments that are never revised	256	4.43	1.43	5	1	7
Management attention ($n = 255$, $\alpha = .815$) (4) Unfavorable budget variances receive the greatest deal of attention from top managers.	256	5.82	1.05	6	2	7
(5) Top managers keep a close eye on budget achievement of the company's business units	255	5.64	1.07	6	1	7
Target difficulty ($n = 256$, $\alpha = .740$) (7) Stretch budgets are the norm	256	5.00	1.27	5	1	7
(6) Budget targets are generally set to be extremely demanding	256	4.87	1.14	5	1	7
(8) Targets incorporated in the budget are typically extremely difficult to reach	256	3.46	1.30	4	1	7
Reward link ($n = 256$, $\alpha = .875$) (12) Achieving budget goals is an extremely important indication of performance of managers and employees	256	5.22	1.07	5	1	7
(10) Financial rewards for managers and employees greatly increase as performance exceeds budget targets	256	4.70	1.29	5	1	7
(9) Compensation for managers and employees is strongly linked to meeting budgets	256	4.63	1.32	5	1	7
(11) The probability of job promotion and advancement increases for managers and employees when performance exceeds budget targets	256	4.51	1.10	5	1	7

Note: Although α is low, the questions for each concepts were created with reference to this in Anderson and Lillis (2011, p. 1370)

were created with reference to this in Anderson and Lillis (2011, p. 1370). Each item was measured on a seven-point scale from "1: not at all" to "4: neutral" to "7: absolutely agree."

Table 3.16 Relationship between company-wide budgeting and budgeting in major organizational units [Q3 (A)]

	n	%
1. Budget systems for major organizational units are implemented based on the company-wide budget system	251	97.3
2. The budget system for major organizational units is implemented completely independently of the company-wide budget system	6	2.3
4. Neither a company-wide budget system nor a budget system for major organizational units is implemented	1	.4
3. A company-wide budget system is not implemented, but a budget system for major organizational units is independently implemented	0	.0

3.4 Business Environment of Major Organizational Units (Question 3)

Many studies have revealed that the business environment affects MCS (Chenhall, 2007). However, since modern Japanese companies have various organizational units, the business environment may differ for each organizational unit. Therefore, respondents to this survey were asked to identify the company's major organizational units.

Then, as shown in Table 3.16, the relationship between company-wide budgeting and budgeting for each major organizational unit was explored. The results show that in almost all companies, each major organizational unit's system is implemented based on the company-wide system for budgeting.

In Question 3, to clarify how the business environment impacts MCS, perceived environmental uncertainty as the external business environment and the importance of a strategy to differentiate the internal business environment was investigated for each major organizational unit.

Table 3.17 shows the results of survey questions on perceived environmental uncertainty. The questions were created with reference to Ekholm and Wallin (2011, p. 158) and Hoque (2004, p. 499). Each item was measured on a seven-point scale of "1: very unpredictable" to "4: neutral" to "7: very predictable." Note that as these questions are reverse scored, the numbers in the table have been reversed.

Table 3.18 reports the results of questions on the importance of differentiation strategies. The questions were created with reference to Anderson and Lillis (2011, p. 1366).[9] The items were measured on a seven-point scale, from "1: not important at all" to "4: neutral" to "7: extremely important."

[9]Anderson and Lillis (2011) conducted an exploratory factor analysis of 11 questions regarding business strategy, from which four factors were extracted. However, this survey only refers to the five-question items that showed high factor loading for the second factor—"innovative products"—which is a subordinate concept of the differentiation strategy (Anderson & Lillis, pp. 1365–1366).

Table 3.17 Perceived environmental uncertainty [Q3 (C)]

	n	Mean	SD	Median	Min	Max
n = 258, α = .791 (3) Deregulation and globalization (R)	260	3.61	1.08	4	1	7
(6) Government regulations and policies (R)	261	3.43	1.09	3	1	7
(7) Economic environment (R)	261	3.25	1.09	3	1	7
(2) Customer demands, tastes, and preferences (R)	261	3.17	1.01	3	1	7
(1) Action of business partners and suppliers (R)	260	3.09	1.00	3	1	6
(8) Industrial relations (R)	261	3.09	1.17	3	1	7
(4) Market activities of competitors (R)	261	2.95	.93	3	1	6
(5) Products, services, and information technology	260	2.91	.94	3	1	7

Note: (R) indicates a reverse-scored item

Table 3.18 Importance of differentiation strategies

	n	Mean	SD	Median	Min	Max
n = 259, *α* = .764 (1) Low cost-in-use	260	5.52	1.04	6	2	7
(2) Advanced product and services features	260	5.36	1.13	5	1	7
(3) Innovation of products and services	260	5.30	1.16	5	1	7
(4) After-sales service	259	4.98	1.16	5	2	7
(5) Technical support	259	4.88	1.23	5	1	7

3.5 Characteristics of Major Organizational Units (Question 4)

Importance has been placed on the relationship between organizational characteristics and MCS (Ferreira & Otley, 2009; Malmi & Brown, 2008). In addition, new concepts and measurement scales have been proposed to capture the characteristics of advanced organizations (Anderson & Lillis, 2011; Simons, 2005).

To clarify the relationship between organizational characteristics and MCS, Question 4 investigates the levers of organizational design and corporate frugality, which are newly proposed concepts, as features of major organizational units.

Table 3.19 presents the results of questions on corporate frugality. Corporate frugality is a concept developed by Anderson and Lillis (2011) to an enduring corporate trait of consistent, disciplined management of spending to achieve long-term strategic objectives and sustainable profits (Anderson & Lillis, p. 1350). This concept is categorized into three sub-concepts: spending discipline, resourceful reuse, and deferred gratification. The questions were created with reference to Anderson and Lillis (2011, p. 1358). Each item was measured on a seven-point scale from "1: not at all" to "4: neutral" to "7: absolutely agree."

Table 3.20 shows the results of survey questions on the levers of organizational design (organizational mechanisms). The questions were created with reference to the description of an interactive network, which was proposed by Simons (2005) as

Table 3.19 Corporate frugality [Q4 (A)]

	n	Mean	SD	Median	Min	Max
Spending discipline ($n = 258$, $\alpha = .853$) *Employees and managers of this company...* (3) Are disciplined in their use of company resources	258	5.18	1.13	5	2	7
(2) Try to get the most from company money	258	5.14	1.15	5	2	7
(4) Work hard to contain costs	258	5.04	1.17	5	1	7
(1) Are careful in how they spend company money	258	4.91	1.21	5	2	7
(5) Plan carefully before spending	258	4.86	1.16	5	2	7
Resourceful reuse ($n = 256$, $\alpha = .836$) *Employees and managers of this company...* (7) Emphasize waste reduction	258	5.19	1.14	5	2	7
(8) Try to reuse or redeploy existing resources rather than buying new resources	258	4.92	1.06	5	1	7
(6) Understand that maintaining company assets saves money in the long run	257	4.75	1.15	5	1	7
(9) In this company there is significant emphasis on recycling and reuse	257	4.55	1.21	5	1	7
Deferred gratification ($n = 257$, $\alpha = .698$) *Employees and managers of this company...* (10) Spend money in the short run to save money in the long run	257	4.47	1.18	5	1	7
(11) Manage costs for the long run, not the short run	258	4.40	1.20	4	1	7

one of the levers of organizational design. Each item was measured on a seven-point scale from "1: not at all" to "4: neutral" to "7: absolutely agree." However, since this concept and measurement scale are not clarified in Simons (2005), Cronbach's alpha coefficient is not reported in Table 3.20.

3.6 Leadership of Managers [Question 5 (A)]

In recent years, several studies have analyzed the relationship between leadership and MCS (e.g., Abernethy et al., 2010). In addition, managers of Japanese companies have adopted various leadership styles (Yokota et al., 2012).

In Question 5 (A), leadership styles of consideration and initiating structure, and transformational leadership were studied to clarify the relationship between leadership and MCS concerning the leadership of organizational unit managers.

Table 3.21 shows the results of survey questions about leadership styles of consideration and initiating structure of managers of major organizational units. The questions were created with reference to Abernethy et al. (2010, p. 14). Table 3.22 shows the results of survey questions about transformational leadership of managers of major organizational units. The questions were created with

Table 3.20 Levers of organizational design (organizational mechanisms) [Q4 (B)]

	n	Mean	SD	Median	Min	Max
(11) Top managers demand a very high standard of organizational objectives from major organizational units	258	5.38	1.05	6	1	7
(10) Actively promoting information sharing with other organizational units within the company will lead to improved business performance of major organizational units	258	5.33	1.08	5	1	7
(7) Even if there is a failure, the next success will lead to recovery in the next internal evaluation	258	5.19	1.01	5	1	7
(2) There is a high level of work-related interdependency with other organizational units in the company	258	4.93	1.32	5	1	7
(5) The success of departments, managers, or employees within major organizational units is evenly distributed	258	4.90	1.04	5	1	7
(8) There is an atmosphere of wanting to implement good ideas in the organization	258	4.84	1.17	5	1	7
(9) There is a high level of self-sufficiency in the management activities of major organizational units	258	4.77	1.30	5	1	7
(6) Rather than acting in the interest of profits for a major organizational unit, actions that take company-wide profits into consideration are valued	258	4.76	1.22	5	1	7
(4) When another organizational unit in the company is having difficulties, value is placed on helping that unit when it is possible to do so	258	4.67	1.20	5	1	7
(3) The transfer of managers and employees to other organizational units is actively promoted	258	4.35	1.34	5	1	7
(1) Transfer prices are set after negotiations with other organizational units in the company and transactions are performed	258	3.72	1.87	4	1	7

reference to Yokota et al. (2012, p. 128). Transformational leadership can be categorized into four sub-concepts: idealized influence, inspirational motivation, intellectual stimulation, and individual consideration. In Tables 3.21 and 3.22, each item was measured on a seven-point scale from "1: not at all" to "4: neutral" to "7: absolutely agree."[10]

[10] Whereas Yokota et al. (2012) and Abernethy et al. (2010) question the subordinates' awareness of the leadership of their superiors, this survey enquired about the awareness of the person in charge of management control regarding the leadership of the managers of major organizational units.

Table 3.21 Leadership styles of consideration and initiating structure of managers of major organizational units [Question 5 (A) First part]

	n	Mean	SD	Median	Min	Max
Consideration ($n = 253$, $\alpha = .874$) (3) I clearly show my attitude to subordinates	254	5.35	1.01	5	1	7
(2) Suggestions from subordinates are incorporated	253	5.21	.96	5	1	7
(4) Subordinates are notified of changes in circumstances in advance	254	5.13	1.01	5	1	7
(1) I try out my ideas with my subordinates	253	5.02	1.00	5	1	7
Initiating structure ($n = 253$, $\alpha = .752$) (8) Subordinates are required to follow standard rules and regulations	254	5.35	1.04	5	1	7
(5) I make sure subordinates understand what is expected of them	254	5.29	.99	5	1	7
(7) Definite performance standards are always indicated	253	5.11	1.14	5	1	7
(6) Subordinates are encouraged to follow the uniform procedures	254	4.92	1.18	5	1	7

3.7 Managerial Behavior [Question 5 (B)]

Managers are central to the concept of MCS, and it is thought that there are various interactions between managerial behavior and MCS (Ferreira & Otley, 2009; Merchant & Otley, 2007). The discussion of the levers of organizational design in Simons (2005) assumes that managerial behaviors play an important role in network construction.

In Question 5 (B), to clarify the relationship between managerial behavior and MCS, behaviors of managers of major organizational units that contribute to network construction were examined.

Table 3.23 shows the results of questions about the degree that managers of major organizational units encourage subordinates to construct personal networks. The questions were created with reference to Takada and Yokota (2010). Table 3.24 shows the results of survey questions on the levers of organizational design (behavior of managers of major organizational units). The questions were created with reference to Simons (2005). Each item in Tables 3.23 and 3.24 was measured on a seven-point scale from "1: not at all" to "4: neutral" to "7: absolutely agree." Since these concepts and measurement scales have not been clarified in previous studies, Cronbach's alpha coefficient was not calculated in either Table 3.23 or Table 3.24.

Table 3.22 Transformational leadership of managers of major organizational units [Question 5 (A) Second part]

	n	Mean	SD	Median	Min	Max
Idealized influence ($n = 253$, $\alpha = .843$) (10) Specifies the importance of having a strong sense of purpose	254	5.23	1.05	5	1	7
(12) Emphasizes the importance of having a collective sense of mission	254	5.14	1.05	5	1	7
(11) Considers the moral and ethical consequences of decisions	253	5.12	1.11	5	1	7
(9) Talks about his/her most important values and beliefs	254	4.69	1.09	5	1	7
Inspirational motivation ($n = 253$, $\alpha = .798$) (14) Talks enthusiastically about what needs to be accomplished	253	5.02	1.02	5	1	7
(16) Expresses confidence that goals will be achieved	254	4.96	1.01	5	1	7
(15) Articulates a compelling vision of the future	254	4.91	1.16	5	1	7
(13) Talks optimistically about the future	254	4.02	1.10	4	1	7
Intellectual stimulation ($n = 254$, $\alpha = .916$) (19) Gets me to look at problems from many different angles	254	4.90	1.14	5	1	7
(18) Seeks different perspectives when solving problems	254	4.87	1.10	5	1	7
(17) Re-examines critical assumptions to question whether they are appropriate	254	4.83	1.06	5	1	7
(20) Suggests new ways of looking at how to complete assignments	254	4.76	1.06	5	1	7
Individual consideration ($n = 253$, $\alpha = .889$) (24) Helps me to develop my strengths	253	5.17	1.02	5	1	7
(22) Treats me as an individual rather than just as a member of a group	253	5.02	1.06	5	1	7
(23) Considers me as having different needs, abilities, and aspirations from others	253	4.83	1.09	5	1	7
(21) Spends time teaching and coaching	254	4.64	1.10	5	1	7

3.8 Conclusion

This study reports the results of a mail-based questionnaire survey conducted to clarify the status of MCS in Japanese companies concerning budgeting, business environment, organizational characteristics, and managerial leadership and behaviors. In the future, the plan is to conduct empirical research to analyze these results in detail.

Table 3.23 Degree that managers of major organizational units encourage subordinates to construct personal networks [Question 5 (B) First part]

	n	Mean	SD	Median	Min	Max
(5) Managers and employees of major organizational units are actively involved in company-wide projects	258	5.23	1.04	5	1	7
(4) Encouraging subordinates to actively share information with other organizational units within the company will lead to improved business performance of major organizational units	258	5.09	.99	5	1	7
(1) Creating personal networks outside the company is encouraged	258	5.04	1.22	5	1	7
(2) People who have broad personal networks outside the company are highly valued	258	4.74	1.20	5	1	7
(3) Mechanisms are created so that subordinates are able to actively create external networks	257	4.32	1.12	4	1	7

Table 3.24 Levers of organizational design (behavior of managers of major organizational units) [Question 5 (B) Second part]

	n	Mean	SD	Median	Min	Max
(8) The level of individual objectives required by the top managers for major organizational unit managers is extremely high	258	5.23	1.02	5	2	7
(7) Managers of major organizational units have a keen interest in the expenses allocated by the head office	258	4.88	1.23	5	1	7
(6) The responsibility held by managers of major organizational units exceeds their authority	257	4.57	1.16	4	1	7

References

Abernethy, M. A., Bouwens, J., & van Lent, L. (2010). Leadership and control system design. *Management Accounting Research, 21*(1), 2–16.

Anderson, S. W., & Lillis, A. M. (2011). Corporate frugality: Theory, measurement and practice. *Contemporary Accounting Research, 28*(4), 1349–1387.

Bouwens, J., & van Lent, L. (2007). Assessing the performance of business unit managers. *Journal of Accounting Research, 45*(4), 667–697.

Chenhall, R. H. (2007). Theorizing contingencies in management control systems research. In C. S. Chapman, A. G. Hopwood, & M. D. Shields (Eds.), *Handbook of management accounting research* (Vol. 1, pp. 163–206). Elsevier.

Ekholm, B. G., & Wallin, J. (2011). The impact of uncertainty and strategy on the perceived usefulness of fixed and flexible budgets. *Journal of Business Finance & Accounting, 38*(1/2), 145–166.

Ferreira, A., & Otley, D. T. (2009). The design and use of performance management systems: An extended framework for analysis. *Management Accounting Research, 20*(4), 263–282.

Hansen, S. C., Otley, D. T., & Van der Stede, W. A. (2003). Practice developments in budgeting: An overview and research perspective. *Journal of Management Accounting Research, 15*, 95–116.

Hansen, S. C., & Van der Stede, W. A. (2004). Multiple facets of budgeting: An exploratory analysis. *Management Accounting Research, 15*(4), 415–439.

Hope, J., & Fraser, R. (2003). *Beyond budgeting: How managers can break free from the annual performance trap*. Harvard Business School Press.

Hoque, Z. (2004). A contingency model of the association between strategy, environmental uncertainty and performance measurement: Impact on organizational performance. *International Business Review, 13*(4), 485–502.

Libby, T., & Lindsay, R. M. (2010). Beyond budgeting or budgeting reconsidered? A survey of North American budgeting practice. *Management Accounting Research, 21*(1), 56–75.

Malmi, T., & Brown, D. A. (2008). Management control systems as a package: Opportunities, challenges and research directions. *Management Accounting Research, 19*(4), 287–300.

Marginson, D., & Ogden, S. (2005). Coping with ambiguity through the budget: The positive effects of budgetary targets on managers' budgeting behaviours. *Accounting, Organizations and Society, 30*(5), 435–456.

Merchant, K. A., & Otley, D. T. (2007). A review of the literature on control and accountability. In C. S. Chapman, A. G. Hopwood, & M. D. Shields (Eds.), *Handbook of management accounting research* (Vol. 2, pp. 785–802). Elsevier.

Miki, R., Masuda, M., & Suzuki, K. (2003). Fact-finding survey of Japan's corporate budgeting system. 2002 (1): Survey tabulation and its bird's eye analysis. *Financial and Cost Accounting, 63*(1), 125–151. (in Japanese).

Moers, F. (2006). Performance measure properties and delegation. *The Accounting Review, 81*(4), 897–924.

Simons, R. (2005). *Levers of organization design: How managers use accountability systems for greater performance and commitment*. Harvard Business School Press.

Takada, A., & Yokota, E. (2010). The development of a network for female physicians' career continuity. *Japanese Journal of Administrative Science, 23*(1), 15–26. (in Japanese).

Van der Stede, W. A. (2000). The relationship between two consequences of budgetary controls: Budgetary slack creation and managerial short-term orientation. *Accounting, Organizations and Society, 25*(6), 609–622.

Yokota, E., Sato, Y., Yoneyama, S., & Senoo, T. (2012). A survey of leadership styles in Japanese companies. *Mita Business Review, 54*(6), 115–136. (in Japanese).

Yokota, E., & Senoo, T. (2011). A survey of leadership styles in Japanese companies. *Mita Business Review, 53*(6), 55–79. (in Japanese).

Chapter 4
A Survey of Performance Management Systems in Japanese Companies

Eri Yokota, Takeyoshi Senoo, Shingo Takahashi, and Yusuke Goto

4.1 Introduction

In recent years, new theoretical frameworks for performance management systems have been proposed, such as the *balanced scorecard* (BSC; Kaplan & Norton, 2004, 2008) and *beyond budgeting* (Hope & Fraser, 2003). However, there are few factual investigations based on previous studies that clarify the overall picture of the performance management systems of Japanese companies. Therefore, to clarify the details of performance management systems in Japanese companies and the factors expected to affect these systems, we conducted a mail-based questionnaire survey.

This chapter reports the main simple tabulation results of the survey. Specifically, this is a report on the results of a survey regarding the organizational structure of major business units (divisional organization, etc.) and the importance of performance measures, the process for setting performance targets and levels, how to use

Reprinted with permission of The Society of Business and Commerce, Keio University. Originally published in *Mita Business Review* 55(6): 67–87, 2013 (in Japanese).

E. Yokota (✉)
Faculty of Business and Commerce, Keio University, Tokyo, Japan
e-mail: yokota@fbc.keio.ac.jp

T. Senoo
Faculty of Commerce, Chuo University, Tokyo, Japan
e-mail: senoo81@tamacc.chuo-u.ac.jp

S. Takahashi
Faculty of Science and Engineering, Waseda University, Tokyo, Japan
e-mail: shingo@waseda.jp

Y. Goto
Faculty of Electronic Information Systems, Systems Engineering and Science, Shibaura Institute of Technology, Tokyo, Japan
e-mail: y-goto@shibaura-it.ac.jp

© Springer Nature Singapore Pte Ltd. 2023

E. Yokota (ed.), *Frontiers of Japanese Management Control Systems*, Translational Systems Sciences 32, https://doi.org/10.1007/978-981-19-9778-5_4

performance management systems and their characteristics, the performance evaluation process at the end of the year, and the factors that are expected to have an impact.

4.2 Survey Method

In November 2009, we conducted a mail-based questionnaire survey of 1700 companies listed on the First Section of the Tokyo Stock Exchange (including 143 major operating companies[1]), entitled "Factual Investigation on Performance Management of Major Business Units in Japanese Companies." The surveys were addressed to the primary representative of each company (such as the president), and we requested a response from those in charge of major business units (such as the general manager of a business division).

The final number of companies responding, including those whose responses were received after the deadline, was 68 (response rate 4.0%). The survey method appears to be problematic because the response rate was low; moreover, the respondents were not responsible for major business units and instead were managers of the Corporate Planning Department or other departments.[2] However, as mentioned above, few surveys have clarified the overall picture of performance management systems in Japanese companies, and thus it is meaningful to publish these results.

This chapter presents the descriptive statistics of the survey results in tables after the previous studies referenced are described. The abbreviations in the table are as follows: "*n*" is the number of valid responses, "Mean" is the mean value, "SD" is the standard deviation, "Median" is the median value, "Min" is the minimum value, and "Max" is the maximum value. Most of the question items were measured using a seven-point scale. The questions in the table are not presented in the order in which they were presented in the questionnaire; rather, they are sorted from high to low using the ratio of the number of responses to the total number of valid answers or the mean value. Most question items were measured on a seven-point scale. In some cases, the respondents were not responsible for major business units, so the survey results for Question 5 about the psychological and behavioral performance of major business unit managers are omitted.

[1]For pure holding company systems, which were identified in advance using company websites, past newspaper/magazine articles, company names, etc., the surveys were sent to the major operating companies and not to the holding company. The company with the largest sales or capital in each corporate group was selected as the major operating company. However, if there were multiple large companies in a corporate group, multiple companies were selected.

[2]When a non-response bias test was performed, non-response bias was confirmed.

Table 4.1 Organizational structure of major business units [Q1 (B)]

	n	%
1. Product/business divisional organization	34	51.5
3. Functional organization	13	19.7
2. Regional divisional organization	9	13.6
4. Matrix organization	4	6.1
6. Major operating company	3	4.5
5. Company in a company system	2	3.0
7. Other	1	1.5
Total	66	100.0

4.3 Importance of Organizational Structure and Performance Measures (Question 1)

In recent years, researchers have focused on the relationship between performance management systems and organizational structures (Ferreira & Otley, 2009; Malmi & Brown, 2008). There is a relationship between the degree to which authority is delegated in the organizational structure and the importance of performance measures (Bouwens & van Lent, 2007). Question 1 investigates the organizational structure of major business units and the importance of performance measures.

4.3.1 Organizational Structure

The results of investigating the organizational structures of major business units are shown in Table 4.1 and indicate that 51.5% of the companies adopted product/business divisional organization. When combined with regional divisional organization (13.6%), 65.1% of companies adopted a divisional organization that is not separated according to function; only 19.7% of the companies adopted functional organization for major business units. This indicates that there is also some use of the "functional division form" (Kagono, 1993), which is a characteristic of the Japanese business division organization. Few companies adopted a matrix organization or company system.

Next, regarding the degree of delegation of authority to those responsible for major business units, question items were developed with reference to Bouwens and van Lent (2007) using a seven-point scale (from "1: I have no authority at all" to "7: I have complete authority"). The results in Table 4.2 show the degree of delegation of authority ranked from higher to lower was as follows: marketing decisions (e.g., pricing decisions), strategic decisions (e.g., development of new products/services, enter and develop new markets), investment decisions (e.g., capital investment, development of new information systems), human resource decisions (e.g., hiring, compensation), and financing decisions (e.g., borrowing, stock issuance). Excluding

Table 4.2 Degree of authority delegated to those responsible for major business units [Q 1 (C)]

	n	Mean	SD	Min	Max	Median
(3) Marketing decisions	68	5.25	1.84	1	7	6
(1) Strategic decisions	68	5.10	1.52	1	7	6
(2) Investment decisions	68	4.75	1.45	1	7	5
(4) Human resource decisions	68	4.56	1.73	1	7	5
(5) Financing decisions	68	3.24	2.03	1	7	3.5

Table 4.3 Importance of performance measures for major business units

	n	Mean	SD	Min	Max	Median
(5) Profit	68	6.74	.51	5	7	7
(3) Profit margin on sales	68	6.26	.92	3	7	7
(4) Sales	68	6.18	.88	4	7	6
(6) Customer-related measures	68	5.81	1.06	3	7	6
(7) Business process-related measures	68	5.81	1.03	3	7	6
(2) Return on capital	67	4.70	1.56	1	7	5
(1) Economic profit	68	4.66	1.43	2	7	5

financing decisions, the mean value is above four points, which indicates there is a tendency to delegate some authority to those in charge of major business units.

4.3.2 *Importance of Performance Measures*

Regarding the importance of performance measures for major business units, the questions refer to Bouwens and van Lent (2007) and Shimizu (2007) and use a seven-point scale (from "1: not important at all" to "7: extremely important"). The results shown in Table 4.3 rank importance from high to low in the following order: sales/profit-related financial measures, such as profit (e.g., operating income, ordinary income, net business income); profit margin on sales (e.g., operating profit margin, ordinary profit margin); sales (ordinary revenue, operating revenue); non-financial measures such as customer-related measures (e.g., market share, customer satisfaction) and business process-related measures (e.g., quality, productivity); and accounting return indicators (Bouwens & van Lent, 2007) such as return on capital (e.g., return on assets (ROA), return on equity (ROE) and economic profit (e.g., economic value added (EVA^{TM}), residual income).

4.4 Process for Setting Performance Targets and Levels

Question 2 investigated the planning stage of the performance management system for each major business unit; specifically, the actual process for setting performance targets and levels.

4.4.1 Performance Target-Setting Process

Questions regarding the process for setting performance objectives were developed with reference to Hartmann and Slapničar (2009) and use a seven-point scale (from "1: not at all" to "7: absolutely agree"). As shown in Table 4.4, the mean value is high for items indicating objective methods that emphasize financial objectives and documenting performance objectives. The mean value is relatively low for items indicating subjective methods that emphasize non-financial (quantitative) or qualitative objectives. This indicates there is a tendency to emphasize objectivity in setting performance targets.

Next, the survey included questions regarding the relationship between performance targets and strategic objectives, with reference to Shimizu (2007) and Yoshida et al. (2009). The results in Table 4.5 show that the importance of financial and non-financial measurement maps, such as strategy maps (Kaplan & Norton, 2004), is relatively low compared to the importance of consistency with strategic objectives.

Questions about the degree of participation in the performance target-setting process were hierarchical and use a seven-point scale (from "1: not at all" to "7: absolutely agree"). As shown in Table 4.6, the degree of participation ranks top management highest, followed by operating managers, and then general employees.

Table 4.4 Process of setting performance targets [Q 2 (A)]

	n	Mean	SD	Min	Max	Median
(2) Emphasis on financial objectives	67	6.57	.68	4	7	7
(1) Document performance objectives	67	6.51	.93	3	7	7
(3) Emphasis on non-financial (quantitative) objectives	67	5.09	1.65	1	7	5
(4) Emphasis on objectives in qualitative terms	67	4.34	1.66	1	7	4

Table 4.5 Relationship between performance targets and strategic objectives [Q 2 (A)]

	n	Mean	SD	Min	Max	Median
(5) Emphasis is placed on aligning the performance targets and strategic objectives of each business unit	67	5.73	1.15	3	7	6
(6) Emphasis is placed on maps showing the relationship between financial and non-financial objectives	67	4.01	1.42	1	7	4

Table 4.6 Degree of participation in the performance target-setting process [Q 2 (A)]

	n	Mean	SD	Min	Max	Median
(7) Top managers participate fully	66	6.27	1.00	3	7	7
(8) Operating managers participate fully	66	5.53	1.34	3	7	6
(9) General employees participate fully	66	4.11	1.70	1	7	4

Table 4.7 Criteria for setting performance targets for major business units [Q 2 (B)]

	n	Mean	SD	Min	Max	Median
(1) Performance target levels are set based on the results of the previous year	67	5.22	1.07	2	7	5
(2) Performance target levels are set at a zero baseline	67	3.72	1.64	1	7	4

Table 4.8 Performance target levels [Q 2 (B)]

	n	Mean	SD	Min	Max	Median
(3) Performance target levels reflect the expectations of shareholders	67	4.81	1.20	2	7	5
(4) Performance target levels are more challenging than those of competitors	67	4.55	1.33	1	7	4
(5) Performance target levels are challenging compared to "other" business units	65	4.34	1.31	1	7	4

This clearly shows that as one rises in an organizational hierarchy, the degree of participation in the performance target-setting process also tends to increase.

4.4.2 *Performance Target Levels*

Regarding performance target levels for major business units, the survey first asked about the criteria used to set the targets using a seven-point scale (from "1: not at all" to "7: absolutely agree"). As shown in Table 4.7, more responses indicate setting the performance target level is based on the results of the previous year, as compared to cases in which the levels are set at a zero baseline.

Next, questions addressed the level of performance target using a seven-point scale (from "1: not at all" to "7: absolutely agree"). Table 4.8 presents these results, which indicate the mean values of the items that reflect shareholder expectations and items that are challenging compared to competitors and other business units are greater than four, which suggests that performance target levels tend to be somewhat high.

Furthermore, the rigidity of performance target levels was investigated using a seven-point scale (from "1: not at all" to "7: absolutely agree"). The results in Table 4.9 show that the mean values of the items that indicate frequent change and being fixed throughout the year are less than four, which indicates that although

Table 4.9 Rigidity of performance targets [Q 2 (B)]

	n	Mean	SD	Min	Max	Median
(7) Performance target levels change frequently to respond to changes in the environment	67	3.81	1.65	1	7	4
(6) Performance target levels are fixed throughout the year	67	3.39	1.84	1	7	3

performance target levels are not completely fixed, the frequency of change is not very high.

4.5 How the Performance Management System and Its Characteristics Are Used (Question 3)

Among Simon's (1995, 2000) four levers of control in performance management systems, there has been an increase in research focusing on differences in how diagnostic control systems and interactive control systems are used (e.g., Widener, 2007). In addition, as a characteristics of performance management systems, it is clear that comprehensive performance measurement systems, such as the BSC, are effective (Hall, 2008). Furthermore, discussions about interactive control systems and the BSC suggest that meetings regarding performance management systems are important (Kaplan & Norton, 2008; Simons, 1995, 2000). Therefore, Question 3 examines how the performance management system is used and its characteristics.

4.5.1 How the Performance Management System Is Used

Questions about how performance management systems are used were set with reference to Widener (2007). Diagnostic control systems were examined using a seven-point scale (from "1: not used at all" to "7: always use") and interactive control systems were surveyed using a seven-point scale ("1: not at all" to "7: absolutely agree"). As shown in Tables 4.10 and 4.11, the mean value of the items in Table 4.11, other than (2) in [Q3 (B)], exceeds 5, which indicates there is a tendency to use the performance management system both diagnostically and interactively.[3]

[3]Cronbach's alpha coefficient for the diagnostic control system, measured with 10 questions, is .903; and Cronbach's alpha coefficient for the interactive control system, measured with seven questions, is .748.

Table 4.10 Diagnostic control system [Q 3 (A)]

	n	Mean	SD	Min	Max	Median
(3) Compare outcomes to expectations	67	6.42	.80	4	7	7
(1) Track progress toward goals	67	6.40	.87	4	7	7
(2) Monitor results	67	5.90	1.21	3	7	6
(9) Enable the entire business unit to focus on common issues	67	5.81	1.16	2	7	6
(7) Provide a common view of the business units	67	5.67	1.05	2	7	6
(5) Enable discussion in meetings of superiors, subordinates, and peers	67	5.48	1.32	2	7	6
(8) Tie the business units together	67	5.39	1.22	2	7	6
(6) Enable continual challenge and debate of underlying data, assumptions, and action plans	67	5.37	1.22	2	7	6
(10) Develop a common vocabulary in the business units	67	5.06	1.42	1	7	5
(4) Review key performance indicators	67	5.01	1.63	1	7	5

Table 4.11 Interactive control system [Q 3 (B)]

	n	Mean	SD	Min	Max	Median
(7) Top management encourages operating managers to achieve their objectives autonomously	67	5.66	1.09	3	7	6
(4) Top management pays day-to-day attention to the performance management system	67	5.60	1.22	1	7	6
(5) Top management interprets the information from the performance management system by themselves	67	5.55	1.17	2	7	6
(1) Top management pays attention to the performance management system only when exceptional matters occur (R)	67	5.39	1.53	1	7	6
(3) Operating managers are involved infrequently and on an exception basis with the performance management system (R)	67	5.30	1.34	2	7	6
(6) Operating managers are frequently involved with the performance management system	67	5.30	1.34	2	7	6
(2) Top management relies heavily on staff specialists in preparing and interpreting information from the performance management system (R)	67	4.28	1.40	1	7	4

Note: (R) indicates reverse-scored items. The numbers in the table have been reversed

4.5.2 Characteristics of the Performance Management System

To examine the extent of comprehensive performance management systems, questions about the characteristics of the performance management system were developed with reference to Hall (2008), using a seven-point scale (from "1: not at all" to "7: absolutely agree"). The results, as shown in Table 4.12, indicate the mean values

Table 4.12 Comprehensive performance management system [Q 3 (C)]

	n	Mean	SD	Min	Max	Median
(6) Links together the activities of your business unit to the achievement of the goals and objectives of the organization	68	5.60	1.20	3	7	6
(3) Provides a diverse set of financial and non-financial measures related to the key performance areas of the business unit	67	5.43	1.16	3	7	5
(7) Provides a variety of information about important aspects of the business unit's operations	68	5.32	1.20	2	7	5.5
(2) Information is fully documented and provides a record for evaluating performance	68	5.26	1.29	2	7	5
(5) Provides information on different dimensions of the business unit's financial and non-financial performance	68	5.15	1.21	2	7	5
(4) Provides links between the current operating performance of your business unit and the long-term strategies of the organization	68	5.15	1.23	2	7	5
(1) Provides a broad range of performance information about different areas of the business unit	68	5.09	1.29	2	7	5
(9) Provides a range of financial and non-financial measures that cover the critical areas of the business unit's operations	68	5.06	1.24	2	7	5
(8) Shows how the activities of your business unit affect the activities of "other" units within the organization	68	4.29	1.43	1	7	1

Table 4.13 Regular and formal meetings [Q3 (D)]

	n	%
1. Are held	63	92.6
2. Are not held	5	7.4
Total	68	100.0

of items other than (8) in Q3 (C) exceed 5, suggesting that performance management systems tend to be somewhat comprehensive.[4]

4.5.3 *Meetings and Performance Management Systems*

We examined whether regular and formal meetings attended by both top managers of major business units and operating managers are held as part of the performance management system. The results, as shown in Table 4.13, indicate that most companies (92.6%) hold regular and formal meetings.

[4]Cronbach's alpha coefficient for the comprehensive performance management system, measured with nine questions, is .916.

Table 4.14 Importance of discussing strategic uncertainty in meetings [Q 3 (E)]

	n	Mean	SD	Min	Max	Median
(1) Changes in product/service technology	63	5.41	1.30	2	7	5
(3) Market tactics of competitors	63	5.40	1.31	1	7	6
(7) Input costs	63	5.37	1.47	2	7	6
(5) Scale effects of products and services	63	5.35	1.26	2	7	6
(8) Internal product and service innovation	63	5.21	1.30	2	7	6
(6) Scope effects of products and services	62	4.87	1.26	2	7	5
(4) Entry of new companies	63	4.33	1.56	1	7	4
(2) Introduction of products and services to adjacent industries	63	4.27	1.56	1	7	4

Table 4.15 Performance evaluation method [Q 4 (A)]

	n	Mean	SD	Min	Max	Median
(2) Emphasis on financial results	67	6.25	.91	1	7	6
(1) Document performance results	67	6.15	1.33	1	7	7
(3) Emphasis on non-financial (quantitative) results	67	4.91	1.42	2	7	5
(4) Emphasis on results in qualitative terms	67	4.31	1.17	1	7	4

Next, regarding the importance of discussing strategic uncertainty (Simons, 2000) in the meetings, questions were set with reference to Widener (2007) using a seven-point scale ("1: not important at all" to "7: extremely important"). The results, as shown in Table 4.14, indicate that the mean values are high for items such as changes in product/service technology, marketing tactics of competitors, and input costs; this indicates there is a tendency to emphasize the three categories of strategic uncertainty identified by Widener (2007): technological, competitive, and operational uncertainty.

4.6 Performance Evaluation Process at the End of the Year (Question 4)

Section 4.4 shows the results of questions about the planning stage of the performance management system. Question 4 examines the evaluation stage of the performance management system of each major business unit; specifically, the performance evaluation process at the end of the year.

Questions about the performance evaluation method were set with reference to Hartmann and Slapničar (2009) and others using a seven-point scale (from "1: not at all" to "7: absolutely agree"). As shown in Table 4.15, the mean value is high for items that indicate objective methods that emphasize financial results and documenting performance evaluation results. The mean value is relatively low for items that indicate subjective methods that emphasize non-financial (quantitative) or

Table 4.16 Importance of processes and results in performance evaluation [Q 4 (A)]

	n	Mean	SD	Min	Max	Median
(6) Performance evaluation is results-oriented	67	5.64	1.03	2	7	6
(5) Performance evaluation is process-oriented	67	4.28	1.37	2	7	1

Table 4.17 Verification of the relationship between non-financial and financial objectives [Q 4 (A)]

	n	Mean	SD	Min	Max	Median
(7) Relationship between non-financial and financial objectives is verified	66	4.35	1.33	1	7	1

Table 4.18 Criteria for performance evaluations [Q 4 (A)]

	n	Mean	SD	Min	Max	Median
(9) Performance evaluation emphasizes comparison with pre-set performance objectives	67	6.01	.93	2	7	6
(8) Performance evaluation is based on formal rules set in advance within the organization	67	5.69	1.43	1	7	6
(10) Performance evaluation emphasizes comparison with competitor performance	67	3.60	1.51	1	7	4
(11) Performance evaluation emphasizes comparison with the performance of "other" business units	67	3.55	1.47	1	7	4

qualitative results. Together, these results indicate that there is a tendency to place more importance on objective evaluations of performance.

Next, the importance of processes and results in performance evaluation was investigated using a seven-point scale (from "1: not at all" to "7: absolutely agree"). The results, shown in Table 4.16, suggest that process is important, but results tend to be more important.

In addition, questions were presented to verify the relationship between non-financial objectives and financial objectives using a seven-point scale (from "1: not at all" to "7: absolutely agree"). The results, shown in Table 4.17, indicate the mean value is above four, suggesting there is some tendency to verify the relationship between non-financial objectives and financial objectives.

Furthermore, the criteria for performance evaluations were investigated using a seven-point scale (from "1: not at all" to "7: absolutely agree"). The results, as reported in Table 4.18, show that there is an emphasis on pre-set performance objectives; the mean value of the items that indicate evaluation is based on formal rules is high, and the mean value is relatively low for items that place importance on comparisons to the performance of competitors and other business units. These results may reflect that it is not always easy to perform a relative performance evaluation.

In addition, feedback on performance evaluation results was examined using a seven-point scale (from "1: not at all" to "7: absolutely agree"). The results, as shown

Table 4.19 Feedback on performance evaluation results [Q 4 (A)]

	n	Mean	SD	Min	Max	Median
(13) Appropriate feedback of performance evaluation results to subordinates	66	5.83	1.10	2	7	6
(12) Performance evaluation results are properly fed back to me	66	5.76	1.23	2	7	6

Table 4.20 Relationship between performance evaluation results and compensation [Q 4 (B)]

	n	Mean	SD	Min	Max	Median
(2) Bonus	67	5.79	1.31	1	7	6
(3) Promotion	66	5.23	1.11	2	7	6
(4) Advancement	65	5.17	1.21	1	7	6
(1) Basic salary	67	4.90	1.49	1	7	5
(5) Internal reputation	66	4.68	1.33	1	7	4

in Table 4.19, indicate there is a tendency to give appropriate feedback to both subordinates and oneself.

Finally, regarding the relationship between performance evaluation results and compensation, questions were developed with reference to Bouwens and van Lent (2007) and others; this was measured using a seven-point scale (from "1: not related at all" to "7: extremely related"). As shown in Table 4.20, the mean value of not only the bonus and basic salary, but all items, exceeds four, which indicates that there tends to be a strong relationship with non-monetary compensation, such as internal reputation.

4.7 Influential Factors (Question 6)

A performance management system is considered to change depending on factors such as the characteristics of the person in charge and the company's business environment. To clarify the actual conditions of performance management systems in Japanese companies, it is necessary to investigate whether the factors that are expected to have an influence actually do have influence. Therefore, Question 6 examines the factors that are expected to influence the performance management systems of each major business unit. Specifically, the question addressed the major business unit manager's degree of understanding regarding information, strategy (Auzair & Langfield-Smith, 2005; Chenhall & Langfield-Smith, 1998), and interdependence between business units (Bouwens & van Lent, 2007).

The factors expected to have an influence were examined using a seven-point scale for the major business unit manager's degree of understanding of the information needed for performance evaluation (from "1: do not understand at all" to "7: completely understand"). Table 4.21 shows that the mean value of all items

Table 4.21 Degree of understanding the information needed for performance evaluation [Q 6 (A)]

	n	Mean	SD	Min	Max	Median
(3) Achievements of the people who evaluate performance	68	5.76	.95	3	7	6
(2) Contents of the work of people who evaluate performance	68	5.74	.91	3	7	6
(1) Performance information flow	68	5.66	1.11	1	7	6
(4) Ability of people to evaluate performance	68	5.50	.92	3	7	6
(5) Career experience of people who evaluate performance	68	5.35	1.10	3	7	5

Table 4.22 Cost leadership strategy [Q 6 (B)]

	n	Mean	SD	Min	Max	Median
(2) Make products/services more cost-efficient	68	5.81	.90	3	7	6
(8) Improve the cost required for coordination of various products/services	68	5.44	1.10	2	7	5.5
(10) Improve the utilization of available assets and equipment	68	5.37	1.04	3	7	5
(5) Achieve lower cost of products/services than competitors	67	5.34	1.29	2	7	5

Table 4.23 Differentiation strategy [Q 6 (B)]

	n	Mean	SD	Min	Max	Median
(3) Provide high-quality products/services	68	6.06	.96	3	7	6
(1) Introduce new products/services quickly	68	5.68	1.07	3	7	6
(4) Customize products/services to customers' need	68	5.66	1.03	3	7	6
(6) Provide products/services that are distinct from that of competitors	68	5.54	1.10	3	7	6
(9) Provide after-sales services and support	68	5.28	1.41	2	7	5
(7) Offer a broader range of products/services than the competitors	68	5.28	1.21	2	7	5

exceeded five, and it is clear that managers of major business units tend to understand a range of information.

Next, questions regarding the strategies of major business units were set with reference to Auzair and Langfield-Smith (2005) and Chenhall and Langfield-Smith (1998), and the importance of strategic objectives based on Porter's (1985) cost leadership strategy and differentiation strategy was explored using a seven-point scale (from "1: not important at all" to "7: extremely important").

The results are shown in Tables 4.22 and 4.23; the mean value of all items exceeds five. Thus, it can be inferred that there is a tendency to emphasize the strategic objectives of both the cost leadership and differentiation strategies.

Furthermore, regarding the interdependence between business units, questions were set with reference to Bouwens and van Lent (2007) and examined using a

Table 4.24 Interdependence between business units [Q 6 (C)]

	n	Mean	SD	Min	Max	Median
(1) Business unit actions impact "other" business units	67	5.19	1.35	1	7	5
(2) The actions of "other" business units impact the business unit	67	4.99	1.32	1	7	5
(3) The business unit operates as a stand-alone business	68	4.50	1.90	1	7	5

seven-point scale (from "1: not at all" to "7: absolutely agree"). As shown in Table 4.24, the mean value of all items exceeds 4; thus, the business units influence each other, but there tends to be a high level of recognition that the main business units are operated as independent businesses.

4.8 Conclusion

This chapter reports the main simple tabulation results of a mail-based questionnaire survey conducted to clarify the actual conditions of performance management systems in Japanese companies and the factors that are expected to influence them. In the future, we plan to conduct a more detailed analysis of the results of this survey.

References

Auzair, S. M., & Langfield-Smith, K. (2005). The effect of service process type, business strategy and life cycle stage on bureaucratic MCS in service organizations. *Management Accounting Research, 16*(4), 399–421.

Bouwens, J., & van Lent, L. (2007). Assessing the performance of business unit managers. *Journal of Accounting Research, 45*(4), 667–697.

Chenhall, R. H., & Langfield-Smith, K. (1998). The relationship between strategic priorities, management techniques and management accounting: An empirical investigation using a systems approach. *Accounting, Organizations and Society, 23*(3), 141–163.

Ferreira, A., & Otley, D. T. (2009). The design and use of performance management systems: An extended framework for analysis. *Management Accounting Research, 20*(4), 263–282.

Hall, M. (2008). The effect of comprehensive performance measurement systems on role clarity, psychological empowerment and managerial performance. *Accounting, Organizations and Society, 33*(2–3), 141–163.

Hartmann, F., & Slapničar, S. (2009). How formal performance evaluation affects trust between superior and subordinate managers. *Accounting, Organizations and Society, 34*(6–7), 722–737.

Hope, J., & Fraser, R. (2003). *Beyond budgeting: How managers can break free from the annual performance trap*. Harvard Business School Press.

Kagono, K. (1993). Functional division form and internal markets. *Journal of Economics & Business Administration, 167*(2), 35–52. (in Japanese).

Kaplan, R. S., & Norton, D. P. (2004). *Strategy maps: Converting intangible assets into tangible outcomes*. Harvard Business School Press.

Kaplan, R. S., & Norton, D. P. (2008). *The execution premium: Linking strategy to operations for competitive advantage*. Harvard Business School Press.

Malmi, T., & Brown, D. A. (2008). Management control systems as a package: Opportunities, challenges and research directions. *Management Accounting Research, 19*(4), 287–300.

Porter, M. E. (1985). *Competitive advantage: Creating and sustaining superior performance*. Free Press.

Shimizu, T. (2007). Survey on business performance management in Japanese companies (Part 1). *Accounting, 59*(8), 74–82. (in Japanese).

Simons, R. (1995). *Levers of control: How managers use innovative control systems to drive strategic renewal*. Harvard Business School Press.

Simons, R. (2000). *Performance measurement and control systems for implementing strategy: Text and cases*. Prentice Hall.

Widener, S. K. (2007). An empirical analysis of the levers of control framework. *Accounting Organizations and Society, 32*(7–8), 757–788.

Yoshida, E., Fukushima, K., & Senoo, T. (2009). Management accounting in Japanese companies (2): Factual investigation of manufacturing industries. *Accounting, 61*(10), 134–140. (in Japanese).

Chapter 5
The Influence of Parent-Performance Management Systems on Subsidiaries' Decision-Making: Process of Parent-Performance Management Systems Use and Subsidiaries' External Embeddedness

Yudai Onitsuka

5.1 Introduction

Multinational companies' operations, including control over subsidiaries, are difficult to manage owing to differences and distances (i.e., physical, geographical, cultural, psychological, and so on) between headquarters and subsidiaries. In addition, market pressures owing to developing globalization urged multinational companies (MNCs) to redesign their strategies, structures, and processes (Ghoshal & Bartlett, 1996; Govindarajan & Gupta, 2000). Globalization forced MNCs to seek competitive advantage in the global market through more standardization and coordination within, while simultaneously needing flexibility and local responsiveness (Ezzamel et al., 1999). Moreover, the information and knowledge that subsidiaries can obtain from local environments are also important in generating a competitive advantage in the global market. Hence, headquarters should delegate decision-making capabilities to subsidiaries and encourage autonomy (McEvily & Zaheer, 1999).

The international business literature argues that to adapt to such complex environmental and managerial difficulties, MNCs developed considerably from a dominant headquarters with hierarchically controlled subsidiaries to a complex set of interdependent, globally dispersed entities structured as multifaceted networks (Dunning & Lundan, 2008; Harzing, 1999). MNCs thus face the challenge of balancing the delegation of decision-making authority to subsidiaries effectively, encouraging subsidiaries' autonomy and independence from headquarters, and coordinating global activities (Busco et al., 2008; Quattrone & Hopper, 2005; Roth & Kostova, 2003).

Y. Onitsuka (✉)
School of Business Administration, Tokai University, Kanagawa, Japan
e-mail: oy320225@tsc.u-tokai.ac.jp

© Springer Nature Singapore Pte Ltd. 2023

E. Yokota (ed.), *Frontiers of Japanese Management Control Systems*, Translational Systems Sciences 32, https://doi.org/10.1007/978-981-19-9778-5_5

When MNCs delegate decision-making authority to subsidiaries and encourage autonomy, headquarters must deploy control mechanisms that align subsidiaries' activities with the MNCs' global strategy and offer relevant information for managerial decision-making, both at headquarters and at the subsidiaries (Doz & Prahalad, 1984; Luo, 2005). Previously, some management accounting studies found that headquarters performance management systems (parent-PMS) are effective mechanisms to control subsidiaries and their activities within the firm's global strategy (Busco et al., 2008; Dossi & Patelli, 2008, 2010; Mahlendorf et al., 2012; Micheli et al., 2011). These studies argue that parent-PMS provide important information for decision-making at all levels because they reflect the firm's global strategy and intentions and allow MNCs to monitor and follow subsidiaries' activities. Parent-PMSs integrate subsidiaries' autonomous activities into overall corporate goals by assisting and influencing subsidiaries' decision-making (Mahlendorf et al., 2012). However, prior research does not completely show the effects of parent-PMS on subsidiaries, especially the mechanisms and processes of the effects of parent-PMSs on subsidiaries' decision-making (Busco et al., 2006). The evidence from prior research is mixed and inconsistent.

These issues can be attributed to two overlooked perspectives. First, prior studies rarely focus on the use of parent-PMS (Dossi & Patelli, 2008; Franco-Santos et al., 2012). While some do consider the use of parent-PMS (i.e., Dossi & Patelli, 2008; Mahlendorf et al., 2012), the results are limited because these studies focus on the purpose of the use of PM but not on the process of parent-PMS use. According to Ferreira and Otley (2009), this aspect is important for PMS research to clarify the effects and mechanisms of the influence of PMS within organizations. Moreover, when examining the influence of PMS on decision-makers, it is important to address the use of PMS (Langfield-Smith, 1997; Simons, 2000). Notwithstanding these arguments, most research focuses on the structural features and aspects of the PMS design, and thus unresolved issues remain about the effects of parent-PMS (Busco et al., 2006; Dossi & Patelli, 2008; Doz et al., 2001; Franco-Santos et al., 2012; Nørreklit & Schoenfeld, 2000; O'Donnell, 2000).

Second, although prior research explains that the effects of parent-PMS relate to the relational attributes of the multinational network (Dossi & Patelli, 2008), which does not sufficiently capture the relationship between headquarters and subsidiaries. Some international business studies argue that when investigating this relationship, it is necessary to focus not only on headquarters' control mechanisms but also on the external network, which influences subsidiaries' activities directly and indirectly (Andersson & Forsgren, 1996; Doz & Prahalad, 1993; Forsgren, 1989). Based on resource dependence theory, the characteristics of the networks of each subsidiary explain the different attributes of an MNC (Ghoshal & Bartlett, 1990, 1993). International business studies have noted that the external networks in which the subsidiaries are embedded, referred as external embeddedness, influence the headquarters' control mechanisms (Andersson & Forsgren, 1996; Andersson et al., 2001, 2005). Similarly, the management accounting literature suggests that the influence of parent-PMS on subsidiaries depends on subsidiaries' external embeddedness (Mahlendorf et al., 2012; Schäffer et al., 2014).

Therefore, this study investigates the influence of parent-PMS on subsidiaries' decision-making and the relationship between the use of parent-PMS and subsidiaries' external embeddedness. In particular, this study analyzes the moderating effects of the subsidiaries' external embeddedness on the cause-effect relation between parent-PMS and subsidiaries' decision-making by combining theoretical perspectives and the results of data analysis.

This chapter proceeds as follows: Sect. 5.2 reviews the PMS and international business literature and establishes the hypotheses, Sects. 5.3 and 5.4 describe the research methods and results, respectively, and Sect. 5.5 discusses the results, conclusion, contributions, limitations, and avenues for future research.

5.2 Theoretical Background and Hypotheses

5.2.1 The Process of PMS Use

In management accounting research, several authors define and categorize the use of PMS. Hopwood (1972) explains that firms use PMS to make use of accounting information to evaluate the performance of the organization and management. Similarly, Bourne et al. (2000) argue that the use of PMS is "split into two main subdivisions; first, the initial use to which they should be put is that of measuring the success of the implementation of that strategy, second, the information and feedback from the measures should be used to challenge the assumptions and test the validity of the strategy" (p. 758).

In addition to these procedural aspects, Simons (2000) explains the processes of the use of PMS by adopting the diagnostic and interactive control aspects of the levers of control concepts suggested by Simons (1995). In his explanation, the processes of the use of PMS relate to accounting information flow; specifically, how information on performance is communicated within organizations when measuring and evaluating performance, the feedback process, and reporting the results of activities to superiors. Henri (2006a) similarly points out that the aspect of accounting information flow is more important in the use of PMS. Moreover, Ferreira and Otley (2009) argue that "the use made of information and controls is a cornerstone of the PMS" (p. 274) and captures the use of PMS as a way to use accounting information and adopt control mechanisms. They also argue that it is more important to capture how and what types of control practices exist within organizations and the information flow processes in investigating the effects of PMS.

However, there is little research on parent-PMS and its use processes. For example, Dossi and Patelli (2008) and Mahlendorf et al. (2012) focus on the purpose of PMS; although, they do not consider accounting information flow and control practices within MNCs. Hence, it is unclear how headquarters can control subsidiaries' decisions and actions by using PMS.

Therefore, in this study, the use of PMS is seen not only in its procedural aspects (i.e., the purpose of PMS, measuring and evaluating performance, and reporting and explaining accountability) but also in its processes. In doing so, we refer to the "diagnostic use of PMS" and "interactive use of PMS" following Simons (1995, 2000) as a typology to capture the processes of PMS use by considering information flow and control practice by headquarters.

5.2.1.1 Diagnostic Use of PMS

Simons (1995) defines diagnostic control as managers' use of information systems to monitor organizational outcomes and correct deviations from pre-set standards of performance. Diagnostic PMS use is the setting of goals and key success factors as opposed to overall strategy, measuring outputs, analyzing variances, and using variance information to adjust activities (Simons, 2000). When managers use PMS diagnostically, they focus on and act to correct business units' and subordinates' activities only when meaningful issues occur and when they identify considerable deviations (Simons, 2000).

Diagnostic PMS use motivates employees to implement organizational strategy and integrate their activities to accomplish the organization's goals (Widener, 2007). Prior research suggests that employees' activities belong to categories that top managers expect or do not expect so employees can understand how to work to accomplish the organization's goals by using PMS diagnostically (Tuomela, 2005). Contrastingly, Henri (2006b) defines the diagnostic use of PMS as a set of formalized procedures that use information to maintain or alter patterns in an organizational activity and argues that the diagnostic use of PMS has important characteristics as a mechanistic control. Firms can enable tight control and elaborate information and communication flow by using a PMS that includes such characteristics, and thus the diagnostic use of PMS enhances decision-making capability (Koufteros et al., 2014).

Although there is no empirical evidence on the diagnostic use of parent-PMS in international business settings, we can assume that the effects of parent-PMS on the relationship between headquarters and subsidiaries correspond with the suggestions above. The headquarters sets global strategy and overall goals in advance and then monitors subsidiaries' activities by using the parent-PMS diagnostically, to integrate subsidiaries' activities into global strategy and the overall goals, similar to a non-international business setting. Hence, the headquarters can use PMS diagnostically to have a positive effect on subsidiaries' decision-making. Therefore, we propose our first hypothesis:

H1. The headquarters' diagnostic use of parent-PMS is positively correlated with the influence of parent-PMS on subsidiaries' decision-making.

5.2.1.2 Interactive Use of PMS

Simons (1995) defines interactive control as managers' use of information systems for their personal involvement in subordinates' decision-making activities. The interactive use of PMS is very different from diagnostic use. When managers use

PMS interactively, they constantly communicate their intent to subordinates and participate in subordinates' decision-making activities to adapt these activities to strategic uncertainties and to find opportunities to grow their business (Simons, 2000). Thus, in organizations in which managers use PMS interactively, all members are constantly interested in information about performance because communicating this information is a daily activity.

The distinct characteristics of the interactive use of PMS include frequent meetings and face-to-face discussions about performance between superiors and subordinates (Bisbe et al., 2007), which allow an organization to deal effectively with problems. Hence, interactively using PMS helps firms make decisions by communicating information about performance to decision-makers and sending signals throughout the organization (Abernethy & Brownell, 1999; Bisbe & Otley, 2004; Henri, 2006b). In addition, empirical evidence suggests that the interactive use of PMS enables headquarters to capture all of the activities and conditions within an organization and enhances decision-making capabilities, resulting in overall improved financial performance (Koufteros et al., 2014).

In MNCs, the headquarters' interactive use of PMS stimulates dialogue between headquarters and subsidiaries and enhances strategic alignment within an organization (Dossi & Patelli, 2010). Conversely, subsidiaries might understand the headquarter's intent, their decision-making, and the behaviors it expects. Therefore, our second hypothesis is as follows:

H2. The interactive use of parent-PMS by headquarters is positively correlated with the influence of parent-PMS on subsidiaries' decision-making.

5.2.2 *Embeddedness Perspective*

As mentioned in Sect. 5.1, we should account for the external network embeddedness, which affects both the subsidiaries' activities and the headquarters' control mechanisms, when investigating the relationship between headquarters and subsidiaries (Andersson & Forsgren, 1996; Doz & Prahalad, 1993; Forsgren, 1989). Polyani (1957) proposed embeddedness theory, which Granovetter (1985) developed further. The concept of embeddedness assumes that social structures have a significant influence on economic behavior. Granovetter (1985) argues that all economic behaviors have structural aspects and that a certain mechanism of one's behavior can be understood by considering the relations with others in social structures. Moreover, Granovetter (1992) argues that because an organization is embedded in social relations, it cannot behave freely like an "atom." Thus, an organization's behavior can be subject to relationships with others in social structures based on the degree that it is embedded in the social structures (Granovetter, 1992).

Most business studies, referring to embeddedness theory, focus on the influence of the network in which the organizations relate and their embeddedness in the network on organizations' behaviors, the structuring processes of resources and capabilities, and performance (Gulati, 1998, 1999). In the past two decades, some studies focused on the relationship between headquarters and subsidiaries concerning embeddedness theory and investigate the influence of subsidiaries' external embeddedness on their behaviors (e.g., Andersson & Forsgren, 1996; Mahlendorf et al., 2012; Schäffer et al., 2014). According to Andersson and Forsgren (1996), subsidiaries' external embeddedness is the extent to which they relate to local counterparts and is embedded in local networks. These studies argue that subsidiaries' external embeddedness significantly influences the effects of the control mechanisms implemented by headquarters to control subsidiaries' behaviors.

5.2.2.1 Interaction Effects of the Use of PMS and Subsidiaries' External Embeddedness

According to network and embeddedness theory, subsidiaries have two criteria when they decide on their behaviors (Forsgren et al., 2005; Ghoshal & Westney, 1993): the control mechanisms implemented by headquarters to integrate subsidiaries' behavior into global strategy and overall goals and the subsidiaries' embeddedness in local networks. When a subsidiary is highly embedded in local networks, it has more information and knowledge peculiar to the local market and behaves based on this information and knowledge. In this situation, the distances between headquarters and subsidiaries are extended, and headquarters will capture and understand subsidiaries' behaviors and norms less, and therefore cannot appropriately control their behaviors (Bouquet & Birkinshaw, 2008; Helliwell, 2002). Thus, it becomes more difficult for headquarters to control subsidiaries' behaviors when they are extensively embedded in local networks (Andersson & Forsgren, 1996).

However, prior empirical management accounting studies show that a subsidiary's higher external embeddedness enhances the influence of parent-PMS on subsidiaries' decision-making (Mahlendorf et al., 2012). This argument can be understood as a suggestion that parent-PMSs are a mechanism to achieve high levels of coordination and integration in highly decentralized MNCs and to successfully combine local autonomy with global goal congruence (Andersson et al., 2002; Busco et al., 2008; Dossi & Patelli, 2008).

However, these effects do not always occur owing to PMS alone. Research on PMS in MNCs suggests that capturing critical areas and key factors and communicating these factors between headquarters and subsidiaries is more important, especially in highly decentralized MNCs (Busco et al., 2008; Dossi & Patelli, 2010; Mahlendorf et al., 2012). Other research also suggests that understanding the business environment well can enhance all decision-making capabilities within highly decentralized MNCs (Aharoni et al., 2010). Contrastingly, subsidiaries' decisions and actions are more uncertain for headquarters when subsidiaries have high embeddedness. In such highly uncertain cases, the interactive use of PMS is more appropriate than diagnostic use (Simons, 1995, 2000).

Based on these studies, we expect that when a subsidiary is extensively embedded, the influence of parent-PMS on the subsidiary's decisions and actions depends on the characteristics of the use of the parent-PMS. While a parent-PMS can affect subsidiaries' decisions and actions when the system can capture the critical factors and when the firm conducts frequent communication, feedback, and follow-up through the parent-PMS, especially in highly decentralized MNCs, the parent-PMS cannot affect subsidiaries' decisions if the parent-PMS lacks a clear process when subsidiaries are extensively embedded. Depending on the different uses of parent-PMS, its influence on subsidiaries' decisions and actions might change when subsidiaries are extensively embedded. Thus, we assume that subsidiary embeddedness positively (negatively) moderates the cause-effect relation between the interactive (diagnostic) use of parent-PMS and the influence of the parent-PMS on subsidiary decision-making.

There are various concepts of embeddedness in business networks (Halinen & Tornroos, 1998). However, investigating all embeddedness is insubstantial and not rational (Kadushin, 2012). Hence, in line with prior research (e.g., Andersson & Forsgren, 1996; Andersson et al., 2001), we focus on subsidiaries' relationships with the local customers and suppliers that influence subsidiaries' products and services and product- and service-related processes. In highly decentralized MNCs, subsidiaries need to flexibly respond to the needs of local counterparts to accomplish the MNC's and subsidiaries' strategy (Forsgren et al., 2005; Martinez & Jarillo, 1989). Therefore, we propose the following hypotheses:

H3a. The subsidiaries' embeddedness with local customers negatively moderates the relationship between the diagnostic use of the parent-PMS by headquarters and the influence of the parent-PMS on subsidiaries' decision-making.

H3b. The subsidiaries' embeddedness with local suppliers negatively moderates the relationship between the diagnostic use of the parent-PMS by headquarters and the influence of the parent-PMS on subsidiaries' decision-making.

H4a. The subsidiaries' embeddedness with local customers positively moderates the relationship between the interactive use of the parent-PMS by headquarters and the influence of the parent-PMS on subsidiaries' decision-making.

H4b. The subsidiaries' embeddedness with local suppliers positively moderates the relationship between the interactive use of the parent-PMS by headquarters and the influence of the parent-PMS on subsidiaries' decision-making.

5.3 Method

5.3.1 Data Collection

Data were collected through a mailed questionnaire-based survey addressed to 1520 top managers of Japanese subsidiaries of foreign MNCs in September 2016. The questionnaires were mailed owing to the large difference in the perception of control and practice of decision-making between headquarters and subsidiaries. Therefore, we cannot observe the real influence of control systems on subsidiaries' decision-making and subsidiaries' external environment, such as subsidiaries' embeddedness directly (Andersson & Forsgren, 1996; Mahlendorf et al., 2012). The total sample is 199 questionnaires (a response rate of 13%) after removing some samples that lacked data. The sample includes both manufacturing and non-manufacturing industries. To test whether respondents and non-respondents have different industries, we use chi-square statistics and find that respondent and non-respondent firms had the same distribution across industries ($p > .10$). Hence, we find no non-respondent bias concerning industry.

5.3.2 Variables

To ensure comparability with other studies and to enhance internal validity of contents, we adopt constructs and measures established by prior research. We altered some constructs and measures slightly to adapt to the MNC setting. Appendix A reports the constructs and measures used in this study and the descriptive statistics.

To measure the diagnostic (DUSE) and interactive (IUSE) use of parent-PMS, which are independent variables, we follow Henri (2006b), Simons (1995, 2000), and Widener (2007). We use 11 items measured on seven-point Likert-type scales (1 = not at all; 7 = to a high extent).[1] Concerning the reliability of the variables, the Cronbach's α of IUSE is .850 and that of DUSE is .639. While DUSE is not highly reliable, it is within a permissible range for analysis (Hair et al., 1998).

To measure subsidiaries' embeddedness with local customers (EMBC) and suppliers (EMBS), which are moderating variables in this study, we measured two items using seven-point Likert-type scales (1 = not at all; 7 = to a high extent) following Andersson and Forsgren (1996). Scale reliability is satisfactory, with a Cronbach's α of EMBC of .700 and EMBS of .890.

To measure the influence of parent-PMS on subsidiaries' decision-making, we refer to Dossi and Patelli (2008) and Mahlendorf et al. (2012) and use 14 items measured on seven-point Likert-type scales (1 = not at all; 7 = to a high extent). Prior studies adopt these items as one variable to analyze. However, it is difficult to adopt this approach owing to the differing contents and aspects of these items.

Hence, we perform an exploratory factor analysis in this study and find that 14 items loaded on three factors (Table 5.1).[2] The first of the three factors include five items concerning control within the subsidiaries (INF-C). The second includes five items about developing products and/or services in subsidiaries (INF-D). The

[1] DUSE includes six items and IUSE includes five items; however, we removed one DUSE item owing to the ceiling effect.

[2] We removed one item because its factor loading was below .50.

Table 5.1 Exploratory factor analysis results: influence of parent-PMS on subsidiaries' decisions[a,b]

	1	2	3
Incentive scheme decisions	***.930***	.023	−.099
Target-setting decisions for employees	***.792***	−.127	.179
Human resource decisions	***.775***	.072	.121
Decisions about performance evaluation	***.733***	.050	−.128
Responsibility accounting decisions	***.514***	.008	.399
Research and development planning and control decisions	.007	***.859***	−.081
Production planning decisions	−.081	***.803***	.067
Making or buying decisions	−.136	***.761***	.201
Investment decisions	.251	***.718***	−.245
Supply chain management decisions	.019	***.625***	.185
Target setting decisions for employees	.021	−.092	***.987***
Distribution channel decisions	.065	.027	***.809***
Pricing decisions about products or services	−.059	.121	***.732***
Cronbach's α	.814	.806	.771

[a] Promax rotation
[b] Contribution rate: 74.771%, eigenvalue: 1.215

final factor includes three items related to decisions about selling processes at subsidiaries (INF-S). The Cronbach's α is .814 for INF-C, .806 for INF-D, and .771 for INF-S, which are satisfactory. Table 5.2 shows the Pearson's correlation coefficients across the variables.

5.4 Results

5.4.1 Main Analyses Results

The six hypotheses in this chapter can be summarized in two basic models:

$$Y_{1,2,3} = \alpha_1 + \beta_1 \text{DUSE} + \beta_2 \text{IUSE} + \beta_3 \text{EMBC} + \beta_4 \text{EMBS} + \Sigma \text{Controls} + \varepsilon \quad (5.1)$$

$$\begin{aligned} Y_{1,2,3} = {} & \alpha_1 + \beta_1 \text{DUSE} + \beta_2 \text{IUSE} + \beta_3 \text{EMBC} + \beta_4 \text{EMBS} + \beta_5 \text{DUSE} \\ & \times \text{EMBC} + \beta_6 \text{DUSE} \times \text{EMBS} + \beta_7 \text{IUSE} \times \text{EMBC} + \beta_8 \text{IUSE} \times \text{EMBS} \\ & + \Sigma \text{Controls} + \varepsilon \end{aligned} \quad (5.2)$$

where Y_1 = the influence of parent-PMS on subsidiaries' internal control decision-making (INF-C), Y_2 = the influence of the parent-PMS on subsidiaries decision-making about developing products and/or services (INF-D), Y_3 = the influence of the parent-PMS on subsidiaries' decision-making about selling processes (INF-C), α

Table 5.2 Correlation matrix

Variables	INF-C	INF-D	INF-S	DUSE	IUSE	EMBC	EMBS
INF-C	1						
INF-D	.310**	1					
INF-S	.658**	.461**	1				
DUSE	.236**	.211**	.158*	1			
IUSE	.366**	.205**	.288**	.705**	1		
EMBC	.073	.249**	.101	.141	.187**	1	
EMBS	.122	.213**	.104	.055	.097	.482**	1

*$p < .05$, **$p < .01$. All tests are two-tailed

Abbreviations: INF-C = the influence of parent-PMS on subsidiaries internal control decision-making; INF-D = the influence of parent-PMS on subsidiaries decision-making about developing products and/or services INF-S = the influence of parent-PMS on subsidiaries' decision-making about selling processes DUSE = diagnostic use of parent-PMS; IUSE = interactive use of parent-PMS; EMBC = subsidiaries' embeddedness in local customers; EMBS = subsidiaries' embeddedness in local suppliers

is the intercept, β_s are regression coefficients, ΣControls = control variables, and ε = error term.

To test these models, we conducted a hierarchical regression analysis. Regression-based methods may be suitable to test these models compared to covariance-based methods because the models and measures in international business research are considered as to be at an early stage of development and lack substantial empirical evidence and because the hypotheses include interaction effects (Schäffer et al., 2014; Venaik et al., 2005).

Table 5.3 reports the analysis results. Model 1 focuses on the main effects of different types of PMS use on subsidiaries' decision-making, and thus focuses on H1 and H2. In Model 1, the direct effects of the diagnostic use of parent-PMS (DUSE) on all independent variables (INF-C, INF-D, and INF-S) are not significant. Therefore, H1 is not supported. For H2, the direct effects of the interactive use of parent-PMS (IUSE) on the influence of parent-PMS on subsidiaries' internal control decision-making (INF-C, standardized β = .411; $p < .001$) and decision-making about selling processes (INF-C, standardized β = .354; $p = .003$) are significant, although the direct effect of the influence of parent-PMS on subsidiaries' decision-making about products and/or services development is not significant (INF-D, $p > .1$). Therefore, H2 is partially supported, and all control variables are not significant.

Model 2 focuses on the interaction effects between different types of PMS use and subsidiaries' embeddedness; thus, Model 2 reflects, H3a, 3b, 4a, and 4b. The results do not confirm a significant interaction effect for H3, so H3a and H3b are not supported. Contrastingly, for H4a, the negative interaction effects between IUSE and EMBC on INF-D (standardized $\beta = -.378$; $p = .021$), and on INF-S (standardized $\beta = -.354$; $p = .031$) are significant. Conversely, the positive interaction effects between IUSE and EMBS on INF-D (standardized $\beta = .263$; $p = .048$) and INF-S

Table 5.3 Hierarchical regression analysis results

		INF-C		INF-D		INF-S	
		Model 1c	Model 2c	Model 1d	Model 2d	Model 1s	Model 2s
Independent variables							
DUSE	H1	−.020	−.034	.156	.146	−.062	−.087
IUSE	H2	***.411****	***.406***	.059	.069	***.354***	***.374***
EMBC		−.074	−.078	.185	.186	.028	.029
EMBS		.153	.141	.109	.097	.114	.095
DUSE × *EMBC*	H3a		−.151		.312		.275
DUSE × *EMBS*	H3b		−.022		−.157		−.208
IUSE × *EMBC*	H4a		−.045		***−.378****		***−.354****
IUSE × *EMBS*	H4b		.191		***.263****		***.325****
Control variables							
ESTType		.093	.105	−.058	−.046	−.080	−.070
ESTYear		−.085	−.100	−.072	−.078	−.064	−.072
SIZE		.086	.068	.071	.041	.016	−.016
INDUSTRY		−.048	−.045	.069	.075	−.037	−.027
R^2		.190	.221	.147	.187	.138	.181
Adj. R^2		.135	.144	.089	.107	.079	.101
F		3.449***	2.894**	2.536**	2.342**	2.355*	2.263**

*$p < .05$, **$p < .01$, ***$p < .001$. All tests are two-tailed

Abbreviations: INF-C = the influence of parent-PMS on subsidiaries' internal control decision-making; INF-D = the influence of parent-PMS on subsidiaries' decision-making about developing products and/or services INF-S = the influence of parent-PMS on subsidiaries decision-making about selling processes DUSE = diagnostic use of parent-PMS; IUSE = interactive use of parent-PMS; EMBC = subsidiaries embeddedness in local customers; EMBS = subsidiaries embeddedness in local suppliers; ESTTYPE = types of establishment of subsidiaries (0 = green-field investment; 1 = M&A); ESTYEAR = past years since subsidiaries have been involved in present MNCs; SIZE = size of subsidiaries; INDUSTRY = industry dummies (0 = non-manufacturing; 1 = manufacturing)

(standardized $\beta = .325$; $p = .015$) are significant. Thus, the results partially support and partially reject H4a and H4b, respectively.

5.4.2 Supplemental Analyses Results

The results above show that some interaction effects are significant. In this analysis, we report the results of a simple slope analysis to clarify and confirm the moderating effects of a subsidiary's EMBC and suppliers. In line with prior research (e.g., Aiken & West, 1991; Cohen et al., 2002), we conducted single slope analyses with PMS as the independent variable and "INF-D" and "INF-S" as dependent variables when EMBC and EMBS scored ±1 SD each. Figure 5.1 illustrates the results of the analyses with a focus on the moderating effect of EMBC. The cause-effect

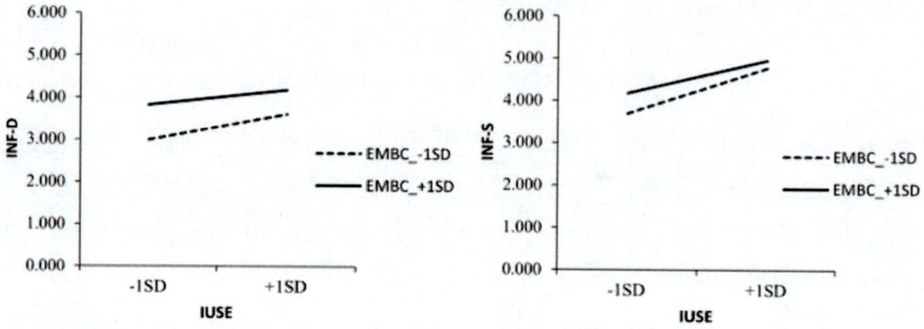

Fig. 5.1 The moderating effects of subsidiaries embeddedness in local customers

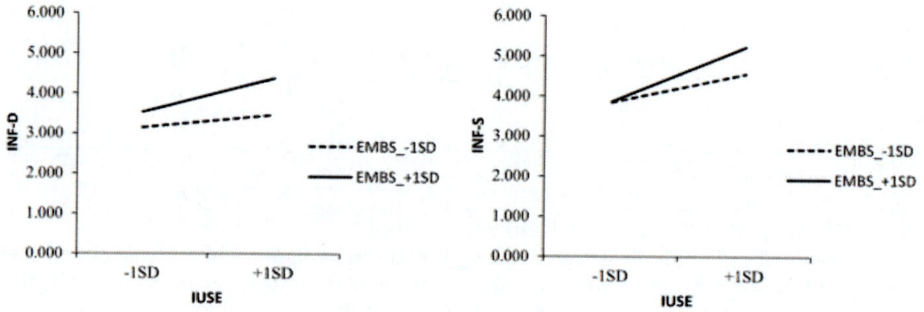

Fig. 5.2 The moderating effects of subsidiaries embeddedness in local suppliers

relationship between IUSE and INF-D is not significant when EMBC is above the mean, though we confirm a significant relationship between IUSE and INF-D when EMBC is below the mean (standardized $\beta = .184$; $p = .047$). Contrastingly, the positive cause-effect relationship between IUSE and INF-S is significant, both when EMBC is above (standardized $\beta = .220$; $p = .029$) and below (standardized $\beta = .302$; $p < .001$) the mean. Thus, the interactive use of parent-PMS is likely to have a high (low) influence when subsidiaries' embeddedness in local customers is low (high).

In contrast, Fig. 5.2 illustrates the results of the analyses of the moderating effect of EMBS. The cause-effect relation between IUSE and INF-D is significant only when EMBS is above the mean (standardized $\beta = .255$; $p = .015$), while the cause-effect relation between IUSE and INF-S is significant both when EMBS is above (standardized $\beta = .386$; $p < .001$) and below (standardized $\beta = .201$; $p = .033$) the mean. These results suggest that the use of parent-PMS is likely to have a high (low) influence when subsidiaries' embeddedness with local suppliers is high (low).

5.5 Discussion and Conclusion

5.5.1 Relevant Findings and Contributions

This study examines the relationships among the use of parent-PMS, subsidiaries' embeddedness, and subsidiaries' decisions, especially the cause-effect relations between the different types of parent-PMS use and subsidiaries' decisions and the moderating effects of subsidiaries' embeddedness on these cause-effect relations. We test six hypotheses using survey data collected from 199 Japanese subsidiary top managers. The results show some relevant findings that extend and contribute to the present discussion about the effects of parent-PMS in MNCs.

First, by reviewing and summarizing relevant studies that focus on the use of PMS, we generate two hypotheses about the effects of the different types of parent-PMS use (H1, H2). The results show the cause-effect relationship between the interactive use of PMS by headquarters and the influence of parent-PMS on subsidiaries' decisions, though we find no significant effect of the diagnostic use of PMS by headquarters. It suggests that the influence of parent-PMS on subsidiaries' decisions is subject to information flow and control practice. Thus, we argue that by using PMS interactively, headquarters can influence subsidiaries' decisions and thus integrate their actions into the company's overall goals. By using PMS interactively, subsidiaries can frequently communicate and share relevant information and thoughts to accomplish the overall strategy with their headquarters (Dirks & Ferris, 2002; Dossi & Patelli, 2010; Maley & Moeller, 2014). Hence, subsidiaries' decisions and actions might coincide with the intentions of headquarters and overall strategy.

Prior research offers empirical evidence about the determinants of the decision-influencing use of a parent-PMS (e.g., Dossi & Patelli, 2008; Mahlendorf et al., 2012), while other studies focus on the interactive use of a parent-PMS by headquarters (e.g., Dossi & Patelli, 2010; Schäffer et al., 2014). However, these studies do not provide evidence on or the implications of how can headquarters control subsidiaries' decisions and actions using PMS. This study overcomes the limitations in prior studies and focuses on the processes of the use of PMS concerning information flow and control practices, and shows how and which types of a headquarters' use of PMS can influence subsidiaries' decisions. Hence, our empirical evidence can complement and extend the findings in prior research. Furthermore, the results support the arguments of prior studies that the effects of PMS within organizations depend on the use of PMS (e.g., Koufteros et al., 2014; Henri, 2006a). Therefore, these findings are an important contribution to PMS research, especially in the MNC setting.

Second, to consider the effects of local networks and counterparts on subsidiaries' decisions and actions from the perspective of embeddedness theory. We test four hypotheses about the interaction effect of parent-PMS use and subsidiaries' external embeddedness (H3, H4). The results show that the subsidiaries' EMBC negatively moderates the positive influence of the interactive use of PMS on subsidiaries' decisions. This result supports empirical evidence in international business research showing that subsidiaries' embeddedness negatively affects the headquarters' control mechanisms (e.g., Andersson & Forsgren, 1996) compared to the PMS research in the MNC setting (e.g., Mahlendorf et al., 2012). We can understand this firm's actions to adapt to local customers' needs via subsidiaries. MNCs should integrate a variety of needs, information, and knowledge of local markets into innovation to acquire competitive advantages in both the global and local markets, especially in Japan (Blahová et al., 2015). In doing so, subsidiaries must be embedded in the local market to obtain this information and knowledge (Johanson & Vahlne, 2009). Consequently, subsidiaries' EMBC might prevail against the parent-PMS. Thus, subsidiaries' EMBC negatively moderates the influence of the interactive use of PMS by headquarters on subsidiaries' decisions.

Contrastingly, we find a positive moderating effect of subsidiaries' embeddedness with local suppliers on the cause-effect relationship between the interactive use of PMS by headquarters and the influence of the parent-PMS on subsidiaries' decisions. This result contrasts the results concerning customer embeddedness. Subsidiaries' embeddedness that influences products and/or services enhance overall organizational performance, which the parent-PMS can capture and influence (Andersson et al., 2005). MNCs can effectively control Japanese subsidiaries' decisions and actions by understanding and adapting to buyer-supplier relationships in the Japanese market (Schlunze, 2004). Hence, the headquarters can capture the relationship between subsidiaries and local suppliers using PMS interactively. Thus, it can communicate important information to subsidiaries. In addition, it may explain the result that the extent to which headquarters' delegate authority for developing products and/or services to subsidiaries is relatively low (Appendix B).

The findings on subsidiaries' embeddedness extend the discussions in both the international business and PMS literature. For PMS research, the empirical evidence in this research helps to reveal the mechanisms and processes of the effects of PMS in combination with the empirical evidence on the use of PMS. These results suggest that the effects of PMS depend not only on the type of PMS use but also on the embeddedness in networks. Although this study investigates only subsidiaries' external embeddedness, other types of embeddedness (i.e., internal embeddedness concerning the dependencies of business units on headquarters) might have important impacts on the effects of PMS. In international business research, few studies classify embeddedness according to local counterparts, though prior research considers many types of embeddedness. Thus, this study helps to extend the discussion on subsidiaries' embeddedness by showing empirical evidence of the impacts of subsidiaries' embeddedness depend on the type of local counterpart. However, future research should investigate why the impacts of embeddedness differ depending on the type of local.

5.5.2 Implications

This study also has implications for MNCs. The results show that by using parent-PMS interactively, the headquarters can affect subsidiaries' decision-making and can obtain goal congruence between headquarters and subsidiaries. More precisely, it is important for highly decentralized MNCs to frequently communicate and discuss both global and local performance with subsidiaries to capture and share critical areas of the business and key factors. This suggestion coincides with Maley and Moeller's (2014) argument that frequent communication, feedback, and follow-up through parent-PMS are important characteristics to integrate subsidiaries' decisions and actions into global strategy. They argue that when the process of PMS use lacks these characteristics, subsidiaries have less trust in headquarters, and might thus disobey the intentions of headquarters.

5.5.3 Limitations and Suggestions for the Future Research

Although this study presents relevant findings, they are subject to some limitations. The first is related to data collection and the target companies. The results can be compared with other studies that focus on similar themes and/or use similar measures in a survey but that obtain different results. This research has some peculiarities because the target of this survey is Japanese subsidiaries. Thus, for subsidiaries in other countries, our results are not applicable. The second limitation is a perception gap between headquarters and subsidiaries. In this study, we investigate the real influence of parent-PMS on subsidiaries' decisions and actions and the extent of the effect of subsidiaries' embeddedness, though because the survey targeted subsidiaries, the results may not reflect the thoughts and intentions of the parent headquarters.

Future research could extend the findings of this study by overcoming these limitations or focusing on other questions. For example, a case study would clarify why and how subsidiaries' embeddedness moderates the influence of parent-PMS. In addition, by focusing on both headquarters and subsidiaries simultaneously, a future study could consider the perception gap between headquarters and subsidiaries. Furthermore, it is necessary to focus on the relationships among the structural features and aspects of the design, purpose, and procedural aspects of PMS use. This study accounts for information flow to reveal the processes of PMS use by headquarters and its influence on subsidiaries. However, we assume that appropriate information flow depends on the design, purpose, and procedural aspects of PMS. There might be a "fit" among these elements, which is a relevant topic for future research to extend the findings.

Appendix A: Constructs, Measures, and Descriptive Statistics

Influence of parent-PMS on decision-making

To what extent does the parent-PMS influence your decision-making on the following items?

(1 = not at all; 7 = to a high extent)

	Min	Max	Mean	SD
Budgeting decisions	1	7	5.05	1.41
Pricing decisions about products or services	1	7	4.65	1.772
Decisions about performance evaluation	1	7	4.64	1.852
Target setting decisions for employees	1	7	4.52	1.941
Incentive scheme decisions	1	7	4.51	1.885
Human resource decisions	1	7	4.38	1.762
Choosing target customer decisions	1	7	4.37	2.005
Responsibility accounting decisions	1	7	4.30	1.930
Distribution channel decisions	1	7	4.12	2.098
Investment decisions	1	7	3.94	2.034
Making or buying decisions	1	7	3.66	2.074
Production planning decisions	1	7	3.65	2.114
Supply chain management decisions	1	7	3.56	2.069
Research and development planning and control decisions	1	7	3.49	2.041

Diagnostic and interactive use of PMS

To what extent do you agree to the following statements about how to use the parent-PMS?

(1 = not at all; 7 = to a high extent)

	Min	Max	Mean	SD
Diagnostic use of PMS				
The parent company uses the PMS to monitor performance and results of your Japanese company's operations	1	7	5.24	1.651
The parent company uses the PMS to track progress of your Japanese company's activities toward goals	1	7	5.24	1.621
The parent company relies heavily on staff specialists in preparing and interpreting information from the parent-PMS	1	7	3.98	1.592
You and/or your Japanese company's employees pay attention to the parent-PMS when exception to the parent-PMS happen	1	7	3.06	1.479
The parent company pays attention to the activities of your Japanese company only when the parent-company knows exception to a plan happened through the parent-PMS	1	7	3.30	1.727
Interactive use of PMS				
The parent-PMS enables continual challenge and debate of underlying data, assumption, and action plan	1	7	4.86	1.642
The parent-PMS enables discussion in meetings with the parent-company and other employees	1	7	4.84	1.584

(continued)

	Min	Max	Mean	SD
The parent-company has paid attention on day-to-day activities of your Japanese company through the parent-PMS	1	7	4.86	1.589
You and/or your Japanese company's employees have paid day-to-day attention to the parent-PMS	1	7	4.86	1.614
Formal meetings are frequently held with the participation of employees in both the parent-company and your Japanese company to discuss the parent-PMS	1	7	4.86	1.708

Subsidiaries embeddedness

To what extent have relationships with the following local Japanese stakeholders caused your Japanese company to change its products/services or operation processes?

(1 = not at all; 7 = to a high extent)

	Min	Max	Mean	SD
Subsidiaries embeddedness in local customers				
Relationships with local Japanese customers have caused changes in products/services	1	7	5.38	1.440
Relationships with local Japanese customers have caused changes in production technologies/service processes	1	7	4.95	1.695
Subsidiaries embeddedness in local suppliers				
Relationships with local Japanese suppliers have caused changes in products/services	1	7	3.63	2.030
Relationships with local Japanese suppliers have caused changes in production technologies/service processes	1	7	3.52	1.962

Appendix B: Descriptive Statistics of Subsidiaries' Decision-Making Authority Delegated by Headquarters

	Min	Max	Mean	SD
Choosing target customer decisions	1	7	6.11	1.149
Target setting decisions for employees	2	7	5.96	1.145
Distribution channel decisions	1	7	5.88	1.303
Responsibility accounting decisions	1	7	5.70	1.234
Human resource decisions	1	7	5.29	1.357
Incentive scheme decisions	1	7	5.15	1.527
Pricing decisions about products or services	1	7	5.07	1.563
Budgeting decisions	1	7	4.82	1.273
Decisions about performance evaluation	1	7	4.71	1.630
Supply chain management decisions	1	7	4.27	1.997
Making or buying decisions	1	7	3.85	2.063
Production planning decisions	1	7	3.40	2.078
Investment decisions	1	7	3.30	1.735
Research and development planning and control decisions	1	7	3.02	1.802

References

Abernethy, M. A., & Brownell, P. (1999). The role of budgets in organizations facing strategic change: An exploratory study. *Accounting, Organizations and Society, 24*(3), 189–204.
Aharoni, Y., Tihanyi, L., & Connelly, B. L. (2010). Managerial decision-making in international business: A forty-five-year retrospective. *Journal of World Business, 46*(2), 135–142.
Aiken, L. S., & West, S. G. (1991). *Multiple regression: Testing and interpreting interactions*. Sage.
Andersson, U., Björkman, I., & Forsgren, M. (2005). Managing subsidiaries knowledge creation: The effect of control mechanisms on subsidiaries local embeddedness. *International Business Review, 14*(5), 521–538.
Andersson, U., & Forsgren, M. (1996). Subsidiaries embeddedness and control in the multinational corporation. *International Business Review, 5*(5), 487–508.
Andersson, U., Forsgren, M., & Holm, U. (2002). The strategic impact of external networks: Subsidiaries performance and competence development in the multinational corporation. *Strategic Management Journal, 23*(11), 979–996.
Andersson, U., Forsgren, M., & Pedersen, T. (2001). Subsidiaries performance in multinational corporations: The importance of technology embeddedness. *International Business Review, 10*(1), 3–23.
Bisbe, J., Batista-Foguet, J. M., & Chenhall, R. H. (2007). Defining management accounting constructs: A methodological note on the risks of conceptual misspecification. *Accounting, Organizations and Society, 32*(7–8), 789–820.
Bisbe, J., & Otley, D. (2004). The effects of the interactive use of management control systems on product innovation. *Accounting, Organizations and Society, 29*(8), 709–737.
Blahová, M., Haghirian, P., & Pálka, P. (2015). Major factors affecting contemporary Japanese business environment. *International Journal of Productivity and Performance Management, 64*(3), 416–433.
Bouquet, C., & Birkinshaw, J. (2008). Weight versus voice: How foreign subsidiaries gain attention from corporate headquarters. *Academy of Management Journal, 51*(3), 577–601.
Bourne, M., Mills, J., Wilcox, M., Neely, A., & Platts, K. (2000). Designing, implementing and updating performance measurement systems. *International Journal of Operations and Production Management, 20*(7), 754–771.
Busco, C., Frigo, M., Giovannoni, E., Riccaboni, A., & Scapens, W. (2006). Integrating global organizations through performance measurement systems. *Strategic Finance, 87*(7), 30–35.
Busco, C., Giovannoni, E., & Scapens, R. W. (2008). Managing the tensions in integrating global organisations: The role of performance management systems. *Management Accounting Research, 19*(2), 103–125.
Cohen, J., Cohen, P., West, G. S., & Aiken, L. S. (2002). *Applied multiple regression/correlation analysis for the behavioral sciences* (3rd ed.). Routledge.
Dirks, K. T., & Ferris, D. T. (2002). Trust in leadership: Meta-analytic findings and implications for research and practice. *Journal of Applied Psychology, 87*(4), 611–628.
Dossi, A., & Patelli, L. (2008). The decision-influencing use of performance measurement systems in relationships between headquarters and subsidiaries. *Management Accounting Research, 19*(2), 126–148.
Dossi, A., & Patelli, L. (2010). You learn from what you measure: Financial and non-financial performance measures in multinational companies. *Long Range Planning, 43*(4), 498–526.
Doz, Y., & Prahalad, C. K. (1993). Managing DMNCs: A search for a new paradigm. In S. Ghoshal & D. E. Westney (Eds.), *Organization theory and the multinational corporation*. St. Martins Press.
Doz, Y. L., & Prahalad, C. K. (1984). Patterns of strategic control within multinational corporations. *Journal of International Business Studies, 2*(Autumn), 55–72.
Doz, Y. L., Santos, J., & Williamson, P. J. (2001). *From global to metanational: How companies win in the knowledge economy*. Harvard Business School Press.

Dunning, J. H., & Lundan, S. M. (2008). *Multinational enterprises and the global economy*. Edward Elgar.

Ezzamel, M., Willmott, H., & Worthington, F. (1999). *Accounting, organisational transformation and work organisation*. In Working Paper Presented at the Accounting, Organisations and Society Conference on Accounting, Organisational Transformation and New Organisational Forms, Los Angeles, November 4–6.

Ferreira, A., & Otley, D. (2009). The design and use of performance management systems: An extended framework for analysis. *Management Accounting Research, 20*(4), 263–282.

Forsgren, M. (1989). *Managing the internationalization process. The Swedish case*. Routledge.

Forsgren, M., Holm, U., & Johanson, J. (2005). *Managing the embedded multinational: A business network view*. Edward Elgar.

Franco-Santos, M., Lucianetti, L., & Bourne, M. (2012). Contemporary performance measurement systems: A review of their consequences and a framework for research. *Management Accounting Research, 23*(2), 79–119.

Ghoshal, S., & Bartlett, C. A. (1990). The multinational corporation as an interorganisational network. *Academy of Management Review, 15*(4), 603–625.

Ghoshal, S., & Bartlett, C. A. (1993). The multinational corporation as an interorganisational network. In S. Ghoshal & E. D. Westney (Eds.), *Organization theory and the multinational corporation*. St. Martins Press.

Ghoshal, S., & Bartlett, C. A. (1996). Rebuilding behavioural context: A blueprint for corporate renewal. *Sloan Management Review, 37*, 23–36.

Ghoshal, S., & Westney, E. D. (1993). Introduction and overview. In S. Ghoshal & E. D. Westney (Eds.), *Organization theory and the multinational corporation*. St. Martins Press.

Govindarajan, V., & Gupta, A. (2000). Analysis of the emerging global arena. *European Management Journal, 18*, 274–284.

Granovetter, M. (1985). Economic action and social structure: The problem of embeddedness. *American Journal of Sociology, 78*(3), 3–30.

Granovetter, M. (1992). Problems of explanation in economic sociology. In N. Nohria & R. G. Eccles (Eds.), *Networks and organizations: Structure for M&A action*. Harvard Business School Press.

Gulati, R. (1998). Alliances and networks. *Strategic Management Journal, 19*, 293–317.

Gulati, R. (1999). Network location and learning: The influence of network resources and firm capabilities on alliance formation. *Strategic Management Journal, 20*, 397–420.

Hair, J. F., Anderson, R. E., Tatham, R. L., & Black, W. C. (1998). *Multivariate data analysis* (5th ed.). Prentice Hall.

Halinen, A., & Tornroos, J. A. (1998). The role of embeddedness in the evolution of business networks. *Scandinavian Journal of Management, 14*(3), 187–205.

Harzing, A. W. (1999). *Managing the multinationals*. Edward Elgar Publishing Limited.

Helliwell, J. F. (2002). *Globalization and well-being*. UBC Press.

Henri, J. F. (2006a). Organizational culture and performance measurement systems. *Accounting, Organizations and Society, 31*(1), 77–103.

Henri, J. F. (2006b). Management control systems and strategy: A resource-based perspective. *Accounting, Organizations and Society, 31*(6), 529–558.

Hopwood, A. G. (1972). An empirical study of the role of accounting data in performance evaluation. *Journal of Accounting Research*, 156–182.

Johanson, J., & Vahlne, J. E. (2009). The Uppsala internationalization process model revisited: From liability of foreignness to liability of outsidership. *Journal of International Business Studies, 40*(9), 1411–1431.

Kadushin, C. (2012). *Understanding social networks: Theories, concepts, and findings*. Oxford University Press.

Koufteros, X., Verghese, A. J., & Lucianetti, L. (2014). The effect of performance measurement systems on firm performance: A cross-sectional and a longitudinal study. *Journal of Operations Management, 32*(6), 313–336.

Langfield-Smith, K. (1997). Management control systems and strategy: A critical review. *Accounting, Organizations and Society, 22*(2), 207–232.

Luo, Y. (2005). Toward cooperation within multinational enterprise: A perspective from foreign subsidiaries. *Journal of World Business, 40*(1), 71–90.

Mahlendorf, M. D., Rehring, J., Schäffer, U., & Wyszomirski, E. (2012). Influencing foreign subsidiaries decisions through headquarters performance measurement systems. *Management Decision, 50*(4), 688–717.

Maley, J. F., & Moeller, M. (2014). Global performance management systems: The role of trust as perceived by country managers. *Journal of Business Research, 67*(1), 2803–2810.

Martinez, J. L., & Jarillo, J. C. (1989). The evolution of research on coordination mechanisms in multinational corporations. *Journal of International Business Studies, 20*(3), 489–514.

McEvily, B., & Zaheer, A. (1999). Bridging ties: A source of firm heterogeneity in competitive capabilities. *Strategic Management Journal*, 1133–1156.

Micheli, P., Mura, M., & Agliati, M. (2011). Exploring the roles of performance measurement systems in strategy implementation: The case of a highly diversified group of firms. *International Journal of Operations and Production Management, 31*(10), 1115–1139.

Nørreklit, H., & Schoenfeld, H. W. (2000). Controlling multinational companies: An attempt to analyze some unresolved issues. *International Journal of Accounting, 35*(3), 415–430.

O'Donnell, S. (2000). Managing foreign subsidiaries: Agents of headquarters, or an interdependent network? *Strategic Management Journal, 21*(6), 525–548.

Polyani, K. (1957). *The grate transformation*. Beacon Press.

Quattrone, P., & Hopper, T. (2005). A 'time-space odyssey': Management control systems in two multinational organisations. *Accounting, Organizations and Society, 30*(7), 735–764.

Roth, K., & Kostova, T. (2003). The use of the multinational corporation as a research context. *Journal of Management, 29*(6), 883–902.

Schäffer, U., Mahlendorf, M. D., & Rehring, J. (2014). Does the interactive use of headquarters performance measurement systems in foreign subsidiaries endanger the potential to profit from local relationships? *Australian Accounting Review, 24*(1), 21–38.

Schlunze, R. D. (2004). Managerial embeddedness of European manufacturing firms in Japan. *Jimbun-Chiri, 56*(5), 64–82.

Simons, R. (1995). *Levers of control: How managers use innovative control systems to drive strategic renewal*. Harvard Business School Press.

Simons, R. (2000). *Performance measurement and control systems for implementing strategy*. Prentice Hall.

Tuomela, T. S. (2005). The interplay of different levers of control: A case study of introducing a new performance measurement system. *Management Accounting Research, 16*(3), 293–320.

Venaik, S., Midgley, D. F., & Devinney, T. M. (2005). Dual paths to performance: The impact of global pressures on MNC subsidiaries conduct and performance. *Journal of International Business Studies, 36*(6), 655–675.

Widener, S. K. (2007). An empirical analysis of the levers of control framework. *Accounting, Organizations and Society, 32*(7–8), 757–788.

Chapter 6
Empirical Study on Capital Budgeting as a Management Process: Evidence from Japanese Manufacturing Firms

Nobumasa Shimizu, Yutaka Kato, Junya Sakaguchi, Takaharu Kawai, and Akiko Tamura

6.1 Introduction

Capital budgeting is critical for firms in regulating the activity of the organization and retaining ample long-term capital. Theoretical research on capital budgeting decision-making started after World War II and had a great influence on management accounting (Hiromoto, 1993). Since prior studies on capital budgeting in management accounting have been strongly influenced by finance theory, the major discussion has been over the use of economic evaluation methods such as payback method, simple rate of return, net present value, internal rate of return, and real options (Sugiyama, 2002). It is prominent in management accounting research on capital budgeting in Japan (Shimizu, 2004).

An early form of this chapter first appeared in *Journal of Cost Accounting Research* 32(2): 1–14 (in Japanese). Republished with permission of Japan Cost Accounting Association.

N. Shimizu
Waseda Business School, Waseda University, Tokyo, Japan
e-mail: s-nobu@waseda.jp

Y. Kato
Doshisha Business School, Doshisha University, Kyoto, Japan
e-mail: ykato@mail.doshisha.ac.jp

J. Sakaguchi
Graduate School of Economics, Nagoya University, Nagoya, Japan
e-mail: ju_sakaguc@soec.nagoya-u.ac.jp

T. Kawai (✉)
Faculty of Commerce, Doshisha University, Kyoto, Japan
e-mail: tkawai@mail.doshisha.ac.jp

A. Tamura
Faculty of Economics, Hosei University, Tokyo, Japan
e-mail: atamura@hosei.ac.jp

© Springer Nature Singapore Pte Ltd. 2023
E. Yokota (ed.), *Frontiers of Japanese Management Control Systems*, Translational Systems Sciences 32, https://doi.org/10.1007/978-981-19-9778-5_6

However, as economic evaluation methods have been the only focus of capital budgeting decisions, the viewpoint of management control has been neglected. The following facts about the capital budgeting management of Japanese firms were discovered from a mail survey sent to Japanese manufacturing firms (Shimizu et al., 2007): (1) economic evaluation methods are used throughout the capital budgeting process; development phase, proposal phase, deliberation phase, authorization phase, and post-investment evaluation phase; (2) economic evaluation methods are used to set capital budgeting targets; (3) the various capital budgeting projects are ranked; and (4) capital spending limits are assigned.

Although these are only a fraction of the facts discovered, it suggests that capital budgeting management in management accounting (i.e., capital budgeting) contains more factors than described in previous studies and textbooks. Therefore, to discuss capital budgeting in management accounting from a practical viewpoint, we should examine not only the investment decision but also a series of management processes; how a capital budgeting project of an actual firm is developed, authorized, and implemented (Maccarrone, 1996; Shimizu, 2006; Toribe, 1997; Yamamoto, 1998).

Therefore, this study examines the management process as a new way to explore capital budgeting in management accounting. We aimed to reveal the realities of capital budgeting practice among Japanese firms. The rest of this study is organized as follows. In Sect. 6.2, we review the previous studies that focused on the management process of capital budgeting to propose our research questions. In Sect. 6.3, we explain the mail survey used in this study, and we report descriptive statistics about the capital budgeting management process. Then, the core component factors of the management process are extracted. The relationship between these core component factors and the efficiency of capital budgeting management is analyzed in Sect. 6.4. Finally, we present our implications and suggest future research directions in Sect. 6.5.

6.2 Literature Review of Capital Budgeting Processes

Studies that focus on the investment decision process have accumulated as a critique of the research that focuses on the economic evaluation method.[1] We review some of these studies in this section.

Studies that focused on the investment project decision appeared in the 1960s. Istvan (1961) noted that management procedures exhibit considerable diversity between firms. Haynes and Solomon (1962) warned that despite the importance of evaluation prior to the economic evaluation stage, the accumulation of studies was inadequate. Bower (1970) showed that the investment decision is not made by an individual but by the systematic activity of the organization and that there is a

[1] See Haka (2007), Marsh et al. (1988), Mukherjee and Henderson (1987), Toribe (1997), and Yamamoto (1994, 1998) for a comprehensive review of research on capital budgeting processes.

political side that contains various factors in the investment decision process. Ackerman (1970) showed that a centralized organization concentrates the capital budgeting process at its headquarters, unlike a decentralized organization.

These studies described the practice itself and brought a lot of research issues to capital budgeting research. More recent studies on the capital budgeting process focus on two aspects. The first captures the investment decision process as optimization of resource allocation. Larcker (1981) and Gordon and Pinches (1984) discuss what type of information is necessary in each of the four phases of the ideal decision-making processes:—“identification,” “development,” “selection,” and “control”—to design a useful decision support system for managers. Moreover, Neale (1991) and Gordon and Smith (1992) examine the effect of “ex-post evaluation” in the capital budgeting process. In addition, Harris and Raviv (1996) and Kim (2006) analyze the actions of headquarters and the proposal division manager in the capital budgeting process by using agency theory. Here, they suggest that headquarters should acquire relevant information to control opportunistic actions of the division manager (maximization of their own division’s budget). In this way, optimal resource allocation can be achieved through information acquisition (equilibrium solution).

These studies examine their issues by using a mail survey and model analysis. They describe headquarters and managers systematically acquiring and analyzing information related to the capital investment.

The second examines the capital budgeting process from the aspect of consensus building within the organization. King (1975) showed that the investment decision process not only develops the investment project but also forms commitment concurrently. Marsh et al. (1988) investigated how top management takes part in the investment decision. Butler et al. (1993) used statistical analysis of interviews with British firms to show that the attributes of the capital budgeting process influence their efficiency. Toribe (1997) surveyed Japanese manufacturing firms by mail and suggested that the evaluation and decision style adopted by a firm was related to the environment within the organization (i.e., the attributes of the investment project, management style, and the decision-making process). In addition, Yamamoto (1998) described the investment decision process and strategy based on a mail survey and interview with Japanese manufacturing firms.

These studies of consensus building within the organization attempt to describe the features of the capital investment process in detail by interview and mail survey. In sum, these studies insist that the capital investment process is not only a rational optimization of resources but also a systematic consensus-forming process because human elements influence the capital budgeting process.

However, the prior studies have notable issues. First, the management of capital investment, and the capital budgeting process itself, is not still understood. Studies of resource allocation optimization define capital investment as only a theoretical decision-making process. They do not reflect the procedures the corporation actually follows. That is, these previous studies of capital budgeting failed to describe “capital investment as a management process” because they did not examine how management implemented this concretely.

Second, researchers failed to examine how each aspect of the capital management process affects the efficiency of the overall capital budgeting process. In previous studies on consensus building in the organization, explanation of the effect of each aspect of capital budgeting are vague, despite a detailed description of the capital budgeting process.

To overcome the issues of previous studies, we examine two research questions: (i) What is the capital budgeting management process in practice? and (ii) How do the core components of this process affect the efficiency of capital budgeting management?

6.3 Research Method and the Core Components of the Capital Budgeting Management Process

6.3.1 *Data Collection*

Our mail survey was sent to Japanese manufacturing firms between September 3 and October 31, 2005. We sent a questionnaire to the production management section or the management planning section of 836 Japanese manufacturing firms listed on the Tokyo Stock Exchange First Section, and we asked them to answer concerning capital investment for their main product. The response rate to the survey was 22.4% (187 of 836 companies), which is fairly high.[2] Responses varied by industry, being somewhat higher in electric appliances (17.6%; 33 companies), chemicals (15.0%; 28 companies), and machinery (14.4%; 27 companies); however, response rates are not significantly biased by industry.[3] Table 6.1 shows the number of respondent firms by industry.

6.3.2 *The Capital Budgeting Management Process*

Previous studies that focused on theoretical principles of the decision-making process, as explained in Sect. 6.2, cannot fully explain a practice of a firm's capital budgeting process. To understand the firm's capital budgeting process, we propose the following model, as shown in Fig. 6.1: development of the project → project proposal → deliberation and authorization → implementation and post-investment

[2]We sent a reminder to improve the response rate. We received answers from 155 firms before the reminder and 32 firms after. We tested the difference between means for important items (total sales and total assets) to confirm that the two groups did not differ. We found no significant difference between groups.

[3]We performed a chi-squared test and confirmed that the respondent firms' distribution by industry was not biased.

Table 6.1 Respondent firms by industry

Foods	Textiles and apparel	Pulp and paper	Chemicals	Pharmaceuticals	Oil and coal products	Rubber commodities	Glass and ceramics products
15 (8.0%)	9 (4.8%)	1 (0.5%)	28 (15.0%)	8 (4.3%)	1 (0.5%)	1 (0.5%)	10 (5.3%)
Iron and steel	Nonferrous metals	Metal products	Machinery	Electric appliances	Transportation equipment	Precision instruments	Other products
11 (5.9%)	3 (1.6%)	11 (5.9%)	27 (14.4%)	33 (17.6%)	18 (9.6%)	3 (1.6%)	8 (4.3%)

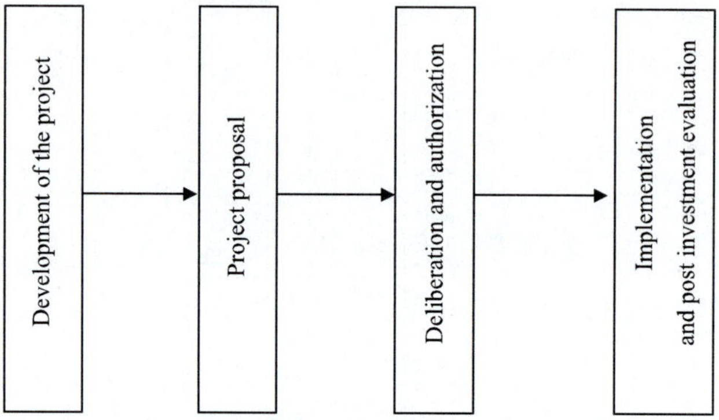

Fig. 6.1 Capital budgeting management process

evaluation. This is based on the strategic capital budgeting planning process presented by Maccarrone (1996, p. 44): development/evaluation → selection → authorization → implementation and control → post-auditing.[4]

Development of the project refers to the desirable capital investment being analyzed as a capital budgeting project. Project proposal refers to the project being proposed to headquarters. Deliberation and authorization refers to the capital budgeting project proposed from the subordinate section of the organization being discussed and finally approved at the highest level. Finally, Implementation and post-investment evaluation refers to the capital expenditure phase and ex-post monitoring of the project.

Next, we constructed 63 question items at each of the four phases of the management process described above, based on interviews we conducted with individual firms (Shimizu et al., 2005), the previous work of Maccarrone (1996), and prior studies in Japan (Kubota & Strategic Capital Investment Committee, 1995; Toribe, 1997; Yamamoto, 1998). Here, we use 13 question items that we consider important for the management of capital budgeting. Table 6.2 presents these 13 question items. We used a five-point Likert scale (1 = *do not agree at all*, 5 = *strongly agree*) for each question item. Table 6.3 reports descriptive statistics of the responses to these question items.

From Table 6.3, we see that "Profitability check" at development phase, "Formalization of deliberation item" and "Profitability check" at proposal phase, and "Profitability check" at the deliberation and authorization phase have relatively high scores. This indicates that the respondent firms tend to conduct their check of profitability at each of the development, proposal and deliberation, and authorization phases, and they follow the prescribed procedure at proposal phase.

[4]See Shimizu (2006) for identification of the capital budgeting management process. However, in our study, "Deliberation of the project" and "Final authorization of the project" were put together into "Deliberation and authorization," and "Implementation of the equipment" and "Post evaluation" were put together into "Implementation and post investment evaluation." We also excluded "Disposal and diversion" from our study.

Table 6.2 Question items for the capital budgeting management process

Phase	Question item	Sentence
Development	"Team organization"	When the development of the investment project begins, the project team is organized
	"Comparison of multiple projects"	When the investment project is developed, two or more ideas are compared
	"Profitability check"	The developer of the investment project is recognizing the level of profitability that should be achieved
Proposal	"Formalization of deliberation item"	When the investment project is proposed, the item that should be deliberated upon is decided
	"Ranking of priority"	The priority is ranked for the proposed project
	"Profitability check"	The profitability of the investment project is evaluated from the financial standard that should be achieved
Deliberation and authorization	"Comparison of implementation plans"	While deliberating on an individual investment project, two or more implementation plans are compared
	"Deliberation frequency"	There are many deliberation frequencies until the investment project is finally approved
	"Profitability check"	While deliberating on the investment project, the profitability level that should be achieved is checked
Implementation and post-investment evaluation	"Monitoring of implementation"	The implementation of investment in equipment is continuously monitored
	"Continuity of evaluation"	After the equipment in which the investment is made is operating at full capacity, post-investment evaluation is conducted continuously
	"Profitability check"	After the equipment in which the investment is made is operating at full capacity, the profitability of the investment project is evaluated
	"Analysis of failed projects"	Analyze the cause of failure of an investment project to reach expected profitability

Table 6.4 displays the results of the factor analysis of 13 question items to search for a potential component factor of capital budgeting management process that cannot be captured from the descriptive statistics of each question item. We use the principal factor method as the factor extraction method and Promax rotation as the factor rotation method. Three factors with eigenvalues greater than one were extracted. The accumulation contribution rate was 57.285%.

From Table 6.4, factor loadings of "Profitability check" at the development phase; "Formalization of deliberation item," "Priority ranking," and "Profitability check" at the proposal phase, and "Profitability check" at the deliberation and authorization phase are relatively high in the first factor. Since these factors are related to evaluation before making investment, we label the first factor *Ex-ante*

Table 6.3 Descriptive statistics of responses by question item

Phase	Question item	*N*	Mean	SD
Development	"Team organization"	171	3.01	1.063
	"Comparison of multiple projects"	171	3.91	0.945
	"Profitability check"	171	*4.43*	0.735
Proposal	"Formalization of deliberation item"	171	*4.09*	0.842
	"Priority ranking"	171	3.73	0.914
	"Profitability check"	171	*4.19*	0.964
Deliberation and authorization	"Comparison of implementation plans"	171	3.46	1.036
	"Deliberation frequency"	171	2.93	0.974
	"Profitability check"	171	*4.23*	0.914
Implementation and post-investment evaluation	"Monitoring of implementation"	171	3.78	0.950
	"Continuity of evaluation"	171	3.65	1.098
	"Profitability check"	171	3.61	1.145
	"Analysis of failed projects"	171	3.60	1.026

Items for which the mean is greater than four are in italics

evaluation. For the second factor, factor loadings of "Monitoring of implementation," "Continuity of evaluation," "Profitability check," and "Analysis of failed projects" at the implementation and post-investment evaluation phase are relatively high. Since these factors are related to evaluation after investment, we label this factor *Ex-post evaluation*. Factor loadings of "Team organization" and "Comparison of implementation plans" at the development phase as well as "Comparison of implementation plans" and "Deliberation frequency" at the deliberation and authorization phase are relatively high for the third factor. Since these items indicate that the project was deliberated upon carefully, we label this factor *Careful deliberation*.

The extracted potential component factors are related to the function achieved through the management process. However, while factor loadings of the first and third factor are relatively high at each phase of development, proposal, and deliberation and authorization, the factor loadings of the second factor are relatively high at the implementation and post-investment evaluation phase. This suggests that these potential component factors have been influenced by each phase, even though it basically relates to the function. In addition, the three component factors related to these functions that are expected to influence the effect of capital budgeting management, such as the acquisition of information, which has been noted by previous studies discussed in Sect. 6.2. Moreover, since the vision for capital budgeting in the organization becomes clearer when such functions are achieved, the appropriate investment timing may become apparent.

In the next section, we analyze the relationship between these potential components and efficiency of capital budgeting management, such as *Acquisition of information* and *Appropriate investment timing*. Table 6.5 presents the question items and descriptive statistics for the efficiency of capital budgeting management.

Table 6.4 Factor analysis of the capital budgeting management process

Phase	Question item	First factor: *Ex-ante evaluation*	Second factor: *Ex-post evaluation*	Third factor: *Careful deliberation*
Development	"Team organization"			0.338
	"Comparison of multiple projects"			0.312
	"Profitability check"	0.884		
Proposal	"Formalization of deliberation item"	0.594		
	"Priority ranking"	0.408		
	"Profitability check"	0.708		
Deliberation and authorization	"Comparison of implementation plans"			0.578
	"Deliberation frequency"			0.660
	"Profitability check"	0.681		
Implementation and post-investment evaluation	"Monitoring of implementation"		0.331	
	"Continuity of evaluation"		1.062	
	"Profitability check"		0.806	
	"Analysis of failed projects"		0.400	

Items for which the factor loading is greater than 0.300 are displayed

Table 6.5 Question items and descriptive statistics for efficiency of capital budgeting management

Question item	Sentence	*N*	Mean	SD
Acquisition of information	Related information necessary for the capital budgeting decision is adequately acquired	171	3.67	0.702
Appropriate investment timing	Equipment can be introduced with appropriate timing	171	3.76	0.740

6.4 The Relationships Between Core Components and the Efficiency of the Capital Budgeting Management Process

This section examines the relationships between the three components extracted in the previous section and the effects of capital budgeting management. Here, we use the following variables in our mail survey to control for environmental factor influences on the efficiency of capital budgeting management process. Since we assume that the capital budgeting management process is influenced by environmental factors, as noted in previous studies (Shimizu et al., 2005), we use the five question items adapted from DeSarbo (2005) that investigated technical or market environment. These items are presented in Table 6.6. The scale used for each question item is a five-point Likert scale (1 = *do not agree at all*, 5 = *strongly agree*). Table 6.7 reports the descriptive statistics of these question items.

From Table 6.7, although the mean of "Difficult to forecast technology" is below 3, and the mean of other question items is over 3.5, there are no distinctive features.

Table 6.6 Question items for environmental variables

Question item	Sentence
"Preferences change through time"	In our kind of business, customers' product preferences change quite a bit over time
"Technological change is frequent"	Technical change in this industry is frequent
"Difficult to forecast technology"	It is very difficult to forecast where the technology in our industry will be in the next two or three years
"Technology changing rapidly"	The technology in our industry is changing rapidly
"New product ideas from technology"	Several new product ideas have been made possible through technological breakthroughs in our industry

Source: adapted from DeSarbo (2005)

Table 6.7 Descriptive statistics: environmental variables

Question item	*N*	Mean	SD
"Preferences change through time"	171	3.57	0.945
"Technological changes are frequent"	171	3.50	0.948
"Difficult to forecast technology"	171	2.60	0.779
"Technology changing rapidly"	171	3.56	1.030
"New product ideas from technology"	171	3.63	0.880

Table 6.8 Factor analysis of environmental variables

Question item	First factor: *Complexity of the environment*	Second factor: *Forecasting difficulty*
"Preferences change through time"	0.665	
"Technological changes are frequent"	0.840	
"Difficult to forecast technology"		0.466
"Technology changing rapidly"	0.823	
"New product ideas from technology"	0.744	

Items for which the factor loading is greater than 0.300 are displayed

We perform the factor analysis for these five question items to investigate potential environmental factors. As with the capital budgeting management process, the principal factor method is used as the factor extraction method, and Promax rotation is adopted as the factor rotation method. We found only two factors with eigenvalues greater than one, with an accumulation contribution rate of 76.00%. Table 6.8 presents the results of this factor analysis.

From Table 6.8, the factor loadings of "Preferences change through time," "Technological changes are frequent," "Technology changing rapidly," and "New product ideas from technology" are relatively high for the first factor, while factor loadings of "Difficult to forecast technology" are relatively high for the second

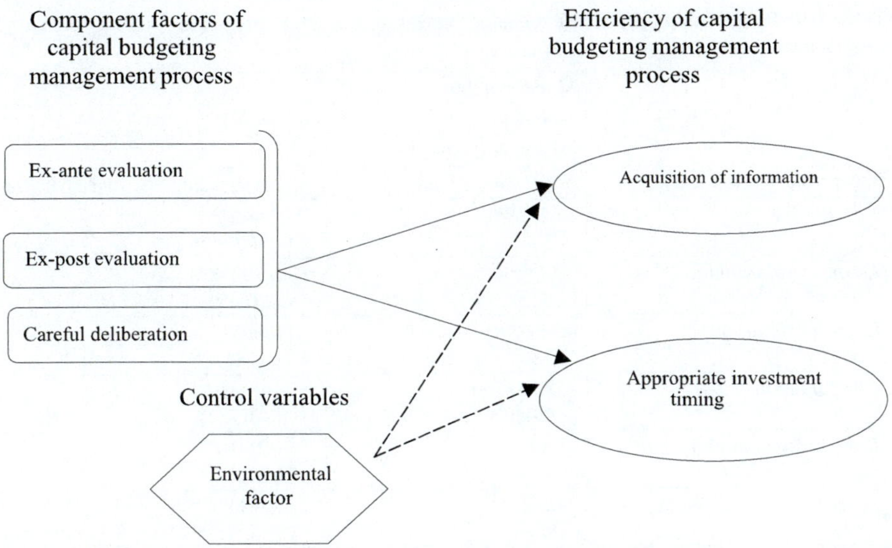

Fig. 6.2 Relationships between the capital budgeting management process and its efficiency: Analytical framework

factor. Therefore, we label the first-factor *Complexity of the environment* and the second-factor *Forecasting difficulty*.

Next, we examine the relationships between the three core components of the capital budgeting management process (*Ex-ante evaluation*, *Ex-post evaluation,* and *Careful deliberation*) and the efficiency of capital budgeting management (*Acquisition of information* and *Appropriate investment timing*), assuming two environmental factors (*Complexity of the environment* and *Forecasting difficulty*) as control variables. Here, each efficiency item for capital budgeting management is regressed on the components of the capital budgeting management process and the environmental factors. Figure 6.2 shows our research framework of the relationship between components of the capital budgeting management process and the efficiency of the capital budgeting management process. Table 6.9 presents the results of this regression analysis.

From Table 6.9, *Ex-ante evaluation* and *Ex-post evaluation* have a significant positive effect on *Acquisition of information*. This suggests that to rank the capital investment project and to check its profitability before making investment decision and to financially evaluate after investment lead to the acquisition of information about capital investment within the organization. *Ex-ante evaluation* has a significant positive effect on *Appropriate investment timing*. This indicates that the firm can carry out more timely capital investment by ranking the priority level of the proposed capital investment project. In addition, *Careful deliberation* has a significant negative effect on *Appropriate investment timing*, indicating that careful deliberation prevents prompt decision-making. Additionally, *Complexity of Environment* has a significant positive effect on *Acquisition of information* and on

Table 6.9 Relationships between the capital budgeting management process and its efficiency: Regression analysis results

	Model number	
	Model 1	Model 2
	Dependent variables	
Independent variables	*Acquisition of information*	*Appropriate investment timing*
Constant	1.651*** (4.348)	2.449*** (5.427)
Ex-ante evaluation	0.343*** (3.685)	0.293*** (2.650)
Ex-post evaluation	0.219*** (3.226)	0.095 (1.183)
Careful deliberation	−0.080 (−1.050)	−0.160* (−1.757)
Complexity of environment	0.112* (1.864)	0.160** (2.241)
Forecasting difficulty	−0.127** (−2.160)	−0.111 (−1.587)
Adjusted R-squared	0.314	0.131
F value	16.57**	6.115**
Number of observations	171	171

Figures in parentheses are t-statistics. *$p < .1$, **$p < .05$, ***$p < .01$. Two-tailed tests

Appropriate investment timing, and *Forecasting difficulty* has a significant negative effect on *Acquisition of information*. These results suggest that the efficiency of capital budgeting management is influenced by not only the capital budgeting management process but also by fierce environment.

Our results link to the practices which were fragmentary mentioned by prior studies of the capital budgeting process. Specifically, understanding of an investment idea can be deepened by a prior profitability check or by post-investment financial evaluation (Bower, 1970; Harris & Raviv, 1996; Kim, 2006; King, 1975; Neale, 1991) priority ranking helps in an intensive examination of a project (Istvan, 1961; King, 1975). Throughout this study, we clearly demonstrate what component factors enhance the efficiency of the entire capital budgeting process, which has been described *ad hoc* by the previous literature.

6.5 Conclusion

In this study, we approached the following two questions by using mail survey: (i) What is the capital budget management process in practice? and (ii) How do the core components of this process affect the efficiency of capital budgeting management?

We extracted three factors as core components of the capital budgeting management process: *Ex-ante evaluation*, *Ex-post evaluation*, and *Careful deliberation*. These components have distinctive features that are related to the functions achieved through the management process. Thus, the contribution of this study is that it describes the functions of a systematic capital budgeting management process applied throughout the entire process.

In addition, we demonstrated the effect of each component of capital budgeting management on its efficiency. Specifically, *Ex-ante evaluation* has a positive effect on *Acquisition of information* and *Appropriate investment timing*, and *Ex-post evaluation* has a positive effect on *Acquisition of information*. Additionally, *Careful deliberation* has a negative effect on *Appropriate investment timing*. The contribution of this study is that it illuminates the fact that the function achieved through the capital budgeting management process is not homogeneous but has differential effects. Perhaps our most significant finding is that extracting the effect of *Ex-ante evaluation* shows that management accounting is useful not only for simply providing the information for decision-making but also to make investment timely.

However, there are limitations to this study. First, since this study is mainly based on a statistical analysis of a mail survey, we could not describe the individual practices within the capital budgeting management process or the relationships among those practices. Moreover, the influence of the hierarchy of the organization, which has often been noted in the previous literature, is not considered here. Further investigations are needed via direct observation, such as interviews within the firm to understand how firms perform post-investment financial evaluation of prior profitability and how they correct the information within the organization during that process.

We should also be careful in interpreting these results because this study is conducted in an exploratory manner. We need to verify the generality of the component factors and empirical results suggested by this study by accumulating experiential knowledge in the future.

Despite these limitations, this study demonstrates that managerial control for capital budgeting is executed not only in the decision phase of the investment but throughout the entire management process. That is, we illustrated that capital budgeting is wider and deeper than described by past studies and textbooks. Therefore, we believe that our study offers the new directions for further research on capital budgeting management in management accounting.

References

Ackerman, R. W. (1970). Influence of integration and diversity on the investment process. *Administrative Science Quarterly, 15*(3), 341–351.

Bower, J. L. (1970). *Managing the resource allocation process: A study of corporate finance and investment*. Harvard Business Press.

Butler, R., Davis, L., Pike, R., & Sharp, J. (1993). *Strategic investment decisions: Theory, practices and process*. Routledge.

DeSarbo, W. S., Benedetto, C. A., Song, M., & Sinha, I. (2005). Revisiting the Miles and Snow strategic framework: Uncovering interrelationships between strategic types, capabilities, environmental uncertainty, and firm performance. *Strategic Management Journal, 25*(1), 47–74.

Gordon, L. A., & Pinches, G. E. (1984). *Improving capital budgeting: A decision support system approach*. Addition-Wesley.

Gordon, L. A., & Smith, K. J. (1992). Postauditing capital expenditures and firm performance: The role of asymmetric information. *Accounting, Organizations and Society, 17*(8), 741–757.

Haka, S. F. (2007). A review of the literature on capital budgeting and investment appraisal: Past, present, and future musings. In C. S. Chapman, A. G. Hopwood, & M. D. Shields (Eds.), *Handbook of managerial accounting research* (Vol. 2, pp. 697–728). London.

Harris, M., & Raviv, A. (1996). The capital budgeting process: Incentives and information. *The Journal of Finance, 51*(4), 1139–1174.

Haynes, W. W., & Solomon, M. B. (1962). A misplaced emphasis in capital budgeting. *The Quarterly Journal of Economics and Business, 2*(1), 39–46.

Hiromoto, T. (1993). *Beikoku Kannrikaikeironn Hattatsushi (History of the United States management accounting theory development)*. Moriyama Shoten. (in Japanese).

Istvan, D. F. (1961). *Capital expenditure decisions: How they are made in large corporations*. Bureau of Business Research, Indiana University.

Kim, D. (2006). Capital budgeting for new project: On the role of auditing in information acquisition. *Journal of Accounting and Economics, 41*(3), 257–270.

King, P. (1975). Is the emphasis of capital budgeting theory misplaced? *Journal of Business Finance and Accounting, 2*(1), 6–82.

Kubota, M., & Strategic Capital Investment Committee. (1995). *Sennryakuteki Setsubitoushi no Jissai: Ishikettei kara Kannsa made (Strategic capital investment in practice: From "decision making" to "audit")*. Nihon Keizai Shimbun Inc. (in Japanese).

Larcker, D. F. (1981). The perceived importance of selected information characteristics for strategic capital budgeting decisions. *The Accounting Review, 54*(3), 519–538.

Maccarrone, P. (1996). Organizing the capital budgeting process in large firms. *Management Decision, 34*(6), 43–56.

Marsh, P., Barwise, P., Thomas, K., & Wensley, R. (1988). Managing strategic investment decisions. In A. M. Pettigrew (Ed.), *Competitiveness and the management process* (pp. 86–136). Basil Blackwell.

Mukherjee, T. K., & Henderson, G. V. (1987). The Capital budgeting process: Theory and practice. *Interfaces, 17*(2), 78–90.

Neale, C. W. (1991). The benefits derived from post-auditing investing projects. *Omega the International Journal of Management Science, 19*(2/3), 113–120.

Shimizu, N. (2004). Nihonn ni okeru setsubitoushiyosann kennkyuu no gennjyou to kadai (Current state and problem of capital budgeting research in Japan). *Momoyama-gakuin daigakuin sogo kennkyuujo kiyo (Momoyama-gakuin University Graduate School General Institute Bulletin), 29*(3), 5–21. (in Japanese).

Shimizu, N. (2006). Kannrikaikei to shiteno shihonnyosann kenkyu no kadai (Problem of capital budgeting research as management accounting). *Sangyokeiri (Industrial Accounting), 65*(4), 42–53. (in Japanese).

Shimizu, N., Kato, Y., Sakaguchi, J., & Kawai, T. (2005). Setsubi toushi manejimennto purosesu to sono eikyou youinn (Capital budgeting management process and its influential factor). *Genkakeisan kenkyu (Cost Accounting Research), 29*(2), 56–65. (in Japanese).

Shimizu, N., Kato, Y., Sakaguchi, J., & Kawai, T. (2007). Setsubi toushi manegimennto no jittai chousa: setsubi toushi manejimennto no zenntaizou (Research of the capital budgeting management: Entire image of capital budgeting management). *Kigyoukaikei (Corporate Accounting), 59*(9), 66–73. (in Japanese).

Sugiyama, Y. (2002). *Toushi Kouritsu wo Takameru Shihonn Yosann (Capital budgeting that improves investment efficiency)*. Chuo Keizai Inc. (in Japanese).

Toribe, S. (1997). *Kigyou no Toushi Koudou Rironn (Theory of firm's investment activity)*. Chuo Keizai Inc. (in Japanese).

Yamamoto, M. (1994). Sennryakuteki toushi kettei to konntoro-ru shisutemu (Strategic investment decision and control system). *Research Annual Report "Economics" (Tohoku University), 56* (2), 121–137. (in Japanese).

Yamamoto, M. (1998). *Sennryakuteki Toushi Kettei no Keizaigaku (Economics of strategic investment decision)*. Bunshindo. (in Japanese).

Chapter 7
Exploring the Use of Balanced Scorecard in Functional Departments: A Case Study of Kirin Brewery Company, Limited

Takeyoshi Senoo

7.1 Introduction

The balanced scorecard (BSC) developed by Kaplan and Norton has evolved from a performance measurement system into a strategic management system (Kaplan & Norton, 2008). In previous studies, a strategic business unit (SBU) has been the basic unit for using a BSC (Hasegawa, 2004; Kaplan & Norton, 2001); hence, whether BSCs are utilized in functional departments—a lower level in the organizational hierarchy—remains somewhat unclear. However, since the functional departments, such as production, supply chain management (SCM), and sales, actually execute the business strategy that the SBU is responsible for, it is important to use a BSC to align them with the SBU's business strategy.

In this study, I developed hypotheses about the importance of using a BSC to align the functional departments with a business strategy by researching leading case studies of BSCs in functional departments.

Reprinted with permission of The Japan Cost Accounting Association. Originally published in *The Journal of Cost Accounting Research* 35(2): 51–61, 2011 (in Japanese).

T. Senoo (✉)
Faculty of Commerce, Chuo University, Tokyo, Japan
e-mail: senoo81@tamacc.chuo-u.ac.jp

© Springer Nature Singapore Pte Ltd. 2023

E. Yokota (ed.), *Frontiers of Japanese Management Control Systems*, Translational Systems Sciences 32, https://doi.org/10.1007/978-981-19-9778-5_7

7.2 Research Framework

7.2.1 *Aligning Functional Departments with a Business Strategy*

Kaplan and Norton (2008) present a BSC-focused strategic management system with six major stages. Of these, the third stage is described as "aligning the organization," in which an organization's diverse organizational units and employees are aligned with its overall business strategy.

Kaplan and Norton (2008) consider the SBU as the basic unit for analysis of line operating departments.[1] To align the SBU with the overall strategy of the company or group for which the corporate division is responsible, they focus on cascading the SBU's BSC, in addition to making vertical and horizontal alignment.

Thus, an SBU is considered a functional organization, and as Ito (2007) suggests, the employees of functional departments, which are further down in the organizational hierarchy, execute the business strategy. Therefore, functional department goals must be aligned with business strategies.

7.2.2 *Effectiveness of a BSC in Functional Departments*

Since an SBU's BSC may be too abstract to be used by functional department employees, the SBU's BSC may be cascaded to use BSCs for functional departments (Kaplan & Norton, 2001; Niven, 2006). However, there is debate about the effectiveness of using a BSC in functional departments.

Sakurai (2008) notes that while it is ideal to develop a BSC for every organizational unit, this poses an issue concerning cost effectiveness, and there is a risk that functional department's BSC may be only partially optimized. In considering how to cascade an SBU's BSC, Ito (2007) notes that it may be more effective to use Hoshin Kanri in departments that are lower (vs. higher) in the organizational hierarchy.

In addition, Grando and Belvedere (2008) considered the effectiveness of a BSC in operations departments such as manufacturing and logistics. Their case study revealed that the main findings of using a BSC in these departments were (1) the operations departments could adapt quickly to changes in management

[1] Only the line operating department is the subject of the analysis. In addition, what is expressed as a "business unit" or "business division" in previous studies may be described as an "SBU" based on the author's interpretation. In such cases, the expressions used in previous studies are noted in brackets. In previous studies, the actual use of BSCs in functional departments has been clarified to some extent in the context of the staff department. For example, Kaplan and Norton (2006) focus on three units: human resources, information technology, and finance, and consider the importance of a BSC in support units.

decision-making and (2) cooperation was promoted among all organizational units related to operations management.

According to these studies, although it is recognized that using a BSC in functional departments may be effective for aligning functional departments with the organization's overall business strategy, the specific method for doing so remains unclear.[2]

7.2.3 Research Questions

The following two research questions indicate the importance of using a BSC in functional departments.

The first research question concerns how an SBU's BSC can be cascaded to functional department BSCs to align functional departments with the business strategy for which the SBU is responsible. However, even within functional departments, there are many cases where there is a hierarchy in place, such as a unit that controls production and factories in the production department and a unit that controls sales and branch offices in the sales department. Therefore, this research question can be divided into two problems: cascading between an SBU and functional departments and cascading between higher and lower organizational levels within functional departments.

The second research question is how to use a BSC to align executing business strategies through collaboration between each of the functional departments, such as production, SCM, and sales. This issue is important because no functional department can execute the SBU's business strategy alone.

This study analyzes and considers the following to establish hypotheses to clarify these two research questions through case studies.

7.3 Research Method

Since there is ample scope for case studies in Japanese management accounting research to develop theory (Yokota et al., 2010), a case study was conducted to establish the hypotheses. The subject of the survey is BSCs for the functional departments of Kirin Brewery Company Limited (hereafter abbreviated as Kirin Brewery).

[2]The general method for cascading a BSC to departments below the SBU has been clarified in previous studies to some extent with case studies of Nova Scotia Power and Mobil NAM&R (Ito, 2007). However, few studies have clarified a specific approach to using a BSC in multiple specific functional departments such as production, SCM, and sales, as is done in this study.

Table 7.1 Outline of interview information (all job titles are as of the interview date)

	Survey date (time)	Interviewees	Interviewer
1st	October 30, 2008 (2 h)	Two people in charge of planning in the Planning Dept. at Kirin Brewery; one person in charge of the Corporate Planning Dept. at Kirin Holdings Company	Author, Eri Yokota (Professor, Keio University)
2nd	March 16, 2009 (1 h)	Two people in charge of planning in the Planning Dept. of Kirin Brewery; one person in charge of logistics and planning at the Logistics Dept. in the SCM Division	As above
3rd	April 30, 2009 (1 h 30 min)	Two people in charge of planning in the Planning Dept. at Kirin Brewery (one of whom was a member of the Sales Department in the Sales Division until March 2009)	As above
4th	August 24, 2009 (1 h 45 min)	One person in charge of planning in the Planning Dept. of Kirin Brewery; one department head at the Production Management Department of the Production Division at Kirin Brewery	Author
5th	December 29, 2009 (3 h)	Two people in charge of planning at the Planning Dept., Kirin Brewery	Author, Eri Yokota

Source: Created by the author

The reasons for choosing Kirin Brewery as the subject of this study are as follows. Kirin Brewery cascades its BSC to its functional departments of production, SCM, and sales. As will be described later, the purpose for this is clear, and some effect has been recognized by aligning the functional departments with the business strategy. The case of Kirin Brewery can be regarded as a leading case study of a BSC in functional departments.

The research was accomplished through interviews; the outline of the interview process is shown in Table 7.1.[3]

[3] A semi-structured interview format was used for all interviews; all interview contents were documented on the same day without a recording, except for the fourth interview. To clarify the content and process of the strategic management system centered on the BSC that is shared within the Kirin Group, prior to the interview with Kirin Brewery, interviews were conducted once with the Business Promotion Group, Group Strategy Department, of the former Kirin Brewery (March 6, 2007) before the pure holding company system was adopted, and twice with the Corporate Planning Department of Kirin Holdings Company (December 4, 2007 and July 29, 2008), for three interviews. Based on these three interviews, Senoo and Yokota (2009) clarified the overall structure of the strategic management system in the Kirin Group. Please refer to Senoo and Yokota (2009) for more information.

7.4 Case Study: The BSC in Functional Departments of Kirin Brewery[4]

7.4.1 Case Study Outline

Kirin Brewery is the core operating company of the Kirin Group, with Kirin Holdings Company, Limited (hereafter abbreviated as Holdings) as a pure holding company. The Kirin Group has implemented a strategic management system centered on a strategy map (BSC).[5]

Kirin Group has adopted a pure holding company system; considering it from the context of the normal BSC (Kaplan & Norton, 2001, 2006, 2008), Holdings corresponds to the corporate division and is responsible for group strategy, while the operating company, Kirin Brewery, corresponds to the SBU and is responsible for the business strategy. In Fig. 7.1, the units for developing strategy maps in the Kirin Group are illustrated based on the context. The dotted line between the corporate level and the SBU level shown in Fig. 7.1 indicates that the operating company's strategy map is not based on that of Holdings but on its own strategic policy.

Consequently, the strategy map of Holdings is abstract. In addition, since Kirin Brewery implements management by objectives at the individual level, a dotted line is also drawn between the functional department and on-site employee levels. However, since this study focuses on analyzing the BSCs in functional departments, the relationship between the company-wide strategy maps of Holdings and Kirin Brewery and management by objectives at the individual level are not included in the analysis.

---

[4]The purpose of this study is to establish hypotheses, add new information based on Yokota and Senoo's case study (2010a, 2010b), and focus the discussion on the case study. The main purpose of Yokota and Senoo (2010a, 2010b) was to describe this case study. Please refer to Yokota and Senoo (2010a, 2010b) for more information.

[5]The Kirin Group, which includes Kirin Brewery, uses various tools, such as index/objective entry sheets and performance evaluation tables that are centered on strategy maps, based on its medium-term management plan. A strategy management system called Kirin Innovative & Strategic Management Action Program has been implemented within the group, and the process of planning, monitoring, and evaluation is performed to execute the strategy. Referring to Hasegawa (2004), who asserts the theory that a BSC is a strategic management system that combines a strategy map and BSC in a narrow sense, this system as a whole can be interpreted more broadly as a BSC. In Kirin Brewery, a strategic management system is implemented for each organizational unit that creates a strategy map, and the main purpose of the strategy map is to specifically describe and clarify the strategy for achieving the future vision in the planning stage through the causal relationships of the four BSC perspectives. For details on the above, see Senoo and Yokota (2009) and Yokota and Senoo (2010a). In the explanation of the Kirin Brewery's case study, except for the description of the effect of the BSC, the term strategy map is generally used instead of BSC. In Kirin Brewery, the expression used is "strategy map of organizational unit manager," such as the strategy map of the president and sales manager. However, the expression used in this study is "strategy map of an organizational unit" to describe strategy maps for the entire company and the sales department to avoid confusion in terminology.

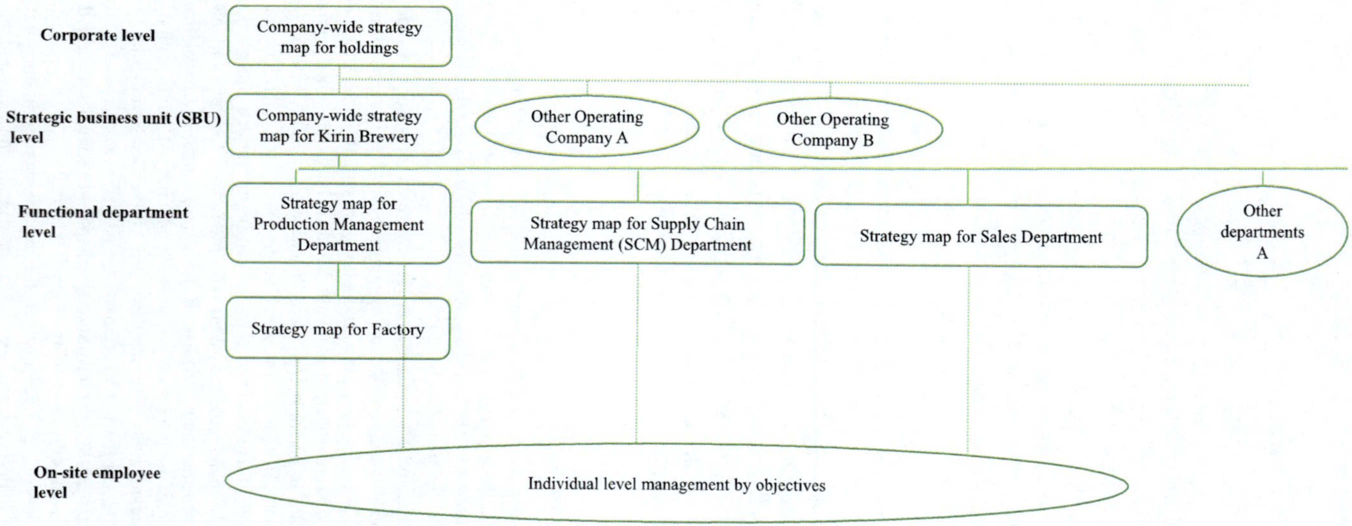

Fig. 7.1 Units for developing strategy maps in the Kirin Group. Source: Created by the author based on the descriptions in Senoo and Yokota (2009) and Yokota and Senoo (2010a)

Kirin Brewery's organizational structure and strategic management system are changed in detail every year to avoid losing substance. As of the end of December 2008, the scope to which Kirin Brewery's organizational structure and strategy maps are commonly used in each organizational hierarchy is shown in Fig. 7.2. This study analyzes the situation that existed when the strategy map for 2009 was developed.

As shown in the areas within the dotted lines in Fig. 7.2, the company-wide strategy map that describes the business strategy is commonly used by the president and general managers of the production division, SCM division, and sales division. Kirin Brewery's business is organized along functional lines, and these three divisions that oversee each functional department are at the highest level of the organizational hierarchy.

The company-wide strategy map is cascaded to the strategy maps of the functional departments such as production, SCM, and sales.[6] The first purpose is to methodically increase customer awareness by developing a customer perspective in each functional department, as they tend to specialize in their own department's functions. Next, to clarify the fairness and responsibility of evaluations, the performance evaluation systems of all organizational unit managers should be unified across the company.

There are various sections in each functional department, and each section is a unit concerning developing strategy maps. To respond to this study's two research questions, the case studies are analyzed and assessed using the production management section and factory as the subject in the production department, the logistics section as the subject in the SCM department, and the sales section as the subject in the sales department, as shown within the framework of the dotted line in Fig. 7.2.

7.4.2 Cascading the BSC

At Kirin Brewery, on-site employees in each functional department are not very aware of the company-wide strategy map and are often aware only of the strategy map of the department to which they belong. Therefore, cascading its BSC is important for aligning the functional departments with the business strategy.

7.4.2.1 Cascading the BSC from the SBU to Functional Departments

Kirin Brewery has implemented the following three initiatives to cascade its BSC from the SBU to the functional departments.

[6] Kirin Brewery has cascaded the strategic map to staff departments such as human resources and public relations; this is not reflected in this study because its purpose is to analyze only the line departments of production, SCM, and sales.

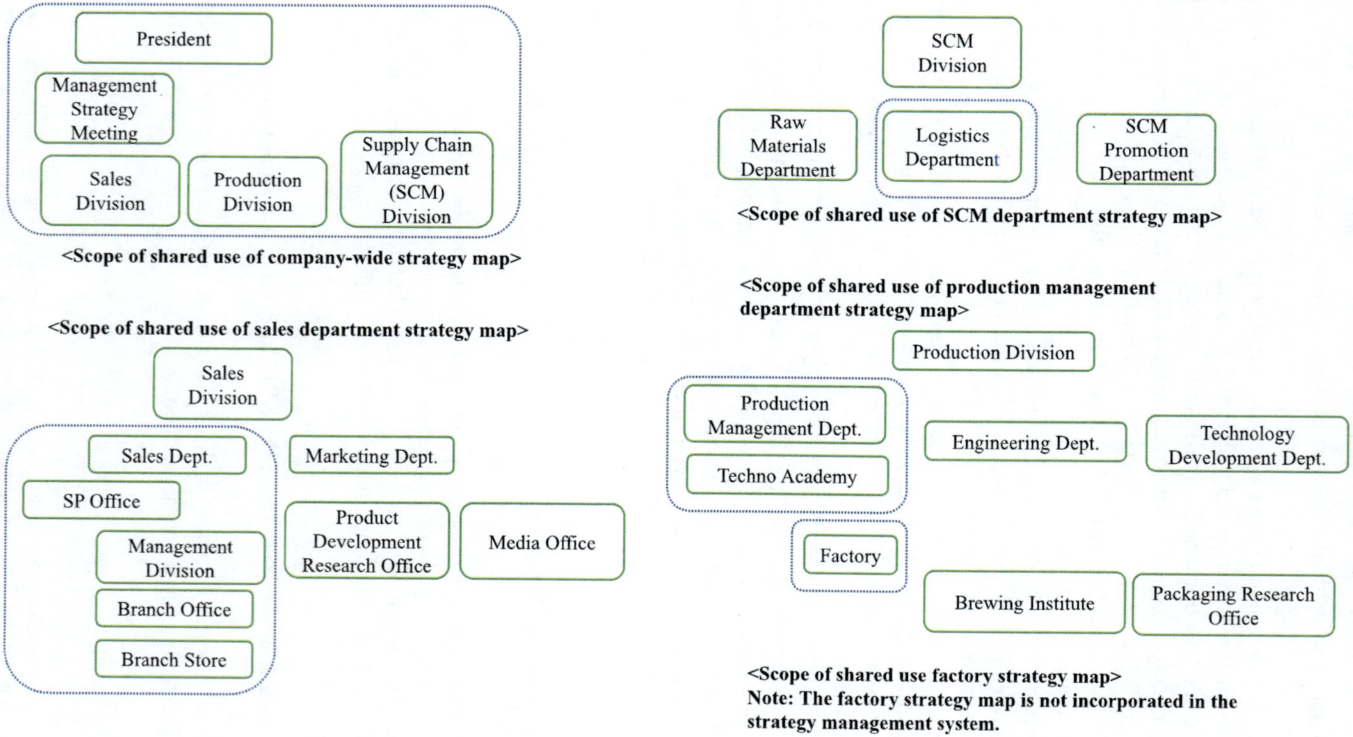

Fig. 7.2 Kirin Brewery organisational structure and scope of shared use of strategy maps (as of the end of December 2008). Source: Created by the author based on a section in Yokota and Senoo (2010a, p. 128)

The first initiative is cascading through strategic themes (Kaplan & Norton, 2008); the strategic themes show commonality with the strategy map of the entire company and the maps of each functional division. Figure 7.3 presents a conceptual diagram of the strategic map of Kirin Brewery's sales department. The four strategic themes of "strengthening customer relationships and technological capabilities," "improving CSR," "improving productivity and cost competitiveness," and "reforming the organizational culture" are the same as those described in the company-wide strategic map.[7] This also applies to the production and SCM departments. Appropriate cascading is possible by describing the strategy maps based on common strategic themes.

The second initiative is to standardize the financial and customer perspectives. For example, in Kirin Brewery's sales department's strategy map shown in Fig. 7.3, the strategic objectives from the financial and customer perspectives are exactly the same as those of the entire company. This is because importance has been placed on the type of objectives that are independently set by the functional departments in the internal processes and learning and growth perspectives, in contrast to the financial and customer perspectives, which are company-wide objectives.

There is a high degree of discretion in setting key performance indicators (KPI) in functional departments from the internal process and learning and growth perspectives.[8] This is done to improve the KPI for the financial and customer perspectives, which are recognized as the collective responsibility of the entire company, such as EVA; in the functional departments, emphasis is placed on the types of KPI that should be set from a perspective below the functions of individual departments.

The contrast between the KPI for the financial and customer perspectives, which are shared throughout the company, and KPI from the internal processes and learning and growth perspectives, which are unique to the functional departments, can be surmised from the weighting of the KPI in performance evaluations. Table 7.2 shows the weighting for each of the BSC perspectives for the performance evaluations of general managers and managers of each functional department. The general manager is allotted the same number of points as the president, and the weight of the financial and customer perspectives is high. For managers that are more involved at sites, such as the production and SCM departments, the points allotted to the weight of internal processes and learning, and growth are high. However, owing to the sales

[7] For a conceptual diagram of Kirin Brewery's company-wide strategy map, see Yokota and Senoo (2010a, p. 131). In Kirin Brewery, instead of "strategic themes," "strategic objectives," and "performance measures," which are usually used in the context of a BSC (Kaplan & Norton, 2001, 2006, 2008), unique terms such as "strategic stem," "strategic issue," and "results measures" are used. The former terms are used in this study to avoid confusion.

[8] However, there are performance measures unique to each functional department from the financial and customer perspectives, and there are performance measures shared among the entire company from the perspectives of internal processes and learning and growth. For specific examples of the BSC performance measures in each functional division of Kirin Brewery, see Yokota and Senoo (2010b).

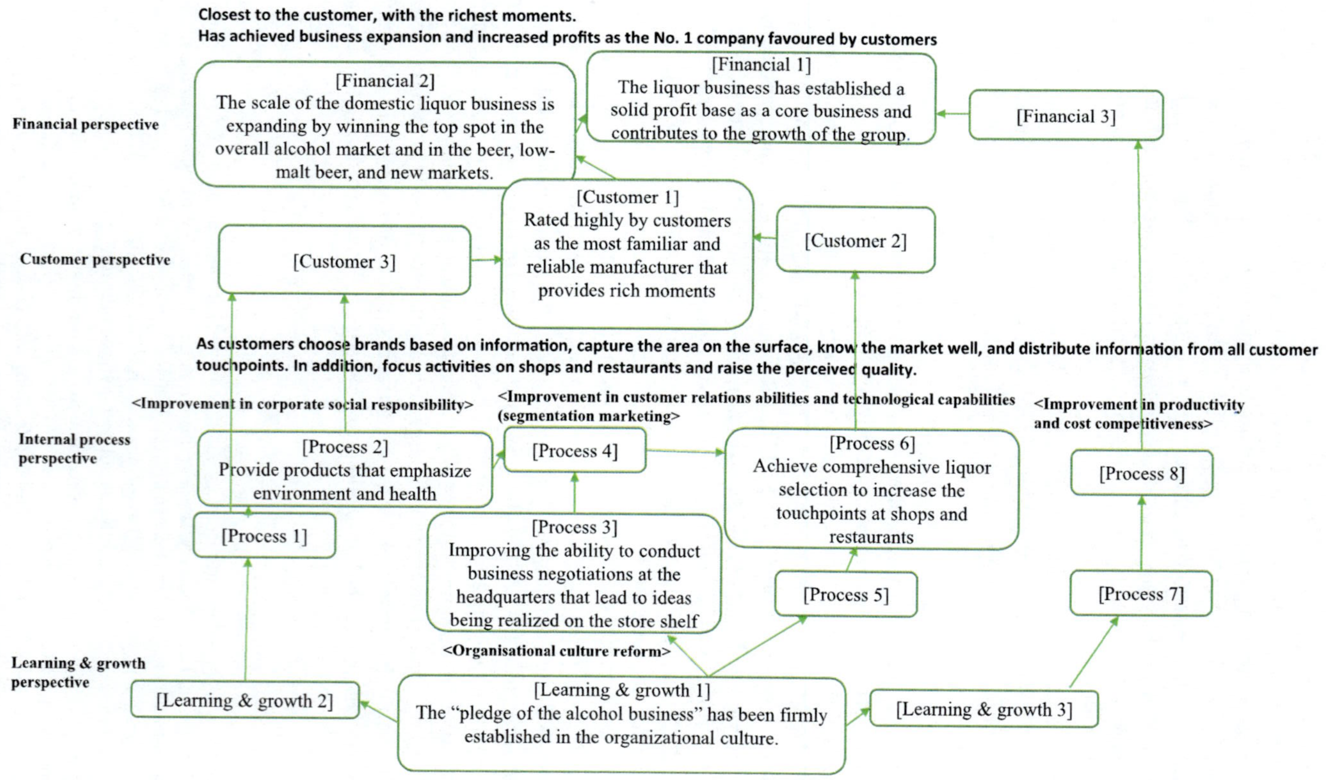

Fig. 7.3 Conceptual diagram of the strategy map of Kirin Brewery's sales department. Source: Created based on Kirin Brewery internal documents and partially modified by the author

Table 7.2 Weighting for each BSC perspective for performance evaluations of general managers and managers of each functional department

<table>
<tr><th></th><th colspan="2">Production Dept.</th><th colspan="2">Supply Chain Management (SCM) Dept.</th><th colspan="2">Sales Dept.</th></tr>
<tr><th></th><th>Production Dept. General Manager</th><th>Production Dept. Manager</th><th>SCM General Manager</th><th>Logistics Manager</th><th>Sales General Manager</th><th>Sales Manager</th></tr>
<tr><td>Financial</td><td>4</td><td>2</td><td>4</td><td>2</td><td>4</td><td>4</td></tr>
<tr><td>Customer</td><td>2</td><td>1</td><td>2</td><td>1</td><td>2</td><td>2</td></tr>
<tr><td>Internal processes</td><td rowspan="2">4</td><td rowspan="2">7</td><td rowspan="2">4</td><td rowspan="2">7</td><td rowspan="2">4</td><td rowspan="2">4</td></tr>
<tr><td>Learning and growth</td></tr>
</table>

Source: Created by the author based on the description from Yokota and Senoo (2010a, 2010b)

function's characteristics, the points allotted to the sales department managers are weighted with an emphasis on results, as is the case with the general managers.

Standardizing the financial and customer perspectives can clarify the relationship between the financial and customer strategic objectives and performance measures, as these are the collective responsibility of the entire company. The strategic objectives and performance measures from the internal processes and learning and growth perspectives can be set at the discretion of the functional department to achieve its strategic objectives. Hence, this is believed to enable appropriate cascading.

The third initiative is frequent communication about strategies between the head office and functional departments. At Kirin Brewery, in response to the strategic objectives in the company-wide strategy map drafted by the head office's planning department, the organizational unit manager plays a central role, listening to the opinions of on-site employees and developing a strategy map for each functional department in cooperation with the head office planning department. In the cascading process, frequent communication between the head office planning department and functional departments is necessary to set, coordinate, and explain strategic objectives and to identify problems. This forms a connection between the strategic objectives of the entire company and the strategic objectives of individual departments, and importance is placed on ensuring the validity of the causal relationship between strategic objectives and performance measures on the strategic map in individual departments. Such discussions primarily deal with strategies. Engaging in frequent communication about strategy using strategy maps requires a great deal of time and effort. However, this process is believed to enable appropriate cascading.

7.4.2.2 BSCs Between Higher and Lower Levels of the Organizational Hierarchies in Functional Departments

Next, to examine the cascading of the BSC between the higher and lower levels of the organizational hierarchies in functional departments, I look at Kirin Brewery's sales and production departments.

As shown in Fig. 7.2, as of the end of December 2008, the sales department had not developed a strategy map for each management division or branch office, and there is shared use of the strategy map for the sales department. When the BSC was introduced in 2003, a strategy map was developed up to the branch office level. However, considering cost effectiveness and the amount of time and effort required to develop a BSC, there was only a small amount of variation in functions between each of the regional branch offices. Because time had passed since the introduction of the BSC, there was an advanced understanding of it even at the branch office level, and the entire sales department now uses a shared strategy map.

By contrast, a strategy map had been developed in the production department not only for the production management section but also for each of the factories. The factory strategic management system differs from the company-wide one; however, unlike the sales department, different strategy maps are used in the higher and lower levels of the production department's organizational hierarchy that have the same function. The reason for this is that the aim is to operate the management system consistently by connecting the business strategy and overall production department's strategy with the issues that should be dealt with by the factory using a shared mechanism.

In an interview with the planning department of the head office, the opinion was expressed that the same strategy map should be used if the functions are the same. Since there is little difference in how organizational units with the same function contribute to the business strategy and a great deal of time and effort is required to cascade the strategy map, my opinion is that the same strategy map should be used within the production department.

7.4.3 Coordination Between Functional Departments Using the BSC

Kirin Brewery highlights that each functional department collaborates to execute business strategies. Therefore, the following two initiatives have been implemented, using its BSC for coordination between functional departments.

In the first initiative, the respective general managers of the production, SCM, and sales divisions at Kirin Brewery share a company-wide strategy map, as shown in Fig. 7.2. Previously, a strategy map was developed for each division. One of the reasons this was discontinued was that the general managers of each functional department shared a company-wide strategic map, which facilitated coordination between functional departments.

In addition, coordination between each of the functional departments in production, SCM, and sales is encouraged in the company-wide strategic map. Thus, it is conceivable that sharing the company-wide strategy map among the highest levels of the organizational hierarchy of each functional department and encouraging coordination since the strategy map makes it possible to coordinate between functional departments to execute business strategies.

In the second initiative, certain strategic objectives and performance measures are shared by functional departments. For example, the SCM department and sales department share performance measures related to "pallet collection." While the SCM department oversees pallet collection because functional departments collaborate to execute business strategies, the sales department is in charge of negotiations with wholesalers (dealers) regarding pallet collection. Although there are a small number of shared strategic objectives and performance measures, this is considered to contribute to executing the business strategy through the collaboration of each functional department.

7.4.4 BSC Effects in Functional Departments

Kirin Brewery recognizes the following two points as the BSC effects on functional departments.

First, the relationships between the functions of each department and the business strategy have been clarified. As mentioned above, functional departments tend to specialize in the functions of their own department, but by cascading the company-wide BSC and developing BSCs for individual departments, the relationship with the business strategy has become clear.

In addition, since an individual department's BSC describes the financial and customer perspectives, which are objectives shared by the entire company, there is strong awareness of how to contribute to achieving those objectives at the discretion of the individual department.

Next, the effect of facilitating coordination between functional departments to execute the business strategy was also recognized; however, it was noted that this was not solely owing to the BSC. The BSC is simply a tool for executing strategies and not something that on-site functional department employees are consistently aware of daily. Concerning daily activities, for example, a Total Cost Reform meeting, which is a meeting where staff from each department at the same site gather, is held every month to adjust. It was pointed out in the interviews that it is important for such activities to be consistent with the BSC.

7.5 Discussion

This case study of Kirin Brewery shows the importance of using a BSC in functional departments; thus, a hypothesis was proposed to clarify the two research questions posed in this study.

The first research question describes the problem of cascading a BSC. The case study suggests that cascading between the SBU and functional departments requires the three initiatives: functional departments can be aligned with business strategies through cascading using strategic themes, standardization of the financial and customer perspectives, and frequent communication regarding the strategies of the head office and functional departments.

The second question considers cascading between the higher and lower levels of the organizational hierarchies in functional departments. Kirin Brewery used one BSC for the same functions in the sales department, whereas the production department used different BSCs for the same function in the higher and lower levels of the organizational hierarchy. As previously mentioned, it is my opinion that cascading a BSC within the same functional department is not necessary, and thus I propose a hypothesis stating the same.

Regarding the problem posed in the second research question about coordinating between functional departments using a BSC, the following two initiatives are required. First, the highest level of the organizational hierarchy in each functional department can share the use of the SBU's BSC; second, the strategic objectives and performance measures can be shared among the functional departments to allow executing business strategies in a coordinated manner. When this is done, the BSC should be consistent with the daily activities of the SBU.

In this case study, use of a BSC in functional departments not only clarified the relationship between the functions of each department and the business strategy but was also shown to considerably contribute to the sharing of strategies between functional departments.

7.6 Conclusion

This study considered the importance of a BSC in aligning functional departments with business strategies through the study of leading cases and presented multiple hypotheses about the problems with cascading a BSC and using it to coordinate between functional departments.

In the future, I would like to conduct additional case studies addressing the hypotheses presented in this study and empirically verify them through quantitative field research with one or several companies as the subject.

References

Grando, A., & Belvedere, V. (2008). Exploiting the balanced scorecard in the operations department the Ducati Motor Holding case. *Production Planning & Control, 19*(5), 495–507.

Hasegawa, K. (2004). Basic theory of the balanced scorecard and strategy map. In T. Shimizu (Ed.), *The strategic management system: The balanced scorecard for companies and non-profit organizations* (pp. 23–62). Toyo Keizai Inc.. (in Japanese).

Ito, K. (2007). *Case study—Management accounting for strategy: Development of a new management system*. Chuokeizai-sha. (in Japanese).

Kaplan, R. S., & Norton, D. P. (2001). *The strategy-focused organization: How balanced scorecard companies thrive in the new business environment*. Harvard Business School Press.

Kaplan, R. S., & Norton, D. P. (2006). *Alignment: Using the balanced scorecard to create corporate synergies*. Harvard Business School Press.

Kaplan, R. S., & Norton, D. P. (2008). *The execution premium: Linking strategy to operations for competitive advantage*. Harvard Business School Press.

Niven, P. R. (2006). *Balanced scorecard step-by-step maximizing performance and maintaining results* (2nd ed.). John Wiley & Sons.

Sakurai, M. (2008). *Balanced scorecard: Theory and case studies, Revised Version*. Dobunkan Shuppan. (in Japanese).

Senoo, T., & Yokota, E. (2009). *Case study of the strategic management system in the Kirin Group, Keio University Commerce Society Discussion Paper FY08, No. 7* (in Japanese).

Yokota, E., Arai, K., Otani, H., Metoki, T., Fukushima, K., Senoo, T., & T. (2010). The validity of field studies in Japanese management accounting research. *Mita Business Review, 53*(2), 101–121. (in Japanese).

Yokota, E., & Senoo, T. (2010a). A case study of strategic management system in Kirin Brewery Co., Ltd. (1). *Mita Business Review, 53*(2), 123–136. (in Japanese).

Yokota, E., & Senoo, T. (2010b). A case study of strategic management system in Kirin Brewery Co., Ltd. (2). *Mita Business Review, 53*(3), 45–58. (in Japanese).

Chapter 8
Discussing the Balanced Scorecard as an Interactive Control System: A Case Study of a Food Company

Eri Yokota and Takeyoshi Senoo

8.1 Introduction

Thirty years have passed since Robert Kaplan and David Norton developed the Balanced Scorecard (BSC) in 1992. The BSC was initially introduced as a performance measurement system that included non-financial measures; however, since then, it has been argued that it should be used as a strategic management system (Kaplan, 2009; Kaplan & Norton, 2001). While several issues have been highlighted, the BSC is also attracting attention in Japan (Hasegawa, 2011) and has been adopted by some Japanese companies, although the number is still low.[1]

During these years, Kaplan and Norton had argued that BSC should be used as an interactive control system (ICS) proposed by Robert Simons (Kaplan, 2009; Kaplan & Norton, 2001). Although the concept of ICS is not clearly defined by Simons, Bisbe et al. (2007) consolidated it into five properties (described below). It is therefore thought that if management control systems (MCS) that include BSC fall within these properties, they are being used as ICS. Is this, however, really the case?

Reprinted with permission of Maki Makoto Foundation. Originally published in the *Melco Journal of Management Accounting Research* 5(1): 3–14, 2012 (in Japanese).

[1] Based on the responses to questionnaires mailed to 1691 companies listed in the first section of the Tokyo Stock Exchange between February and March 2010 (responses were received from 221 companies for a response rate of 13.1%), 10.5% of companies use BSC (Yokota & Senoo, 2011a, pp. 62–63).

E. Yokota
Faculty of Business and Commerce, Keio University, Tokyo, Japan
e-mail: yokota@fbc.keio.ac.jp

T. Senoo (✉)
Faculty of Commerce, Chuo University, Tokyo, Japan
e-mail: senoo81@tamacc.chuo-u.ac.jp

© Springer Nature Singapore Pte Ltd. 2023

E. Yokota (ed.), *Frontiers of Japanese Management Control Systems*, Translational Systems Sciences 32, https://doi.org/10.1007/978-981-19-9778-5_8

After examining the case of a company that previously used BSC under the firm leadership of top management in the context of the five ICS properties identified by Bisbe et al. (2007), we analyzed why the company decided to discontinue using BSC, which had seemingly been used as an ICS, and considered what the requisites are for using BSC as an ICS.

8.2 Research Framework

8.2.1 General Properties of the ICS

Simons (1995, 2000) expanded on the existing concept of MCS and proposed a control framework comprising belief systems, boundary systems, diagnostic control systems (DCS), and ICS. Of these four control levers, recent MCS studies have concentrated on DCS and ICS as concepts focusing on the use of MCS rather than its design. In particular, there has been an increase in quantitative and qualitative empirical research on ICS (e.g., Bisbe & Otley, 2004; Tuomela, 2005; Widener, 2007). Simons argues that in businesses with high strategic uncertainty, strategies emerge from learning through debate and dialogue between top management and operating managers using MCS as ICS (Simons, 2000). In case studies, Marginson (2002) classified units of analysis into MCS properties, including ICS, influence on strategic activity at the individual level (manager), and strategic outcomes at the firm level. The effect of ICS at the individual level has been analyzed by Marginson (2002) and within some qualitative empirical research; however, the numbers are limited with few findings. For example, as Simons (1995, 2000) argues, it is not entirely clear whether ICS brings out managers' innovative activities. However, the effect of ICS at the firm level has been clarified to a degree in multiple cases of quantitative empirical research. For example, Bisbe and Malagueño (2009) and Bisbe and Otley (2004) identify various positive and negative effects of ICS on product innovation.

Bisbe et al. (2007) questions the ambiguity of conceptual definitions of ICS in existing research and performed thematic analysis of 108 quotations defining the features of ICS within Simons' seven studies.[2] From this, They defined ICS as a multidimensional construct containing all of the following five properties (Bisbe et al., 2007).[3]

[2] Bisbe et al. classified the coded quotations into three groups according to the classifications by Marginson (2002) mentioned earlier. The effect on strategic activity and strategic outcomes at the firm level show the effect and not the ICS concept itself; thus, they were excluded from analysis, and only the codes relating to the ICS properties were used for conceptual definitions (Bisbe et al., 2007).

[3] Bisbe et al. (2007) also argue that in some cases conceptual definitions are more suitable where the relationship between the construct and the measurement indicator is viewed as a formative model (relationship where the construct is composed of indicators) or an emergent model

The first of the five properties of ICS in Bisbe et al. (2007) is "an intensive use by top management."

The second is "an intensive use by operating managers." This means that both top management and operating managers devote a significant part of their limited time and attention span to MCS. The ICS management style is the opposite of management by exception. Bisbe et al. (2007) view the operating manager level as the middle-management level.

The third is "a pervasiveness of face-to-face challenges and debates." Here, top management and operating managers engage in face-to-face challenges and debates through direct, continuous, and frequent interchange and dialogue. Simons identifies "information generated by the system is an important and recurring agenda addressed by the highest levels of management" as a characteristic of ICS (Simons, 1995, p. 97) and Bisbe et al. (2007) views operating managers as the middle-management level. Thus, we can interpret that these dialogues are exchanged within the highest levels of the organization.[4]

Fourth is "a focus on strategic uncertainties." This refers to the properties relating to the content and nature of ICS communication. As ICS is a lever for controlling strategic uncertainty, there is a need to gather and provide information on the impact of strategic uncertainties that are threats or opportunities with the potential to invalidate existing business strategies.

Fifth is "a non-invasive, facilitating, and inspirational involvement." Under ICS, personal involvement by top management must be empowering and not intervening. That is, there is a need for a positive informational environment that brings out dialogue and encourages information sharing. Therefore, the type of involvement is essentially different from hands-on management.

Of course, as argued by Bisbe et al. (2007), ICS does not necessarily have to satisfy all of these five properties. Moreover, the ICS originally proposed by Simons may contain properties other than these. Nonetheless, empirical research on ICS published after Bisbe et al. (2007), including Bisbe and Malagueño (2009) and Widener (2007) often refer to the definition by Bisbe et al. (2007); therefore, in this sense, it has become the authoritative definition. However, there are few

(two-dimensional formative model) and not as a reflective model (relationship where the indicators reflect the construct) or a latent model (two-dimensional reflective model) in management accounting and MCS research. In addition, it is argued that ICS is a multidimensional construct and should be viewed as an emergent model comprising five dimensions (Bisbe et al., 2007).

[4]However, Simons also considers "demands frequent and regular attention from operating managers at all levels of the organization" in his 1995 book (Simons, 1995, p. 97), and "must be used by managers at multiple levels of the organization" in his 2000 book (Simons, 2000, p. 220) as characteristics of ICS; thus, it should be noted that Simons does not necessarily downplay its use by lower-level managers.

previous studies that include the definition of all of these five properties in their analysis of ICS.[5]

8.2.2 *BSC as an ICS*

The developers of BSC—Kaplan and Norton—argue that BSC should be used as an ICS. For example, Kaplan and Norton (2001) argue that BSC fits the four characteristics of ICS described in Simons (1995) and Simons (2000). Kaplan (2009) states that when BSC was originally developed in 1992, it was envisioned as a performance measurement system that included non-financial measures, which equated to DCS, but became an ICS when BSC evolved into a strategic management system (Kaplan, 2009).

However, the books and studies by Kaplan and Norton rarely give a strict definition of BSC as ICS. For example, in Kaplan and Norton (2008), the use of BSC at strategy review meetings is expressed as ICS (Kaplan & Norton, 2008); however, other than this, there are few descriptions examining BSC specifically as ICS.

There is also quantitative and qualitative empirical research on ICS that looks at BSC as one of the typical MCS (Bisbe & Malagueño, 2009; Bisbe & Otley, 2004; Tuomela, 2005).[6] However, these studies do not examine all five properties of ICS described by Bisbe et al. (2007). Consequently, there is considerable scope for examination of the suitability of the five properties regarding BSC as ICS.

8.2.3 *Relationship Between the BSC as an ICS and Other MCS*

According to Simons, MCS such as BSC can be used either as DCS or ICS; however, except for special cases, specific MCS at a given company are used only as DCS or only as ICS. Moreover, generally at a given company, there is only one MCS used as ICS, and all other MCS are used as DCS (Simons, 1995, 2000).

However, as noted by Bisbe and Malagueño (2009), Tuomela (2005), Widener (2007), that specific MCS including BSC at a given company can function as both

---

[5]For example, questions regarding ICS by Bisbe and Malagueño (2009) and Bisbe and Otley (2004) only consider properties 1–3 (Bisbe & Malagueño, 2009). Questions by Widener (2007) only consider properties 1 and 2.

[6]However, strictly speaking, BSC in Bisbe and Malagueño (2009) and Bisbe and Otley (2004) is not limited to the BSC described by Kaplan and Norton but is a more general term covering a performance measurement system that includes both financial and non-financial performance measures of multiple perspectives (Bisbe & Malagueño, 2009; Bisbe & Otley, 2004).

DCS and ICS.[7] Arae (2008) examined the cases of Tuomela (2005) and argues that the BSC measures that relate to strategic uncertainties should be used as ICS, and the others should be used as DCS.

Nonetheless, regardless of whether BSC is used as ICS only or used as both DCS and ICS, if BSC is used as ICS, other MCS are fundamentally used as DCS. Since there is little previous research that examines the relationship of BSC and other MCS from a DCS and ICS perspective, there is considerable scope for study regarding this aspect.

8.3 Research Method

In this study, we examine a case study regarding the use of BSC as ICS based on previous research on ICS by Bisbe et al. (2007) and others. The study aims at the BSC of a food company (Company X).[8] As will be discussed later, Company X was seemingly using BSC to meet the five properties of ICS described in Bisbe et al. (2007); however, this is a distinctive outlier in that it later discontinued its use of the BSC. Thus, we consider this a suitable case study to examine the concept of BSC as ICS—an area where there remains inadequate theoretical study (Merchant & Van der Stede, 2006; Yokota et al., 2010).

We conducted unstructured interviews totaling 11 h as shown in outline in Table 8.1 to understand Company X's BSC.[9] In addition, we used published studies related to Company X and confirmed the contents with the company to enhance the objectivity of the statements.[10] We also obtained statements from Company X internal material, such as presentation material used by Company X President when BSC was introduced and being used, and BSC-related presentation material by divisions that received company awards.

[7] Bisbe and Malagueño raised the following three possibilities as reasons that such views are held. First, only one MCS is analyzed, making identification by dividing certain MCS as DCS and other MCS as ICS virtually impossible. Second, the nature of the MCS analyzed, such as performance management systems, is too wide-ranging; thus, there are many internal subsystems that can be used as DCS or ICS. The third is that there is no strict conceptualization of the properties that make up ICS (Bisbe & Malagueño, 2009).

[8] We used the name Company X because the company wished to remain anonymous.

[9] In this study, we sought to document, as much as possible, the information disclosed to us to improve the validity of the case study described in Yokota et al. (2010). We have not, however, described the theoretical foundation. The reason for this is that the theoretical foundation of the ICS concept analyzed in this study itself is not clear, as Bisbe et al. (2007) showed by way of an example of the practice-defined concept.

[10] To ensure the anonymity of Company X, we cannot list the details of references relating to Company X, but the published articles we referred to include Nikkei Information Strategy and Nikkei Sangyo Shimbun.

Table 8.1 Summary of interview data

Round	Survey date (time)	Interviewee's position at time of interview	Interviewee's primary position when company was using BSC	Recorded: Y/N
1	April 16, 2010 (2 h)	Corporate officer A, production division	Factory manager	N
2	November 12, 2010 (2 h)	Director B, management division	Company manager	N
3	November 16, 2010 (1.5 h)	Factory manager C	Manufacturing director of manufacturing subsidiary Y	Y
4	November 16, 2010 (1.5 h)	Subsidiary factory manager D	Manufacturing director of manufacturing subsidiary Y	Y
5	November 16, 2010 (1.5 h)	Director E, technology management department, production division	Factory manager	Y
6	December 14, 2010 (1.5 h)	Corporate officer A, production division	Factory manager	Y
7	January 20, 2011 (1 h)	Director B, management division Branch store manager F	Company manager Branch store manager	Y

Y = yes. N = no

8.4 Case Study: Use of the BSC at Food Company X

Founded after World War II, Company X is a major company in the food industry and today distributes its products to all parts of Japan. The company introduced BSC in 2003 and stopped using it entirely in 2010. In this section, we describe the background and details of the company's introduction of BSC, and the process by which it was used.

Considering the purpose of this study is to examine the use of BSC by Company X from the perspective of BSC as ICS and also in view of the issue of availability of information in that we were unable to obtain sufficient information on the details of the strategic map through the interviews, description of the design aspects of BSC at Company X is kept to the minimum.[11]

[11] Yokota and Senoo (2011b), who describe the processes from BSC introduction to discontinuation at Company X, cover to a degree the design aspects of BSC at Company X, including diagrams of the strategy map. The reader should also refer to it.

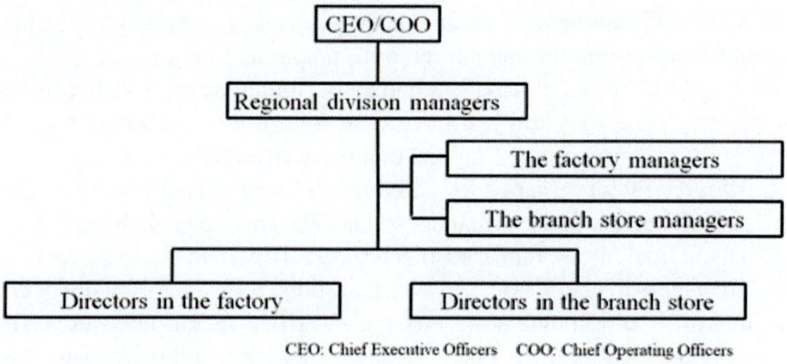

Fig. 8.1 Organizational chart

8.4.1 Overview of the Business and BSC at Company X

8.4.1.1 Business Environment, Business Strategy, and Introduction of the BSC

Over recent years, Company X has been facing increasingly fierce competition from its rivals. Pursuing originality, Company X built up a solid customer base; however, the impact of globalization and diversifying sales channels generated intense competition, not just from its existing rivals but also from new entrants into the market. Conscious of the limitations of its existing workplace-centered performance measures and in response to these changes to the business environment, in 2003, Company X top management introduced BSC as a tool for clarifying the links between each measure and long-term financial performance, and for managing the execution of corporate strategy under a universal structure throughout the company. In introducing BSC, top management were fully and repeatedly briefed by experts and business consultants and fully absorbed their views. Company X's introduction of BSC was therefore top-down based on the strong leadership of top management. When drawing up the BSC, the company strategically examined its product and business outlook 3–5 years into the future. Company X's strength was in its originality; thus, it strategically focused on aspects of uncertainty, including gaining an understanding of new product trends among rivals that could threaten the competitive edge of its own products.

8.4.1.2 Organizational Structure of Company X When Using the BSC

When introducing BSC, top management was deeply conscious of its three-tiered organizational structure. The three tiers were top management (Chairman of the Board of Directors and President), regional division managers, and the workplace, in particular factory and sales division directors. Figure 8.1 shows an outline of the organizational structure of Company X at that time.

Profit centers within regional companies were classed as Strategic Business Units (SBUs), and factories and branch stores were positioned under each of the regional divisions. Regional division managers had authority and responsibility in both sales and profit, and while they did not have total investment authority, they did hold partial authority for strategic operations to a predetermined extent.

Contrastingly, factory managers and branch store managers were classed as division staff. That is, factory managers had no cost responsibility, and branch store managers had no revenue responsibility. Top management required both classes of managers to check both types of measures; thus, factory managers verified business measures and branch store managers verified factory measures. However, factory managers and branch store managers held no authority over workplace operations.

Those who held authority and responsibility over workplace operations were factory division directors and sales division directors. Managers were positioned directly beneath division managers; therefore, the responsible officers at the workplace where BSC was used were not the factory or branch store managers but the division managers.

8.4.1.3 Overview of the BSC

Company X used a strategy map as a system chart within BSC. The strategy map was cascaded to the regional division as a priority so subordinates could grasp the general thinking of top management. It also specified challenging targets and was reviewed every six months.

Company X set performance measures for each of the four BSC perspectives of financial, customer, business processes, and learning and growth. The company set 45 measures. Each measure was managed in real time or weekly through a data system, and because multiple graphs on a single computer screen provided advanced visualization, BSC was referred to as the cockpit. Managers could view the measures relevant to them from the groupware. Clicking on the measure number also enabled the user to drill down to sub-measures in search of causes. The system was structured so that the gathering of data was as automatic and as prompt as possible.

8.4.2 Use of the BSC

This was how the BSC introduced by Company X was structured, but in 2010, Company X stopped using it entirely. The interviews revealed that among the reasons the company stopped using the BSC were problems relating to its design aspects, including the suitability and several measure options. There were, however, also views from both the factories and branch stores that perhaps the problem was in how BSC was used rather than how it was designed.

> I think the problem was with how BSC was used. My staff and I in the latter stages could use BSC effectively. Because the BSC sheet was drawn up from the viewpoint of how the targets should be set and what can be done to improve efficiency, it was effective since the vectors were facing in the same direction (Director E, Technology Management Department, Production Division).

> I think the purpose of the BSC was good. [...] The key is how it is used. [...] It may have worked out better if the use of the BSC had been more flexible and less rigid, (Director B, Management Division).

So how did Company X use BSC? Here, we describe the process by which BSC was used from the perspective of top management and operating managers.

8.4.2.1 Use of the BSC by Top Management

Top management at Company X had a detailed understanding of the data system and were also enthusiastic about using BSC. On their own computers, top management could rapidly reflect changes in conditions and grasp the local operational state through the cockpit as it showed numerical values and graphs of the BSC measures. They and their managers could quickly determine whether the measures for each of the products, regions, stores, and affiliated wholesalers were improving or dropping. Through the BSC measures, top management had their own data on hand to ascertain the situation at the factories and branch stores. If a measure value changed significantly, top management would pass on to the relevant regional division managers their own hypotheses on what should be done in response to the change. From this, regional division managers would then hold meetings with local staff and division directors about the BSC; thus, in most cases, the strategy map was adjusted, and the will of the top management reflected in the following six-month period.

Top management also raised any problems or discussed any issues uncovered by BSC that needed clarification at the monthly meetings with regional division managers. At these meetings, top management would question regional division managers about; for instance, why there were more customer claims or why the freshness measure was dropped, and they asked what was being done to resolve the problem. Top management also routinely raised problems detected from information gained from the cockpit at the weekly meetings attended by the President, Tokyo-based directors, corporate officers, and management staff.

Top management therefore spent considerable time using BSC to improve business operations. In Company X, regional division managers held all authority and responsibility for their local operations and were required to control both factories and branch stores in their respective regions. For their part, top management were interested not just in the broad strategic side of the business but in the details as well, including the day-to-day running of operations, and explored causes for any problems through the data and discussions at meetings.

8.4.2.2 Use of the BSC by Operating Managers

Managers of Company X companies, which are SBUs with functions similar to those of independent companies, the regional division managers occupying the next tier down, and factory and branch store managers, who were classed as regional division staff, used the BSC in the following way.

Regional division managers, their subordinate factory and sales division directors, and factory and branch store managers all had constant computer access to the BSC measure data and were required to check these data before their weekly meetings.

Regional division managers often required factories and branch stores and their own staff to draw up analyses and responses using specified briefing material in preparation for the monthly and weekly meetings with top management and to check any business issues that may have arisen within their respective divisions. Factory and branch store managers, as division staff, were required to check each other's measures. At the internal division business meetings, factory and branch managers and other division staff, together with factory and sales division directors, who were responsible for local operations, worked face-to-face to prepare briefing material explaining weekly and monthly data trends for head office staff. This was very time-consuming, and some even spent their days off preparing the material.

With a view of top management intentions expressed at the regional division-wide meetings, the regional division managers focused their internal business meetings on responses to improve problem measures. However, at times, discussions also turned to business strategies covering areas such as production and sales of new products and responses to rival companies. Because measures were checked in detail at short intervals of a week, though, on more than a few occasions matters dealing with the day-to-day running of the business dominated the meetings. Therefore, in many cases, these meetings became a mixture of discussions on long-term strategies and day-to-day routine. This had the tendency to lead to a degree of neglect for discussion on business operations that were fundamental to the factories, and also for discussion on existing key products that accounted for the bulk of sales revenue.

Frontline employees working in the factories or branch stores only had access to computer data that were directly related to their jobs according to necessity; thus, employees went about their work as usual with little awareness of anything to do with BSC. Managers at division director level and above, however, had to monitor the BSC measure trends at least weekly, and they devoted a huge amount of their time to prepare related briefing material.

Staff at factories and branch stores performed their normal routine operations; however, in addition to this, they were also involved in business activities connected with BSC. Essentially, the factories would acknowledge their current state of business operations and draw up their objectives based on this, whereas the BSC was based on the concept of what the business should be, and it was the role of the division directors to bridge this gap between these goals and the BSC. However, in most cases, the factories had little idea of which of the BSC strategic objectives and measures related to their operations. Even when a strategy map was prepared from the bottom up and presented to top management, at times top management required that the maps be revised.

8.4.2.3 Other Business Management Systems

In addition to BSC, Company X also adopted the following business management systems. The company had been implementing Total Productive Maintenance (TPM) from before it introduced BSC, and one of its factories was even awarded a TPM prize. Several of the factories were performing 5S activities, and this was later expanded to the national level.

Similar to Company X, manufacturing subsidiary Y had adopted BSC; however, in its case, it separated its management systems so that the execution of strategies was managed under BSC, and the day-to-day operations were managed under 5S activities. Thus, their use of BSC tended to be less rigid than that of Company X. However, as described earlier, there was the opinion at some of Company X's factories and branch stores that day-to-day operations were affected and hindered by BSC, which essentially looks at strategies.

The rewards system is another business management system connected with BSC. Company X linked BSC outcomes with personnel performance evaluation for SBU division directors and above. It was structured so that the higher the BSC-based performance evaluation score, the larger the bonus; thus, after introduction, the relationship between BSC and rewards gradually grew stronger. Evaluation measures related to bonus were characterized by the large number of process-related measures, such as number of claims at the factories and, at the branch stores, store product freshness,[12] and sales promotion rate. The amount of bonus was set objectively based on an evaluation formula rather than being determined by a subjective evaluation by a superior. However, the definition of the evaluation formula changed frequently and was quite complex. Because the evaluation formula was not open, no one knew whose business performance had improved and whose had not.

8.4.3 Impact of the BSC

Company X had originally emphasized business processes; however, with the introduction of the results-focused BSC, structurally, this gave rise to the situation in which both processes and results were emphasized. There was also mention of problems whereby the factories and branch stores gradually felt that top management

[12] Store product freshness was a measure unique to Company X and was designed to measure how long products were kept on shelves. The measure showed a percentage of products in the store that were more than one month old.

was increasingly caught up in managing the business processes. That is, to the employees, management became more centralized following the introduction of BSC. Obviously, this was the case when the BSC-based business evaluation result was poor; however, even when it was good, the standard of business processes was questioned by top management.

From the factory viewpoint, even though the correlation between strategic objectives was linked by the strategy map, it was felt that this was not always linked to local measures; thus, factories and branch stores at times became confused when the cause-and-effect relationships between strategic objectives or the actual objectives themselves were changed.

There was the view that when the organization changed to a three-tiered structure and the factory managers and branch store managers became classed as staff, the motivation of the factory managers dropped significantly, but because the branch store managers still felt they still had a practical responsibility for sales operations, they were not as affected by the change.

8.4.4 Discontinuation of the BSC and the Situation After

An internal questionnaire sent out to company employees when the new Chairman and President took over in spring 2009 revealed through self-assessment that employees felt "little motivation." Externally, Company X was highly regarded, but the internal assessment was quite low. Business was controlled in detail through a range of measures and data centered on BSC; however, with too many measures, it was impossible to look at all of them, and it became easy to lose sight of what each of the numerical values actually meant. There was also the risk that with attention focused entirely on processes, evaluation of the results could be neglected.

On January 1, 2010, regional companies were abolished and formed into four regional business headquarters. To reinforce head office functions, head office adopted a headquarter system under which product planning was established within the marketing headquarters, and a domestic business headquarters and an overseas business headquarters were also established. Factory managers and branch store managers were given authority and responsibility as line managers.

The new top management focused on costs, full-scale expansion into overseas markets, and raising the return on development investment. To this end, the company had another look at who would be responsible for what measures and shifted the perspective to how best to achieve the desired outcomes. The company also reviewed and streamlined the key performance indicators. Specifically, greater weight was given to evaluation of financial measures, with managers responsible for sales and profit and the factories and stores responsible for cost aspects.

Since product freshness had already been guaranteed, daily checking of product freshness data was scaled down, and renewal of product freshness data in the business visualization system finished with the data of February 2010. And in March 2010, use of the BSC system came to an end.

8.5 Discussion of the Case

In this section, we examine the case of Company X's use of BSC from the perspective of BSC as ICS. Specifically, we examine the five properties of ICS described by Bisbe et al. (2007); then, we examine the relationship with other MCS and the effect of ICS on strategy emergence.

8.5.1 Examination of the Five ICS Properties in the Use of the BSC

This example of BSC use in Company X, on the surface, seems to satisfy the five ICS properties described by Bisbe et al. (2007). Our examination of the use of BSC from the perspective of the five properties suggests that there are two key points in BSC as ICS.

First is the level of managers using the BSC and the content of their dialogue. When we apply the five properties of ICS to the use of BSC, top management from the first property and their operating managers from the second property use BSC intensively, and from the third property, both engage in face-to-face challenges and debates. From the fourth property, it can be inferred that the content of dialogue by both top management and operating managers focus on strategic uncertainties.

In the use of BSC by Company X, BSC was used frequently not just by regional division managers but by managers more closely positioned to the factories and branch stores, and the weekly meetings between regional division managers and managers resulted in frequent and close dialogue. However, as well as the substantial burden of preparing the material for these meetings, there was always the strong possibility that discussions at these meetings would be a mixture of business strategy and routine business operations. It can be considered that in business operations with high strategic uncertainties, top management will deal with this by devising strategies (Simons, 1995, 2000). Therefore, using BSC as ICS is based on the premise that the highest echelons of the organization; that is, top management and their subordinate operating managers will engage in dialogue focusing on the strategic uncertainties. Contrastingly, it is likely that the confusion could have been avoided if BSC-based dialogue between regional division managers and their managers had focused on details regarding routine business operations, thereby using BSC as DCS rather than as ICS. Kaplan and Norton (2008) also argue for a clear differentiation between operational review meetings dealing with routine business and strategy review meetings dealing with corporate strategy, and as discussed earlier, the use of BSC in the latter is positioned as ICS.

The second is that the fifth property of non-invasive, facilitating, and inspirational involvement by top management is critical in the use of BSC as ICS. In Company X's use of BSC, the regional division managers and managers were seemingly given a degree of authority, but they had a low feeling of empowerment. The reason for this was that although the organization was structured in a way that the regional division managers functioned as regional division managers, top management could access information directly connected with the day-to-day running of the factories and branch stores through the BSC, resulting in unidirectional control of processes by top management. Therefore, even using BSC, the regional division managers and managers felt a widening gap between strategy and frontline work, and there is the likelihood that this brought about the feeling of "little motivation."

There is also the view that it is possible to judge whether BSC is being used as ICS quantitatively by the frequency of dialogues or the number of meetings; however, this standard is not necessarily valid. Unless it is known exactly who used BSC for what purpose and how there is no way of judging whether BSC is used as ICS or not.

8.5.2 Examination of the Relationship with Other MCS

As mentioned earlier, Simons (1995, 2000) does not argue that all MCS should be used as ICS; thus, if BSC is to be used as ICS, there is a need to consider the relationship with other MCS used as DCS. In this respect, the cases of Company X and manufacturing subsidiary Y suggest the following three points.

First, as described in the previous section, a separation of the use of BSC as ICS by the highest echelons of the organization—top management and operating managers—and its use as DCS by the lower tiers of management. It is considered that for this differentiation to function, a process by which the BSC of the upper tiers can cascade properly to the lower tiers is essential.

Second, as suggested by the case of manufacturing subsidiary Y, there is a need to clearly differentiate between the execution of strategies managed under BSC as ICS or as combined ICS and DCS and routine business operations managed under DCS by way of TPM or 5S activities.

The third is related to the connection between rewards and outcomes. According to Simons (2000), the rewards system (pay and bonus) is normally formularized in the relationship between DCS and incentives. However, ICS incentives are not formularized and are evaluated subjectively regarding individual effort for and contribution to innovation. Simons points to promotion of the learning effect and information sharing as advantages of subjective evaluation and time burden as a disadvantage (Simons, 2000, pp. 224–225). Kaplan and Norton also argue that subjective evaluation is desirable for BSC-based incentives (Kaplan & Norton, 1996). We thus infer that the formularization of the rewards system at Company X was not suitable if Company X's purpose in using BSC was as ICS.

8.5.3 *Examination of Strategy Emergence Through the ICS*

Simons (2000) argues that incentives should not be formularized in ICS. When MCS is used as ICS to produce innovative outcomes, strengthening the relationship between outcomes and rewards itself inhibits the operating managers' intrinsic motivation, possibly leading to a loss of willingness for innovative activities (Yokota, 1998, 2011). Discussions on BSC also emphasize intrinsic motivation (Kaplan & Norton, 1996, 2008). When using BSC as ICS, carefully constructing the relationship with rewards and constructing an information environment that promotes the autonomy of subordinates—one of the ICS properties introduced by Bisbe et al. (2007)—becomes critical for determining whether it is possible to promote the intrinsic motivation of operating managers.

Company X used BSC for the management of both routine business operations and strategic activities. The company also strengthened the relationship between BSC outcomes and rewards. Moreover, top management kept throwing their own unidirectional hypotheses at the operating managers. It is surmised that such a structure and actions by top management may have hindered the intrinsic motivation of operating managers and led them to sense a shift toward centralization. This may hindered strategy emergence, which was raised by Simons as an effect of ICS.

8.6 Conclusion

In this study, we showed through case study that even though characteristics such as frequent dialogue or responses to strategic uncertainties and the way in which top management is involved in the business, or empowerment, may make the situation seem like ICS, this does not necessarily mean that BSC is in fact being used as ICS. The use of MCS as ICS is not a matter of information usage or frequent dialogue but is closely connected with how a top management intends to use MCS like BSC and for what purpose. Although our focus was frequently on strategic uncertainties under the strategy map, if top management looked at the performance measures for monitoring purposes, then this is not ICS but rather DCS.

ICS is attracting much attention, but further examination is essential on the requisites and properties that ICS should have as a system for producing the innovative outcomes that Simons originally had in mind.

References

Arae, T. (2008). Using the balanced scorecard as a interactive control system. *The Accounting Research, 51*, 218–230. (in Japanese).

Bisbe, J., Batista-Foguet, J., & Chenhall, R. (2007). Defining management accounting constructs: A methodological note on the risks of conceptual misspecification. *Accounting, Organizations and Society, 32*(7–8), 789–820.

Bisbe, J., & Malagueño, R. (2009). The choice of interactive control systems under different innovation management modes. *The European Accounting Review, 18*(2), 371–405.

Bisbe, J., & Otley, D. T. (2004). The effects of the interactive use of management control systems on product innovation. *Accounting, Organizations and Society, 29*(8), 709–737.

Hasegawa, K. (2011). Questions of balanced scorecard. *Financial and Cost Accounting, 70*(4), 61–72. (in Japanese).

Kaplan, R. S. (2009). Conceptual foundations of the balanced scorecard. In C. S. Chapman, A. G. Hopwood, & M. D. Shields (Eds.), *Handbook of management accounting research* (Vol. 3, pp. 1253–1269). Elsevier.

Kaplan, R. S., & Norton, D. P. (1996). *The balanced scorecard: Translating strategy into action*. Harvard Business School Press.

Kaplan, R. S., & Norton, D. P. (2001). Transforming the balanced scorecard from performance measurement to strategic management: Part II. *Accounting Horizons, 15*(2), 147–160.

Kaplan, R. S., & Norton, D. P. (2008). *The execution premium: Linking strategy to operations for competitive advantage*. Harvard Business School Press.

Marginson, D. E. W. (2002). Management control systems and their effects on strategy formation at middle-management levels: Evidence from a UK organization. *Strategic Management Journal, 23*(11), 1019–1031.

Merchant, K. A., & Van der Stede, W. A. (2006). Field-based research in accounting: Accomplishments and prospects. *Behavioral Research in Accounting, 18*, 117–134.

Simons, R. (1995). *Levers of control: How managers use innovative control systems to drive strategic renewal*. Harvard Business School Press.

Simons, R. (2000). *Performance measurement and control systems for implementing strategy: Text and cases*. Prentice Hall.

Tuomela, T. S. (2005). The interplay of different levers of control: A case study of introducing a new performance measurement system. *Management Accounting Research, 16*(3), 293–320.

Widener, S. K. (2007). An empirical analysis of the levers of control framework. *Accounting, Organizations and Society, 32*(7–8), 757–788.

Yokota, E. (1998). *Management and psychology of flattening organizations: Management control in an era of change*. Keio University Press. (in Japanese).

Yokota, E. (2011). A think of management control systems for contribution to innovation. *Mita Business Review, 54*(3), 95–108. (in Japanese).

Yokota, E., Arai, K., Otani, H., Medoki, T., Fukushima, K., & Senoo, T. (2010). The validity of field studies in Japanese management accounting research. *Mita Business Review, 53*(2), 101–121. (in Japanese).

Yokota, E., & Senoo, T. (2011a). A survey of management control systems in Japanese companies. *Mita Business Review, 53*(6), 55–79. (in Japanese).

Yokota, E., & Senoo, T. (2011b). Discussing the use of balanced scorecard: A case study of a food company. *Keio University Commerce Society Discussion Paper FY11, No. 1* (in Japanese).

Chapter 9
A Management Control Package for Associating Customer Satisfaction with Financial Performance: A Case Study on Customer Satisfaction Management at Hoshino Resorts

Sakichi Otomasa and Takahito Kondo

9.1 Introduction

Many companies in the manufacturing and service industries are engaged in diverse management efforts to achieve high levels of customer satisfaction. Companies that engage in improving customer satisfaction likely do so to improve their profits by increasing the number of repeat and word-of-mouth customers while decreasing the marketing costs that they incur to acquire customers.

Studies in the management accounting and marketing fields have exhibited substantial interest in clarifying the causal relationship between customer satisfaction and financial outcomes. However, previous studies in these fields have not produced consistent results regarding whether improving customer satisfaction is associated with future financial performance. Industry and contextual factors can influence the relationship between customer satisfaction and financial outcomes. Therefore, a question arises as to how the relationship between customer satisfaction and financial outcomes, which is academically ambiguous, is managed in practice.

Consequently, this study's objective is to clarify how improving customer satisfaction can be managed to lead to financial outcomes. To examine this from the perspective of the management control package, we demonstrate a case study where

Reprinted with permission of the Japanese Association of Management Accounting. Originally published in the *Journal of Management Accounting* 23(1): 43–60, 2015 (in Japanese).

S. Otomasa (✉)
Faculty of Commerce, Otaru University of Commerce, Hokkaido, Japan
e-mail: otomasa@res.otaru-uc.ac.jp

T. Kondo
Faculty of Business Administration, Kyoto Sangyo University, Kyoto, Japan
e-mail: k4769@kyoto-su.ac.jp

© Springer Nature Singapore Pte Ltd. 2023
E. Yokota (ed.), *Frontiers of Japanese Management Control Systems*, Translational Systems Sciences 32, https://doi.org/10.1007/978-981-19-9778-5_9

a Japanese resort company has implemented organization-wide efforts to improve customer satisfaction, placing emphasis on profitability.

9.2 Previous Studies on the Relationship Between Customer Satisfaction and Financial Outcomes

9.2.1 Previous Studies in the Management Accounting and Marketing Fields

The top section of Table 9.1 summarizes previous studies on the relationship between customer satisfaction and financial outcomes in the management accounting field.[1] Panel A (management accounting field) of Table 9.1 shows that previous studies in the management accounting field have generally shown good results regarding the relationship between customer satisfaction and financial outcomes. However, Ittner and Larcker (1998) found that there are threshold and industry differences in the relationship between customer satisfaction and financial outcomes. In addition, Maiga and Jacobs (2005) found no significant results between customer satisfaction and financial performance and indicated that the lack of significant results might be owing to a time lag. Furthermore, Banker and Mashruwala (2007) demonstrated the effect of concentrated competition on the relationship between customer satisfaction and financial outcomes. In addition to examining the relationship between customer satisfaction and financial outcomes, Banker et al. (2000) examined performance impacts of incorporating non-financial measures of customer satisfaction in incentive contracts.[2]

Panel B (marketing field) of Table 9.1 summarizes previous studies on the relationship between customer satisfaction and financial outcomes in the marketing field. First, Anderson et al. (1994) showed that although customer satisfaction positively influences financial outcomes, the returns provided by improved customer satisfaction are not realized quickly; rather, the effect is cumulative. In addition,

---

[1]Regarding the 'Survey Method' in Table 9.1, "Archival" indicates that the study used quantitative data about the study's subject. Similarly, "Survey" is a study that examined the relationship between the constructs using questionnaires, and "Case" is a study that mainly relies on qualitative data from the informants. For each of these, the term "Time-series" is used when data spanning multiple years are used. The "Analysis level" indicates whether the unit of aggregation of variables related to customer satisfaction and financial outcomes is at the customer level, business unit level, or company level.

[2]The hotel chain studied has changed their managers' bonus assessment from a profit-only based method to a profit and customer satisfaction-based method. The importance of customer satisfaction to financial performance was recognized by managers even before the transition to the new bonus assessment method. However, the managers did not focus their efforts on improving customer satisfaction until the transition to the new bonus assessment system, even though the time lag between improved customer satisfaction and increased profits was only six months.

Table 9.1 Previous studies on the relationship between customer satisfaction and financial outcomes

Studies	Method	Sample/data	Analysis level	The examined relationship between (non-financial and financial) indicators	Results
Panel A: Management accounting field					
Ittner and Larcker (1998)	Archive	Electronic communications company	Customer	The relationship between customer satisfaction and customer retention (and change in revenue)	Threshold in positive effect of customer satisfaction
	Archive	Financial company	Business unit	The relationship between customer satisfaction and unit-level financial performance (revenue, expenditure, and gross profit margin)	Threshold in positive effect of customer satisfaction
	Archive	American Customer Satisfaction Index (ACSI)	Corporation	The relationship between customer satisfaction and corporate value	Positive effect of customer satisfaction and its industry differences
Banker et al. (2000)	Archive (Time series)	Hotel chain (U.S.)	Business unit	The relationship between customer satisfaction (likelihood of return and number of complaints) and financial performance (revenue, cost profit)	Positive effect of customer satisfaction
Smith and Wright (2004)	Archive (Time series)	Large company (PC World/PC Magazine) (U.S.)	Corporation	The relationship between the determinations of customer loyalty and the loyalty, and financial performance (sales growth rate, average price, and ROA)	Direct/indirect effects of customer loyalty on the financial performance
Maiga and Jacobs (2005)	Survey	Company and faculty implementing TQM	Business unit	The relationship between the determinations of quality and the quality The relationship between customer satisfaction and financial performance	No relationship between customer satisfaction and financial performance
Matsuoka (2006)	Archive	Hotel chain (Japan)	Customer	The determinations of customer satisfaction, the relationship between customer, satisfaction and customer loyalty, the effects of customer satisfaction and loyalty on financial performance	Positive effect of customer satisfaction and customer loyalty

(continued)

Table 9.1 (continued)

Studies	Method	Sample/data	Analysis level	The examined relationship between (non-financial and financial) indicators	Results
Banker and Mashruwala (2007)	Archive (Time series)	Department store chain	Business unit	The context factors influencing the relationship between non-financial indicators (customer satisfaction and employee satisfaction) and financial indicator (profit)	The non-financial indicators preceding the financial ones in high competitive environment
Panel B: Marketing field					
Anderson et al. (1994)	Archive (Time series)	Swedish Customer Barometer (SCSB)	Corporation	The relationship between the determinations of customer satisfaction and the satisfaction and financial performance (ROA) and market share	Positive effect of customer satisfaction on financial performance, in which the long-run nature of the economic returns from improving customer satisfaction
Anderson et al. (1997)	Archive (Time series)	Swedish Customer Barometer (SCSB)	Corporation	The relationship between customer satisfaction and productivity The relationship between customer satisfaction and productivity, and financial performance	In the service industry, the negative effect of customer satisfaction on productivity, and the negative effect of interaction between customer satisfaction and productivity on financial performance
Reinartz and Kumar (2000)	Archive (Time series)	An established U.-S. catalog retailer	Customer	The relationship between transaction period with customers and financial performance in non-contract transaction	Long-term customers are not necessary high profitable
Kamakura et al. (2002)	Archive	State-owned bank (Brazil)	Customer/ business unit	The relationships in service profit chain (from investment in the operations to attribute performance perceptions, behavioral intentions, customer behavior, and profit)	Negative effect of investment in operations on profit Focusing on either efficiency of operations or customer retention is not effective in (terms of) profit
Mittal et al. (2005)	Archive (Time series)	American Customer Satisfaction Index (ACSI)	Corporation	The effect of strategic enhancement (revenue, cost, and both (of them)) on the relationship between customer satisfaction and financial performance (Tobin's q)	Attaining both (high) customer satisfaction and efficiency simultaneously is not good for the short-term financial effect, but desirable for long-term financial success

Morgan and Rego (2006)	Archive (Time series)	American Customer Satisfaction Index (ACSI)	Corporation	The relationship between customer-related indicators (average satisfaction, Top2Box, proportion of customers complaining, repurchase likelihood, number of recommendations) and financial performance (e.g., Tobin's q)	The positive effects of average satisfaction, Top2Box, proportion of customers complaining, and repurchase likelihood on financial performance No significant relationship between customer-related indicators (net promoters and number of recommendations) and financial performance

Anderson et al.'s (1997) empirical results indicated that the simultaneous pursuit of customer satisfaction and productivity improvement becomes difficult when service customization is important for meeting customer needs.

Rucci et al. (1998) discussed Sears, where a 5% improvement in employee satisfaction drove a 1.3% improvement in customer satisfaction, leading to a 0.5% improvement in revenue growth. However, although not reported in Panel B of Table 9.1, Brown (2000) estimated that when Sears earns a profit of two cents on each dollar of sales, the amount invested in employees to increase sales exceeds the additional amount of profit that would be earned.

The fact remains that the cost and investment incurred to increase customer satisfaction cannot be ignored. Based on their examination of the service-profit chain (Heskett et al., 1994), Kamakura et al. (2002) argued that to increase profits, the focus must be on both operational efficiency and customer retention. Mittal et al. (2005) also demonstrated the need to simultaneously achieve customer satisfaction (profit-oriented) and efficiency (cost-oriented) in the long term, even if they do not provide expected financial results in the short term.[3]

9.2.2 Perspectives for Addressing the Research Question

As previously noted, the findings on the relationship between customer satisfaction and financial outcomes lack consistency in both the management accounting and marketing fields. The empirical results regarding the relationship between customer satisfaction and financial outcomes differ depending on the industry studies, how the variables are measured, and whether time lags or contextual factors are considered. One of the reasons for the lack of consistency may be the diversity of research designs, such as differences in the industries surveyed and the measurement of variables.

Regarding the diversity of research designs, Dikolli and Sedatole (2007) examine the refinement of research on the causal relationship between financial and non-financial indicators from five perspectives: measurement methods for non-financial indicators, time lags, interactions, functional forms, and mediation. Identifying the causal relationship between financial and non-financial indicators is an important research topic that will continue to be refined in the future because of its implications for both methodology and practice.

However, refining the causal relationship alone cannot fully clarify how the relationship between customer satisfaction and financial outcomes is understood in

---

[3]In addition, Reinartz and Kumar (2000) examined the relationship between the duration of the customer transaction and financial performance and found that customers with long-term relationships do not necessarily pay higher prices or reduce service costs and are not necessarily profitable. Furthermore, Morgan and Rego (2006) examined the predictive ability of customer-related indicators on future financial performance and found that some indicators have a positive effect on financial performance, while others have no relationship.

practice and how an organization's improvement in customer satisfaction leads to better financial outcomes. Although the causal relationship between customer satisfaction and financial outcomes is unclear, there are still companies that advocate for customer satisfaction management. Thus, it is not only necessary to refine research on the causal relationship but also to consider how the relationship between customer satisfaction and financial outcomes is managed in practice.

To our knowledge, no previous studies exist on how to manage the relationship between customer satisfaction and financial outcomes. Although academic researchers and business practitioners have paid much attention to the causal relationship models such as the service-profit chain and balanced scorecard (Kaplan & Norton, 2001), there are no consistent empirical results regarding the relationship between customer satisfaction and financial outcomes. Therefore, relying only on these models is insufficient when considering how to manage the relationship between customer satisfaction and financial outcomes in practice.

Performance measurement systems are supposed to play a central role in managing the relationship between customer satisfaction and financial outcomes. For example, Hall (2008) surveyed senior managers in strategic business units in an Australian manufacturing company and found that the comprehensiveness of information provided by strategic performance measurement systems does not directly affect managers' performance and job satisfaction but rather affects managerial performance and job satisfaction by improving psychological empowerment[4] and role clarity. Nevertheless, the effect of information comprehensiveness is not always clear in situations where causality is ambiguous.

Therefore, it is useful to examine managing the relationship between customer satisfaction and financial outcomes from the perspective of a management control package (hereafter referred to as a control package); this is a more comprehensive concept, including performance measurement systems based on a causal relationship model. Based on criticisms of the traditional views (of management control) where many researchers have emphasized that accounting-based controls such as budgeting play a central role in (implementing) management control, a control package attempts to expand the conceptual framework of management control by considering non-accounting controls (e.g., Abernethy & Chua, 1996; Merchant & Van der Stede, 2007; Malmi & Brown, 2008).

A control package consists of accounting-based controls plus other controls such as human resource management and culture. However, the types of individual controls that are components of a control package have not been shared in previous studies. For example, Malmi and Brown (2008) indicated five types of controls: planning, cybernetics, rewards and compensation, administrative, and cultural. Using a longitudinal study of reform at a public hospital, Abernethy and Chua (1996) identified four types of controls: board composition, governance, accounting

[4]Psychological empowerment consists of meaning (importance of work), ability, self-determination, and influence.

controls, and organizational culture. Merchant and Van der Stede (2007) discussed three types of controls: results, action, and personnel/culture.

This study examines a case study about managing the relationship between customer satisfaction and financial outcomes. The control package presented by Malmi and Brown (2008) is used. In our study, their classification of the components of a control package provides a useful research framework for our better understanding of how to manage the relationship between customer satisfaction and financial outcomes in practice.

9.3 Case Study

9.3.1 Research Method and Survey Summary

The subject of this case study is Hoshino Resorts Co., Ltd. (hereinafter referred to as Hoshino Resorts). The company was chosen for the case study because it has attracted attention from the business community owing to its track record of achieving financial outcomes through continuous improvement in customer satisfaction. This is particularly notable in an industry characterized by a unique governance structure, low failure aversion, high turnover, high fixed costs, a magnitude of demand volatility, service extinction, and capacity constraints (Dittman et al., 2008). The aim of this study is to accumulate knowledge and develop a theory within a single case about management that can both improve customer satisfaction and produce financial results.

In conducting the research, a case was first created based on secondary sources in the literature related to Hoshino Resorts, centering on the series of studies[5] in the magazine, *Leisure Industry Data Monthly*.[6] Next, interviews were conducted with the company's public relations contact on May 24 and June 20, 2011, to have them confirm the content of the case that was prepared and to ask additional questions.[7]

The interviews, which lasted about 180 min, were conducted using semi-structured questions. The contents of the interviews were recorded with a digital voice recorder and documented immediately after they were conducted. All descriptions of Hoshino Resorts in this report, except that in the "Discussion" section, are taken from secondary sources, mainly from *Leisure Industry Data Monthly*;

---

[5] *Leisure Industry Data Monthly* published articles on Hoshino Resorts every month from the February 2004 issue to the June 2007 issue.

[6] For details, see Otomasa and Kondo (2011).

[7] The details of the interview survey are shown in Otomasa et al. (2012a, 2012b). Although we cannot reveal their name, we express our gratitude again to the public relations contact at Hoshino Resorts, who kindly cooperated in the survey despite their busy schedule. The description of Hoshino Resorts' practices in this paper is limited to the content before the survey. It does not reflect any changes in practice at the resort after July 2011.

although, some parts have been revised based on confirmation of the contents by the company's public relations contact.

9.3.2 *Overview of Hoshino Resorts*

Based in Karuizawa in Nagano Prefecture, Hoshino Resorts is a general resort management company that operates resorts and inns throughout Japan. The company's origins date back to the development of Karuizawa in 1904 and the opening of the Hoshino Onsen Ryokan (Hoshino Hot Spring Inn) in 1914. In 1991, the current president, Mr. Yoshiharu Hoshino, became the fourth-generation president, and the name was changed to Hoshino Resorts in 1995.

Normally, a resort business is operated through the integration of "development," "ownership," and "operation" (Think!, 2006, p. 38). Hoshino Resorts also developed, owned, and operated as a resort when it was a long-established hot spring inn. However, with the enactment of the Resort Law (Comprehensive Resort Area Development Law) in 1987, the company began to specialize in the "operation" of its own business.

To coexist and grow with the major companies entering the resort industry in a severely competitive environment, Yoshiharu Hoshino pushed for the reform of Hoshino Onsen. The company aimed to become "resort management experts" to grow into a company that could undertake the "operation" of inns and resorts outsourced by their owners (*Leisure Industry Data Monthly*, 2003, pp. 38–39).

9.3.3 *Customer-Oriented Management*

9.3.3.1 Management Reform and Vision Setting

The customer-oriented management of Hoshino Resorts began when Mr. Yoshiharu Hoshino, who became increasingly concerned about the construction and opening of large-scale resorts after the enactment of the Resort Law, undertook drastic management reform to break away from the conventional, facility-oriented style of management. To promote management reform, Mr. Yoshiharu Hoshino first shifted from resort management that integrated development, ownership, and operation, from the era of well-established hot spring inns to specializing in operation as the company's area of business. Simultaneously, the company set forth its management vision of becoming resort management experts.

The management vision of being resort management experts is not just an abstract management philosophy or slogan. The degree to which the management vision is achieved is made clear through the degree to which its targets are achieved using three indicators: customer satisfaction, the ordinary income ratio, and reduction in environmental impact (ecological points).[8] The targets for the three indicators that measure the degree to which the management vision is achieved are a customer satisfaction score of 2.50 points, an ordinary income ratio of 20%,[9] and a score of 24.3 points[10] for ecological points. To become resort management experts, the company is attempting to simultaneously achieve these three extremely high benchmarks.

9.3.3.2 Pursuit of Customer Satisfaction

Under a clear management vision, the first step taken to reform Hoshino Onsen was to conduct a customer satisfaction survey (Kiriyama, 2008). All guests were surveyed. The questionnaire distributed to guests contained about 30 questions, including questions about the rooms, meals, and facilities. Customers evaluated each item on a seven-point scale from *very satisfied* (+3 points) to *very dissatisfied* (−3 points). While the average score of customer satisfaction for general leisure facilities in Japan is around "0 (normal)," the company's target was set at the extremely high level of +2.5 (Leisure Industry Data Monthly, 2004a, p. 149).

The company attempted to use the data obtained from the customer satisfaction survey to shed light on the mechanism that increases repeat customers (Leisure Industry Data Monthly, 2004a). For example, a specific analysis was performed to evaluate whether improving the quality of dinner by using more expensive ingredients leads to repeat use and, if so, what kind of customer was likely to come back. In addition, items that have a significant effect on repeat use and items that are not expected to have an effect were identified and prioritized according to their importance.

Furthermore, from the accumulation of past data, we know that there is a large difference between the results "very much want to use (+3)" and "want to use (+2)" when responding to the question, "Do you want to use this service again?" Therefore, for items that are effective in improving the repeat rate, resources are invested until the level of "very satisfied" is reached. This is because if the level of "very

[8]Based on the Hoshino Resorts website (http://hoshinoresort.com).

[9]In the *TKC Management Index* published by TKC National Federation, the 2010 industry average of the ratio of ordinary income to sales in the "accommodation and food service industry" is 3.1% (TKC Group website: http://www.tkc.jp/). According to the *Fiscal and Financial Statistics Monthly No. 702* published by the Ministry of Finance, Policy Research Institute, the 2009 industry average of the ratio of recurring profit to sales in the "accommodation industry" was −0.9% (Ministry of Finance, Policy Research Institute website: http://www.mof.go.jp/). Hoshino Resorts, which specializes in "management," has made it its mission to earn the returns expected by resort owners (investors). Therefore, the company has set a high target for the ordinary income ratio and is thoroughly reviewing its operations to achieve said target.

[10]Hoshino Resorts has considered the ability to "operate with a low environmental impact" as part of its strategy. To measure ecological points, the Eco-Challenge Hotel Inns entry from the Green Purchasing Network (http://www.gpn.jp/) is used. The maximum score is 25 points.

satisfied" is not reached, the item may even become a factor that puts pressure on the management.

In recent years, to achieve the target value of +2.5 points for customer satisfaction, Hoshino Resorts has been working on more advanced practices (Leisure Industry Data Monthly, 2004a). For each questionnaire item, the "Top Box 50%" was defined as an indicator where 50% of all customers answered "+3 (very satisfied)." To achieve the Top Box 50%, the company is engaged in detailed efforts to increase individual customers' satisfaction, rather than the satisfaction of the entire customer base.[11]

9.3.3.3 Top Management's Perception of Customer Satisfaction

The company, which specializes in operating the business, aims for customer satisfaction that maximizes profits. The following reflects the perception of the company president, Mr. Yoshiharu Hoshino, regarding the position of customer satisfaction in resort and inn management.

First, he speaks about the relationship between customer satisfaction and revenue (profit):

> The logic is that increased customer satisfaction leads to an increase in repeat use, which reduces marketing costs and therefore increases profits. However, the issue is that the mechanisms of customer satisfaction and increase in repeat customers are not clear (Leisure Industry Data Monthly, 2004a, p. 149).

---

[11] 'Hoshinoya' is the core brand of Hoshino Resorts, which is only awarded to inns that offer an overwhelming sense of the extraordinary and provide the same level of service as the world's top-class resorts do. To raise the level of satisfaction of each customer, a system called the Better Spec Sheet (BSS) has been introduced. The purpose of the BSS is to approach 100% satisfaction by gradually customizing the contents of the service to each customer with every repeat stay. To implement the BSS, the company has been developing a database of customer information. Each time a customer visits the resort, information such as the purpose of the trip and whether the customer uses various services is collected. In addition to information from the customer satisfaction survey, the collected customer data are used for customer relationship management (CRM). Moreover, the company operates an information system called CRM Kitchen for customer relationship management. When a repeat customer arrives at the inn, the system automatically displays the service content tailored to the individual customer. The staff confirms the content of the service and meals based on the information in the system at a preliminary meeting and changes the process of service provision as necessary to improve service for repeat customers. In addition, the ideas and results obtained through the CRM Kitchen will be laterally deployed to other facilities. The CRM Kitchen is also used to create new repeat customers. For example, after staying at a Hoshinoya resort for the first time, customers are offered events and accommodation plans that match their preferences via e-mail. In addition, customer information is shared among the facilities that use CRM Kitchen. Therefore, even if a customer who stayed in Karuizawa visits Kyoto for the first time, he or she can enjoy detailed services as a repeat visitor. Because it requires advanced employee skills to implement BSS, it was initially assumed that BSS would be introduced only at 'Hoshinoya'. However, it was judged to be a useful model for other facilities as well, and expansion of the model to facilities that are outsourced to Hoshino resorts for operation is planned for the future.

Next, he states the following about the relationship between customer satisfaction and cost:

> Since information is inevitably concentrated in the hands of managers and executives, this is immediately passed onto those working on site. When this is done in half measures, they pursue customer satisfaction rather than profit; so, things develop in the direction of spending more and more money. However, if you give them the tools to think for themselves and be able to realize when an idea is good but not profitable, they will develop the habit of thinking about profitability. Everyone works to make their own household profitable; so, naturally, everyone possesses this skill. All that is needed is for the company to disclose everything about its situation and the information (Leisure Industry Data Monthly, 2004e, p. 134).

In addition, in view of the situation where customer satisfaction and profit are not always compatible, he talks about how to instill cost consciousness in the workplace as follows:

> Managing costs does not equal reducing costs. . .In the revitalization of resorts, I believe that the method of uniformly reducing costs across the board poses a risk. If there is an atmosphere within the company that says, "cost reduction is the top priority," then things that should actually be used will be cut. I believe that the first cost-reduction measures should be implemented directly by management, looking for specific places to make cuts, and allowing employees to focus on a customer-oriented organization and marketing activities. I think that a better approach would be to introduce a structure with solid cost awareness and management methods once the revitalization is already on track to some degree (Leisure Industry Data Monthly, 2003, p. 39).

Finally, he states the following about the relationship between customer satisfaction and employee satisfaction:

> If the staff do not enjoy their work, they cannot make the customers feel happy (Leisure Industry Data Monthly, 2004c, pp. 165–166).

9.3.4 *Management of the Relationship Between Customer Satisfaction and Financial Outcomes*

9.3.4.1 Organizational Structure[12]

At Hoshino Resorts, each section, such as the front desk/lounge, hotel food preparation, bridal promotion, and finance and accounting, is divided into a separately named unit (Leisure Industry Data Monthly, 2004c), with about ten members per unit. All employees, whether they are part-time or full-time, belong to a unit.

In the unit system, employees are not anchored to a single unit. It is possible for an employee to be transferred to other units according to the challenge the employee wants to engage in. The system is designed to produce results as a team, with

[12] Descriptions of the unit system and UD in this section are based on Kiriyama (2008, pp. 131–132), unless otherwise specified.

everyone on a level playing field, rather than being controlled or controlling others according to one's individual rank. The units can also be integrated if necessary and integration of units is performed from time to time to improve profitability and customer satisfaction. As they are in constant contact with customers, each unit is encouraged to work autonomously.

Each unit has a leader called the unit director (UD) who serves as the coordinator. Since the UD reports directly to the president or manager of each facility,[13] it is easy for the UD to make a direct proposal to the president or manager. In addition, the UD is also given a significant amount of authority. The UD can propose new services and review the prices of existing services at his or her own discretion. The UD is required to know how to work together with the other members as the team captain, how to increase customer satisfaction, how to be aware of cost management, and how to reform and improve the operation efficiency (Leisure Industry Data Monthly, 2006).

It is not the president or human resources department in the company that appoints the UD. The UD is appointed based on an appointment method referred to as a candidacy system (Think!, 2006). Under the candidacy system, all employees are invited to nominate candidates for UD every year. Anyone with a new business plan or proposal for reform can become a candidate for a UD position. Candidates present their ideas in a presentation competition, and if they receive a certain level of evaluation from the president, manager, and employees in the audience, they become the new UD.

9.3.4.2 Strategy Development[14]

Each of the facilities operated by Hoshino Resorts holds an "all-staff training" program once a year (Nakazawa, 2010). The all-staff training program is an important opportunity for the president to directly communicate to the employees the organization's strategy and specific measures for implementing it. Then, each facility formulates a strategy for itself through discussions at a "strategy meeting," which includes the UDs who work on site and anyone who wishes to participate voluntarily. In the strategy meeting, the participants continue discussions, considering the data from the customer satisfaction survey. Occasionally, the results of market trends and customer needs surveys conducted by external research organizations are considered in these meetings.

The strategy meeting is a forum for thorough discussion. By including those who wish to participate voluntarily in the meetings, the aim is that not only the marketing

[13] There are basically three accounting management layers at Hoshino Resorts: the president, the manager of each facility, and UDs. However, managers of the facilities that have been entrusted with operations also belong to the company that is the owner of the facility. Although the UD in the head office reports directly to the president, for large-scale fields such as sales, there is a manager who unifies the units.

[14] Statements in this section regarding the development of strategies are based on *Leisure Industry Data Monthly* (2004b, pp. 162–163), unless otherwise specified.

team and management but also the entire staff will understand and gain experience with the strategy.[15]

9.3.4.3 Annual Planning[16]

Following the strategy development, each facility develops an annual plan for implementing the strategy. First, the manager encourages the UDs to develop proposals for their units that are in alignment with the facility's strategy and policies. Next, the UD formulates a detailed plan with the participation of the members of the unit. Finally, the manager compiles the proposals from all units and, after adjusting in coordination with the units, develops an annual plan for the entire facility. The annual plan for the entire facility is also discussed between the manager and the president.

In the annual plan planning process, target values are set for all facilities for customer satisfaction, the ordinary income ratio, and ecological points, which are three indicators used to measure the degree to which the management vision is achieved. In setting the target values, it is important to update the previous year's results while considering the impact of the rapidly changing market environment. Therefore, the target value is set at a level that is not easily attainable and requires a great deal of ingenuity and effort.

In addition to the three indicators, each facility sets its own targets and indicators that are important for implementing its strategy, such as reducing overtime hours, according to the manager's judgment. The facility's targets, including target values for the three indicators, are expanded to each unit and even to individual members within a unit.[17]

After the planning process described above, the financial aspects of each facility's annual plan are finally presented as an estimated income statement, an estimated balance sheet, and an estimated cash flow statement in accordance with hotel accounting standards.

---

[15] Mr. Yoshiharu Hoshino, as a manager, checks the discussions of front-line staff from the following five perspectives: (1) What is the purpose of the idea? (2) After investigating the competitors are their strengths and weaknesses understood? (3) Are the needs of the customers met? (4) Are costs and risks understood? and (5) Is it based on a strategic idea? It does not matter what concept or service is proposed if it has gone through the appropriate discussion process. This is because a new attempt is evaluated numerically in the results of a profit report or a customer satisfaction survey.

[16] Based on the authors' interview survey.

[17] In Hoshino Resorts, the amount of capital investment is rarely limited by the budget in general. After carefully examining each project, the company will make the necessary capital investment when it is deemed necessary. Whether capital investment is necessary is judged by whether it attracts customers, except for capital investment to ensure a minimum level of comfort, such as repairing leaks.

9.3.4.4 Performance of Duties[18]

To improve work efficiency, the company tracks a unique indicator called "operational efficiency." In resorts and inns, employees perform various tasks and depending on the employee, sometimes there is downtime. Downtime must be completely eliminated because it implies zero productivity. Operational efficiency is considered important in each of the company's facilities because it indicates the degree of downtime and the facility's overall efficiency.

For business management purposes, all company employees enter the details of their daily work into the company intranet using 30-min increments. When an employee enters data, the efficiency of the operation can be calculated using categories such as per customer, per employee, and per hour. If the actual results deviate significantly from the standard operational efficiency set for each facility, a specialized team that operates on a company-wide basis uses a root-cause analysis to take remedial measures.[19]

The company is not this thorough in its operation management simply to reduce costs. In general, there is a high level of uncertainty in operating inns and resorts. Throughout the day, employees are faced with unexpected tasks, and the workload range varies greatly. Therefore, efforts are made to equalize the amount of daily work as much as possible by reviewing how work is performed and the time required to perform it. If the workload can be equalized, employees can devote themselves to each task with more planning, and unnecessary overtime can be reduced. In turn, this enables the employees to provide their customers with even higher quality services.

9.3.4.5 Comparison of Targets and Actual Results

In achieving the numerical targets, Hoshino Resorts holds a meeting referred to as the "situation report meeting" (Kiriyama, 2008, pp. 131–132). At the resort hotels, the situation report meeting is held monthly at each facility. Inns that are relatively small-scale meet at the Tokyo office and hold their situation report meeting as a group.

A situation report meeting is basically a meeting that involves the UD and the manager. The UD reports on the unit's operational performance at this meeting. Reports are presented, mainly on the last month's results; current month's sales, cost of sales, labor costs, and departmental profit; current month's forecast regarding reservation status and sales; and the unit's issues and problems (Leisure Industry Data Monthly, 2004b).

---

[18] Based on the authors' interview survey.

[19] Hoshino Resorts has long been working on work management through standardization, measuring the time required for each task with a stopwatch and observing the movements of workers as they perform their tasks to reduce downtime. The company's experience in standards management led to the construction of its current intranet.

Everyone is welcome to participate in the company's regular internal meetings. Non-UD staff are welcome to participate, ask questions, or raise issues if they are interested. In addition, the meeting inevitably reveals which units are performing well or, conversely, which units are performing poorly. By participating in the meeting and generating ideas for improvements and new projects, the non-UD staff have an opportunity to become a candidate for the UD position.

In the meeting, Mr. Yoshiharu Hoshino generally does not make the decisions, even for important matters such as revising the price of a service (Nikkei Information Strategy, 2006). Decisions are made through discussions among the staff. There is a higher level of agreement if the decision does not come from the top down but is instead made collectively. It can also increase the motivation for work.

However, sufficient information must be provided to each staff member to enable them to make autonomous decisions. The company makes efforts to share information by making the management decision-making process more transparent in meetings. Concurrently, to support each staff member in making decisions on their own, the company has established methods of providing information to staff members, including through internal e-mails (Leisure Industry Data Monthly, 2004b). Information necessary for decision-making, such as the results of market surveys, customer satisfaction surveys, employee satisfaction surveys, and financial information, is fed back to all employees as needed.[20]

9.3.4.6 Personnel Systems

In general, the employee retention rate in the hotel industry is low. According to a survey by the Ministry of Health, Labour and Welfare, the turnover rate in the accommodation and food services industry in 2009 was 32.1%.[21] In contrast, the company's current turnover rate is 7%. The low turnover rate is supported by the company's personnel system.

The company's personnel system first incorporates diversity in its work system (Nakazawa, 2009). The company has developed a series of unique work arrangements to adapt the work system to the needs of its employees. For example, an employee can choose to work from home as one working arrangement. An employee can also become a "holiday employee" who works only on weekends, giving the

[20] In addition, at present, the feedback of various survey results and financial information to all employees is devised in such a way that it can be understood by anyone, rather than disclosing the detailed and voluminous data as it is. For example, in the case of financial data, it is difficult to understand the meaning of the figures without specialized knowledge, and it is also difficult to make comparisons between facilities of different sizes and environments. Therefore, the degree of achievement of each indicator is indicated by using symbols such as □, △, and X so that all employees can intuitively understand the meaning of the values. If more detailed data is required, the employee is free to contact a specialist.

[21] The overview of the results of the 2009 Survey of Employment Trends was referred to from the Ministry of Health, Labour and Welfare website (http://www.mhlw.go.jp/).

employee more days off. There is also a "Gnu" system that allows employees to change their work location according to the season. In addition, there is an option called "Educational Leave" that allows employees to take a leave of absence for up to one year.

Next is a description of the job structure and compensation system (Leisure Industry Data Monthly, 2004d). The positions of the company's staff are divided into three categories: director, Picasso, and player. UDs fall within the category of "director," while specialists with high ability in specific fields such as research, IT, and legal affairs are classified as "Picasso." All other staff members are "players," which are further subdivided into four levels from I to IV, according to their abilities.

In this company, UDs, who are in director positions, are positioned as leaders of change, and therefore, the kind of change they can accomplish over several years is the subject of a performance evaluation. In general, a UD's salary is based on an annual salary, which is set between 6 million and 12 million yen. A UD will move up in the annual pay scale depending on the nature of the change they are driving.

In addition to the annual salary, the "value of change" is added to a UD's compensation. After estimating the cash flow for the next five years produced by the changes made by the UD, the company provides 5% of the total cash flow, discounted to the present value. The calculation of cash flow is based on the UD's self-assessment. A compensation system based on the value of change is adopted because the candidacy system allows for the UD to be replaced. If the compensation is not paid at the time the change occurs, it would be difficult to replace the UD. Additionally, it can be assumed that this might demotivate the employee to take on the challenge of UD again after they have been replaced.

Each "player" staff member is evaluated twice a year on a five-point scale from A to E, for 11 competence items, including achievement orientation, team behavior, calculation management, and customer orientation.[22] The result of the evaluation determines the player's rank. Even if a staff member belongs to level III, if he or she receives an evaluation (points) worthy of the II level, his or her rank will immediately increase. Similarly, their rank may be lowered according to the result of the evaluation. Salaries also increase and decrease depending on the player's rank. Only if they continue to be ranked at the same level will their salary increase with seniority. A staff member who is a "player" may run for UD regardless of rank.

The third aspect of the personnel system is the company's employee training. The company has an in-house business school, Rokuson Juku, as a support measure to enhance its employees' business skills (Leisure Industry Data Monthly, 2004b). The role of Rokuson Juku is to provide the knowledge and skills necessary to lead reform in the work area each employee is responsible for. Although the curriculum is reviewed from time to time, participants can acquire not only the knowledge necessary for management, such as marketing, finance, and strategic planning but

[22] However, it is not evaluated unilaterally from above. Individual assessments are determined in discussion with the UD. In evaluations, the fairness of evaluations among UDs is examined by an Agreement Committee to ensure uniformity in evaluation standards for evaluators among UDs.

also practical skills such as presentation and logical thinking (Leisure Industry Data Monthly, 2005a). The company's president, Mr. Yoshiharu Hoshino, is also a lecturer at Rokuson Juku, and lectures on marketing, in addition to other subjects (Nakazawa, 2010; Nikkei Top Leader, 2010). The course is held throughout the year, and even part-time workers can take the course if they wish (Leisure Industry Data Monthly, 2005a).

The final component is recruiting human resources. As the company manages an expanding number of lodging facilities, it is trying to increase its staff by hiring mid-career employees. There are many people who change jobs from industries unrelated to hotels and inns. Additionally, in April 2007, Wakuwaku Ryokan, a Japanese inn management company, was established as a solution to the difficulty of securing new university graduates and immediately effective mid-career workers (Leisure Industry Data Monthly, 2007). Wakuwaku Ryokan is positioned as a parent organization that supplies human resources to the facilities that Hoshino Resorts is entrusted to manage. The purpose of establishing Wakuwaku Ryokan is to secure talented people by providing an attractive workplace for revitalizing hot spring inns rather than for employment at a particular inn.

9.3.5 Considerations

In Hoshino Resorts, it is generally recognized that if customer satisfaction is improved, it will lead to an increase in profit. However, the company also fully understands that there is a cost to improving customer satisfaction. Although research and analysis are conducted as necessary, at the time of this writing, the mechanism of the causal relationship between customer satisfaction and financial outcomes remains unclear. The following discussion from the perspective of a control package is regarding the management of Hoshino Resorts at a time when the mechanism of the causal relationship between customer satisfaction and financial outcomes remains unclear.

Malmi and Brown (2008), in emphasizing the need for control package research, presented five types of controls that are the components of a control package, as shown in the "Elements" and "Definitions" columns of Table 9.2. The right column of Table 9.2 summarizes the content of the control practices at Hoshino Resorts based on the components of the control package presented by Malmi and Brown (2008).

Furthermore, Fig. 9.1 illustrates how the five types of controls form relationships in Hoshino Resorts. In Fig. 9.1, the company holds all-employee training sessions to ensure that every employee is familiar with the management vision to be resort management experts. Through strategy meetings and annual planning, the strategies and plans for becoming resort management experts are put into practice (arrow 1). The degree to which the management vision is achieved can be clarified by the degree to which the targets of each of the three indicators (the ordinary income ratio, customer satisfaction, and ecological points) is achieved (arrow 2).

Table 9.2 Control package components and Hoshino Resorts' control practices

Elements	Definitions	Components in Hoshino Resorts
Planning controls	An ex ante form of control: First, it sets out the goals of the functional areas of the organization, thereby directing effort and behavior; second, it provides the standards to be achieved in relation to the goal, making clear the level of effort and behavior expected; third, it enables congruence by aligning goals across the functional areas of an organization, thereby controlling the activities of groups and individuals	All-staff training Strategy meeting Participatory annual planning
Cybernetic controls	Five characteristics of cybernetic control: First, there are measures that enable quantification of an underlying phenomenon, activity, or system. Second, there are standards of performance or targets to be met. Third, there is a feedback process that enables comparison of the outcome of the activities with the standard. This variance analysis arising from the feedback is the fourth aspect of cybernetic control systems. Fifth, there is an ability to modify the system's behavior or underlying activities	Ordinary income ratio Customer satisfaction (Top2Box 50%) Ecological points Work efficiency Situation report meeting Establishing methods for sharing information
Reward and compensation controls	Motivating and increasing the performance of individuals and groups through attaching rewards to control effort direction, effort duration, and effort intensity	Personnel evaluations for players Performance appraisals for director A variety of work styles
Administrative controls	Administrative control systems are those that direct employee behavior through the organization of individuals (organization design and structure); the monitoring of behavior and who employees are made accountable to for their behavior (governance); and the process of specifying how tasks or behaviors are to be performed or not performed (policies and procedures)	Unit system Candidacy system Rokuson Juku Wakuwaku Ryokan
Cultural controls	The values, beliefs, and social norms that are established influence employees' behavior	Management vision: being "resort management experts"

The "Elements" and "Definitions" columns of this table are based on Malmi and Brown's (2008, p. 292) description of a control package

In addition to the three indicators, target values for operational efficiency and indicators are set independently by each facility at strategy meetings and annual planning sessions that include voluntary participants (arrow 3). Since updating the previous year's results is important in setting target values, arrow 3 is a two-way arrow that considers the feedback from the cybernetic control.

In the hospitality industry, including resorts, the actions and decisions of employees who provide services have a direct impact on customer satisfaction. Regarding arrow 4, Hoshino Resorts has established a flat organization based on a

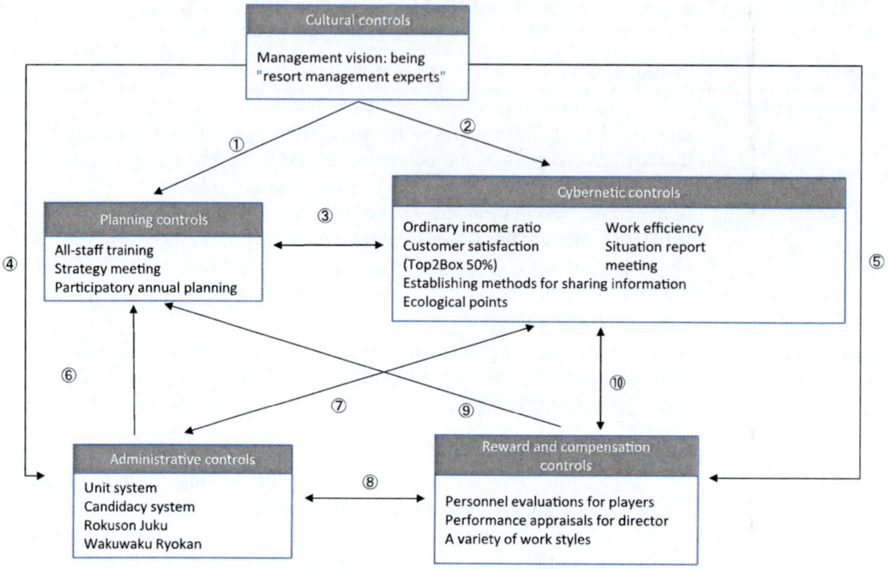

Fig. 9.1 Management of the relationship between customer satisfaction and financial outcomes at Hoshino Resorts

unit system to encourage all employees to act and make decisions autonomously to achieve the management vision. In addition, in achieving the management vision, the organization is constantly revitalized through its practice of the candidacy system and development of human resources who can lead change through Rokuson Juku. Furthermore, in the hospitality industry, where it is difficult to secure human resources, the company is actively engaged via Wakuwaku Ryokan to secure talented people who can contribute to achieving its management vision.

Employees who are encouraged to act and make decisions autonomously under the unit system, or those who attend the Rokuson Juku, actively participate in open meetings such as the strategy meetings and situation report meetings (arrows 6 and 7). In addition, meetings are run in a way that anyone can "say what they want, to the person they want to say it to, when they want to say it." Arrow 7 is shown as a two-way arrow because participation in the situation report meeting or providing various information, including financial information, promotes employees' creation of ideas for reform, which activates the candidacy system.

Personnel evaluations and performance appraisals at Hoshino Resorts reflect the management vision of being resort management experts (arrows 5 and 10) and are linked to the unit and candidacy systems (arrow 8). Each of the three job categories established under the unit system is subject to different personnel evaluations and performance appraisals according to its role in line with the management vision. As for directors, there is a plan that uses a compensation system that adds the value of change for five years in addition to an annual salary to avoid hindering the operation of the candidacy system to become a director.

For rewards and compensation controls, various service systems are also part of the rewards and compensation. Providing a variety of work styles creates a sense of empathy and security among employees. Employees' empathy and sense of security are the foundation for the operation of the unit and candidacy systems, as they reduce Hoshino Resorts' turnover rate (arrow 8). Furthermore, it can be linked to the recruitment of talented people through Wakuwaku Ryokan.

Personnel evaluation and performance appraisals that are related to monetary compensation increase employees' motivation to work. Increased motivation for work not only leads to participation in open meetings such as strategy meetings and situation report meetings but also encourages employees to be proactive in speaking up (arrows 9 and 10). In addition, the compensation system encourages behaviors such as participation in Rokuson Juku and the candidacy system to demonstrate higher ability (arrow 8).

However, performance evaluation issues related to customer satisfaction, as previously mentioned by Banker et al. (2000), were not recognized in this company. Even if the value of change achieved by a UD is measured based on cash flow, improvement in customer satisfaction is not to be neglected. This is because any short-sighted behavior by a UD is inhibited by the shared management vision (arrow 5), the comments of participants in open meetings such as strategy meetings and situation report meetings, and the transparency of the organization, which is enhanced by establishing methods for sharing information (arrows 9 and 10).

Finally, regarding Fig. 9.1, improving work efficiency through standardization and equalization is used as the basis for setting up various work systems (arrow 10).

Under these multiple controls, cost-conscious customer satisfaction is being improved at Hoshino Resorts facilities. For example, the head chef of Hoshinoya, one of the company's luxury inns, said of the company's generous food service, "Our first priority is to increase satisfaction, not to think about the cost of sales ratio. Therefore, we keep the price lower than the price calculated based on cost" (Leisure Industry Data Monthly, 2005b, p. 177). While prioritizing an increase in customer satisfaction, the company does not neglect costs.

In summary, while Hoshino Resorts generally recognizes that improving customer satisfaction will lead to increased profits, at present, it does not necessarily fully understand the mechanism of the causal relationship between customer satisfaction and financial outcomes. However, through the interrelationship of multiple controls centered on culture, planning, and cybernetics, employees operate autonomously under management control while clearly recognizing their own roles. In addition, employees' autonomous activities are supported by information sharing, a high level of business skills, and motivation, which are mainly fostered by cybernetic, administrative, and rewards and compensation controls. Furthermore, any shortsightedness in employees' autonomous behavior is curtailed by controls other than rewards and compensation.

Similar to Hall's (2008) results, the performance of Hoshino Resorts has been improved through the clarity of employees' roles and autonomy. However, it comes from not only the comprehensiveness of the information provided by the performance measurement system that brings about employee role clarity and autonomy but also the control package that includes the performance measurement system. Even in a situation where the causal relationship between customer satisfaction and financial outcomes is unclear, the employees of Hoshino Resorts, through role clarity and autonomy brought about by the control package (the interrelationship among multiple controls), including the performance measurement system, are engaged in efforts to simultaneously achieve customer satisfaction and increase profits while maintaining cost consciousness.

9.4 Conclusion

The purpose of this study is to clarify through a case study how the practice of achieving financial outcomes by improving customer satisfaction is managed given that the relationship between customer satisfaction and financial outcomes is unclear.

The subject of the case study, Hoshino Resorts, generally recognizes that improving customer satisfaction will lead to increased profits; however, at present, it does not necessarily fully understand the mechanism of this causal relationship. Although the causal relationship between customer satisfaction and financial outcomes is unclear, it is apparent that the employees, through their role clarity and autonomy brought about by the control package (the interrelationships among multiple controls) are engaged in efforts to simultaneously achieve customer satisfaction and increase profits.

The conclusions of this study suggest that when studying the management of the relationship between non-financial and financial indicators, consideration must be given not only to what non-financial and financial indicators are used but also to how using performance indicators relates to other controls in the organization. However, our findings also have limitations.

First, the validity of the classification of control packages presented by Malmi and Brown (2008) has not been verified. Even if several controls are interrelated, there is still a possibility that the controls used in Hoshino Resorts may be described using different classifications. In addition, this study does not examine the process by which a control package is formed or the factors that affect the formation of a control package. Therefore, at the time of this writing, it is not possible to state whether the control package used by Hoshino Resorts is optimal for managing the unclear relationship between customer satisfaction and financial outcomes.

Second, although Hoshino Resorts draws out the autonomous activities of employees under the interrelationship of multiple controls, it is necessary to further examine what role accounting information plays in autonomous behavior and decision-making. Specifically, it should be clarified how each employee positions accounting information as part of the set of information provided in performing his or her job or how accounting information is used and interpreted in discussions at meetings.

Finally, the conclusions drawn in this study are based on a single case study and are therefore difficult to generalize. Consequently, it is necessary to accumulate cases on management in situations where the causal relationship between customer satisfaction and financial outcomes is unclear, including in the manufacturing industry, to verify the current findings.

References

Abernethy, M. A., & Chua, W. F. (1996). A field study of control system 'redesign': The impact of institutional processes on strategic choice. *Contemporary Accounting Research, 13*(2), 569–606.

Anderson, E. W., Fornell, C., & Lehmann, D. R. (1994). Customer satisfaction, market share, and profitability: Findings from Sweden. *The Journal of Marketing, 58*(3), 53–66.

Anderson, E. W., Fornell, C., & Rust, R. T. (1997). Customer satisfaction, productivity, and profitability: Differences between goods and services. *Marketing Science, 16*(2), 129–145.

Banker, R. D., & Mashruwala, R. (2007). The moderating role of competition in the relationship between nonfinancial measures and future financial performance. *Contemporary Accounting Research, 24*(3), 763–793.

Banker, R. D., Potter, G., & Srinivasan, D. (2000). An empirical investigation of an incentive plan that includes nonfinancial performance measures. *The Accounting Review, 75*(1), 65–92.

Brown, M. G. (2000). *Winning score: How to design and implement winning scorecards*. Productivity Press. (Translated by Hiroyoshi Umezu. 2002. Winning balanced scorecards—Performance evaluation based on MB award criteria. Japan Productivity Centre).

Dikolli, S. S., & Sedatole, K. L. (2007). Improvements in the information content of nonfinancial forward-looking performance measures: A taxonomy and empirical application. *Journal of Management Accounting Research, 19*(1), 71–104.

Dittman, D. A., Hesford, J. W., & Potter, G. (2008). Managerial accounting in the hospitality industry. In C. S. Chapman, A. G. Hopwood, M. D. Shields, & G. Potter (Eds.), *Handbooks of management accounting research* (Vol. 3, pp. 1353–1369). Elsevier Ltd.

Hall, M. (2008). The effect of comprehensive performance measurement systems on role clarity, psychological empowerment and managerial performance. *Accounting, Organizations and Society, 33*(2/3), 141–167.

Heskett, J. L., Jones, T. O., Loveman, G. W., Sasser, W. E., Jr., & Schlesinger, L. A. (1994). Putting the service-profit chain to work. *Harvard Business Review, 72*, 164–174.

Ittner, C. D., & Larcker, D. F. (1998). Innovations in performance measurement: Trends and research implications. *Journal of Management Accounting Research, 10*(2), 205–236.

Kamakura, W. A., Mittal, V., de Rosa, F., & Mazzon, J. A. (2002). Assessing the service-profit chain. *Marketing Science, 21*(3), 294–317.

Kaplan, R. S., & Norton, D. P. (2001). *The strategy-focused organization: How balanced scorecard companies thrive in the new business environment*. Harvard School Press.

Kiriyama, H. (2008). *Regeneration of the inn: The story of people reviving a long-established business*. Kadokawa Shoten.

Leisure Industry Data Monthly. (2003). Hearing about [business revitalization] strategy. *Leisure Industry Data Monthly, 36*(8), 34–44.

Leisure Industry Data Monthly. (2004a). Increasing customer satisfaction and creating repeat customers through 'Hoshino style marketing'. *Leisure Industry Data Monthly, 37*(2), 148–152.

Leisure Industry Data Monthly. (2004b). The ideal organization for achieving customer satisfaction and the creation of autonomy: Information sharing and an open corporate culture to create a workplace with job satisfaction. *Leisure Industry Data Monthly, 37*(3), 160–164.

Leisure Industry Data Monthly. (2004c). The revitalization and reconstruction of 'risonare' (Vol 1): A dynamic management method that blends a revolution in staff consciousness and flexibility. *Leisure Industry Data Monthly, 37*(6), 164–167.

Leisure Industry Data Monthly. (2004d). The 'evaluation system' that promotes a revolution in staff consciousness: The process of equating compensation with the degree of contribution to the organization. *Leisure Industry Data Monthly, 37*(9), 194–197.

Leisure Industry Data Monthly. (2004e). The revitalization of alpha resort Tomamu begins already in motion (part 2): Tomamu's philosophy aims to return to the origin of snowy mountains in the 'declaration of the liberation of winter mountains'. *Leisure Industry Data Monthly, 37*(12), 128–134.

Leisure Industry Data Monthly. (2005a). Roles of the specialist group 'sky' (5). *Leisure Industry Data Monthly, 38*(5), 110–115.

Leisure Industry Data Monthly. (2005b). The people who made 'Hoshinoya Karuizawa'. *Leisure Industry Data Monthly, 38*(9), 172–177.

Leisure Industry Data Monthly. (2006). Revitalization initiated for 'Furumaki Hot Springs and Shibusawa Park' and 'Oirase Gorge Hot Springs'. *Leisure Industry Data Monthly, 39*(1), 138–141.

Leisure Industry Data Monthly. (2007). Establishment of an inn management company 'Waku Ryokan'. *Leisure Industry Data Monthly, 40*(9), 132–138.

Maiga, A. S., & Jacobs, F. A. (2005). Antecedents and consequences of quality performance. *Behavioural Research in Accounting, 17*(1), 111–131.

Malmi, T., & Brown, D. A. (2008). Management control systems as a package-opportunities, challenges and research directions. *Management Accounting Research, 19*(4), 287–300.

Matsuoka, K. (2006). An empirical study on the relationship between customer satisfaction, customer loyalty and financial performance. *Osaka University School of Economics, 55*(4), 106–126.

Merchant, K., & Van der Stede, W. A. (2007). *Management control systems* (2nd ed.). Prentice Hall, Pearson Education Limited.

Mittal, V., Anderson, E. W., Sayrak, A., & Tadikamalla, P. (2005). Dual emphasis and the long-term financial impact of customer satisfaction. *Marketing Science, 24*(4), 544–555.

Morgan, N. A., & Rego, L. L. (2006). The value of different customer satisfaction and loyalty metrics in predicting business performance. *Marketing Science, 25*(5), 429–439.

Nakazawa, K. (2009). *Case files of Hoshino Resorts: Why do their customers come again?* Nikkei BP. (in Japanese).

Nakazawa, Y. (2010). *Hoshino Resorts case file: Why did the customer come back?* Nikkei Business Publications, Inc.

Nikkei Information Strategy. (2006). Facilitation for successful reform. *Nikkei Information Strategy, 15*(5), 44–53.

Nikkei Top Leader. (2010). Management with determination: The importance of the 'textbook approach' for small companies. *Nikkei Top Leader*, 42–53. (in Japanese).

Otomasa, S., & Kondo, T. (2011). *Hoshino Resorts: Customer-oriented organisation management*. Otaru University of Commerce Discussion Paper 133. (in Japanese).

Otomasa, S., Kondo, T., & Sakashita, M. (2012a). *Hoshino Resorts customer satisfaction management (A): Establishing the foundation to become resort management experts*. Keio Business School.

Otomasa, S., Kondo, T., & Sakashita, M. (2012b). *Hoshino Resorts customer satisfaction management (B): Becoming resort management experts*. Keio Business School.

Reinartz, W. J., & Kumar, V. (2000). On the profitability of long-life customers in a noncontractual setting: An empirical investigation and implications for marketing. *Journal of Marketing, 64*(4), 17–35.

Rucci, A. J., Kirn, S. P., & Quinn, R. T. (1998). The employee-customer-profit chain at Sears. *Harvard Business Review*, 83–97.

Smith, R. E., & Wright, W. F. (2004). Determinants of customer loyalty and financial performance. *Journal of Management Accounting Research, 16*(1), 183–205.

Think! (2006). Learning from 'resort management experts' how to think beyond logic to revitalize hot spring inns. *Think!, 17*, 36–41.

Chapter 10
Institutional Isomorphism of Corporate Social Responsibility Performance Measurement: A Case of a Japanese Homebuilding Firm

Yasushi Onishi and Eri Yokota

10.1 Introduction

The performance measurement of corporate social responsibility (CSR) activities provides an important foundation to ensure sustainable corporate management (Contrafatto & Burns, 2013). Growing interest in the social and environmental aspects of corporate activities has facilitated management accounting research that focuses on the measurement of CSR performance[1] (Lisi, 2015; Guenther et al., 2016).

The CSR performance measurement literature in management accounting includes conceptual and technical studies of the balanced scorecard (BSC) with CSR performance indicators (Hansen & Schaltegger, 2016; Ito, 2014; Oka, 2010) and empirical research on the effect of CSR-oriented management control systems (MCSs)[2] on CSR and financial performance (Henri & Journeault, 2010; Lisi, 2015).

An early form of this chapter first appeared in *Melco Journal of Management Accounting Research* 13(2): 35–48 (in Japanese). Republished with permission of Maki Makoto Foundation.

[1] In this study, CSR performance is defined as the "performance related to the management of CSR aspects" by modifying the definition of ISO 14031 (ISO, 2021) on environmental performance evaluation.

[2] In this study, CSR-oriented MCS is defined as "a package that allows an organization to ground its future-oriented, operational and strategic management decisions on the collection and evaluation of

Y. Onishi (✉)
School of Accountancy, Kansai University, Osaka, Japan
e-mail: yonishi@kansai-u.ac.jp

E. Yokota
Faculty of Business and Commerce, Keio University, Tokyo, Japan
e-mail: yokota@fbc.keio.ac.jp

© Springer Nature Singapore Pte Ltd. 2023

E. Yokota (ed.), *Frontiers of Japanese Management Control Systems*, Translational Systems Sciences 32, https://doi.org/10.1007/978-981-19-9778-5_10

In addition, several studies have qualitatively analyzed CSR-oriented MCSs by drawing from Simons' (1995) framework (Gond et al., 2012; Battaglia et al., 2016).

However, how companies measure CSR performance and use it in their control activities has not been extensively investigated. In particular, sustainability, a key goal of CSR activities, has been criticized as an unclear and polysemous concept (Bebbington & Larrinaga, 2014). As such, it is not easy to identify and manage a firm's CSR performance, and the relationship between CSR performance and financial performance is not clear (Lisi, 2015; Ito, 2016).

CSR performance measurement methodologies through various performance indicators and procedures have been developed within CSR reporting guidelines such as the Global Reporting Initiative (GRI, 2016). The GRI (2016) proposes that performance indicators be set for important CSR issues after assessing the materiality of various CSR issues through stakeholder engagement to select content for CSR reporting. CSR performance measurement items are selected based on the subjective opinions of various stakeholders (GRI, 2016).

Therefore, it is not easy for firms to identify CSR performance that affects their financial performance, and the selection of CSR performance indicators for external reporting purposes is potentially influenced by various stakeholders. A question arises as to how firms measure CSR performance when the institutional environment (such as regulations and norms)[3] encompassing their CSR performance measurement practice is highly uncertain.

To address this issue, we focus on institutional isomorphism in neo-institutional theory (DiMaggio & Powell, 1983). Institutional isomorphism implies that an organization in an uncertain institutional environment becomes similar (isomorphic) to other organizations belonging to the same organizational field, such as a specific industry (DiMaggio & Powell, 1983). However, organizations undergoing institutional isomorphism may not be identical in all aspects. Specifically, it has been proposed that decoupling may occur between formal organizational structures and specific activities (Meyer & Rowan, 1977).

Several environmental management accounting studies have employed institutional isomorphism as a framework for analyzing CSR-oriented MCSs (Wijethilake et al., 2017; George et al., 2016). However, they do not focus on the selection of CSR issues and the determination of measurement scales in performance measurement.

This study aims to explore how firms assess the materiality of their CSR issues and set and use CSR performance indicators when the institutional environment surrounding their CSR activities is uncertain. Using the case of a Japanese homebuilding company, we present two findings. First, we find that the practice of materiality assessment of CSR issues became isomorphic with the GRI (2016) and

CSR information covering all company functions and the entire value and supply chain" by modifying Guenther et al.'s (2016) definition on environmental management control systems.

[3]Uncertainty in the institutional environment refers to situations in which the stability and understandability of the regulatory environment, professional norms, and cognitive context surrounding the firm are problematic (Suchman, 1995).

the practices of other companies in the same industry while introducing materiality assessment. Later, decoupling from GRI-based procedures is observed owing to the internal management purpose. Second, we present examples of CSR activities that can refer to industry-based performance indicators and those that cannot. We then explore the degree of coupling between activities and indicators. These findings provide empirical evidence on the measurement of CSR performance and are expected to contribute to management accounting research and practice.

The rest of this study is organized as follows. Section 10.2 reviews studies on management accounting and social and environmental accounting on CSR performance indicators, and Sect. 10.3 presents the analytical framework based on neo-institutional theory. Section 10.4 describes the research methodology. Section 10.5 presents the case study of Misawa Homes Co., Ltd. (hereinafter, Misawa), and Sect. 10.6 discusses the case study. Finally, Sect. 10.7 presents the conclusions.

10.2 Literature on CSR Performance Measurement

An important issue related to CSR performance measurement is how CSR performance influences the strategic and financial performance of firms.[4] To address this issue, several studies apply CSR performance indicators to BSCs to develop environmental management accounting tools (Hansen & Schaltegger, 2016; De Villiers et al., 2016; Kerr et al., 2015; Ito, 2014; Oka, 2010).

Empirical studies based on quantitative methodologies have been conducted on how CSR-oriented MCSs, including CSR performance measurement systems, relate to CSR and financial performances (Henri & Journeault, 2010; Lisi, 2015; Kajiwara, 2011). For example, Henri and Journeault (2010) reveal the relationship between environmental MCS and environmental performance but note that the relationship with financial performance is partial. Moreover, Lisi (2015) finds that environmental performance measurement positively influences environmental performance, which positively influences financial performance.

In empirical studies based on qualitative methodologies, case studies have been conducted on the relationship between CSR-oriented MCS and financially-oriented MCS. In particular, the levers of control framework presented by Simons (1995) has been used in several studies. For example, Arjaliès and Mundy (2013) investigate the CSR-oriented MCS practices using questionnaires and interviews, categorizing and clarifying them using the levers of control framework. Similarly, several qualitative studies use Gond et al.'s framework (2012), which presents an analytical model on the degree of cohesion between sustainability control system and MCS based on the framework of Simons (1995). For example, Battaglia et al. (2016) investigate the adoption and decline of sustainability-oriented MCS in Italian food cooperatives.

[4] See also Ando (2015) for a literature review related to MCS on CSR.

George et al. (2016) explore the adoption of CSR performance measurement in oil and gas companies.

Furthermore, employing the old economic institutional theory, Contrafatto and Burns (2013) reveal a case in which environmental performance measurement was established through the introduction of social and environmental accounting and reporting but there was no considerable change in the financially-oriented MCS. In addition, based on the actor-network theory, Jollands et al. (2015) find that the establishment and abolition of a sustainability-focused core value has a significant impact on the use of environmental performance measures. Jollands et al. (2018) find that companies facing demands from external groups would mobilize multiple control systems, such as performance measures, in addition to environmental reporting to legitimate themselves.

As seen above, the quantitative studies on CSR performance measurement present a partial association between CSR performance and financial performance. The evidence from qualitative studies on CSR-oriented MCS shows that it is not easy to construct strong relationship between financially oriented and CSR-oriented MCSs. Therefore, it appears difficult to set CSR performance indicators which contribute to financially oriented strategies.

Several qualitative studies on CSR performance measurement and CSR-oriented MCS include their research subject in CSR reporting (e.g., Contrafatto & Burns, 2013; de Villiers et al., 2016; Jollands et al., 2018; Kerr et al., 2015). Considering that material CSR performance indicators are disclosed on CSR reports, the practice of CSR reporting needs to be included in analyzing CSR performance measurement practices. The GRI (2016) argues that the materiality of CSR issues should initially be assessed through stakeholder engagement to determine the disclosure content of CSR reports. Then, performance indicators should be set for the issues identified as material (GRI, 2016). Following these suggestions, this study focuses on the two stages of CSR performance measurement, assessing the materiality of CSR issues and setting indicators for individual activities.

The CSR performance measurement process has not been fully explored in terms of the prioritization of and the relationship among various CSR issues, such as the environment, human rights, and labor. The GRI (2016) does not strictly specify the materiality of each CSR issue that companies should manage and report on. This means that the assessment of material CSR issues is influenced by the diverse opinions and positions of stakeholders. There may be considerable uncertainty associated with CSR performance measurement in the institutional environment (Meyer & Rowan, 1977). In other words, it is not always possible to predict the indicators that should be measured and disclosed in the CSR report. Therefore, this study seeks to identify how firms assess the materiality of CSR issues and set and use indicators in an uncertain institutional environment surrounding their CSR activities.

10.3 Analytical Framework

This study focuses on the practice of CSR performance measurement when rational decision-making is difficult owing to uncertainty in the institutional environment. Therefore, to analyze corporate behavior under institutional uncertainty, this study employs the institutional perspective, specifically, the institutional isomorphism of the neo-institutional theory (DiMaggio & Powell, 1983).

DiMaggio and Powell (1983) argue that organizations become similar to one another (isomorphism) within an organizational field such as an industry.[5] According to DiMaggio and Powell (1983), isomorphism is expected to be promoted through coercive, mimetic, and normative processes.[6] Therefore, if institutional isomorphism is applied to the practice of CSR performance measurement, it is expected that firms' practices of assessing the materiality of CSR issues and setting and using performance indicators for specific CSR activities will be similar to those of their peers.

Several studies investigate CSR performance measurement concerning institutional isomorphism. Wijethilake et al. (2017) found that an apparel manufacturing company in Sri Lanka used a sustainability MCS to strategically respond to institutional pressures, such as the government and customers. George et al. (2016) identified barriers and enablers in the process of integrating CSR-oriented and traditional MCSs at the oil and gas company with high external pressures. Although these studies shed light on the practice of CSR-oriented MCS, studies that focus on the CSR performance measurement process are limited. Further studies that investigate the CSR performance measurement process are needed. Therefore, this study contributes to the literature on CSR performance measurement by presenting qualitative evidence on the practice of CSR performance measurement from the perspective of institutional isomorphism.

Despite a series of seminal works in neo-institutional theory, the applicability of institutional isomorphism has been subject to continuous debate (Greenwood et al., 2015). Meyer and Rowan (1977) proposed that actual activities may decouple from the formal organizational structure when there is isomorphic change in the organizational structure (Meyer & Rowan, 1977). The weaknesses (Meyer & Rowan, 1977) and strengths (Sauder & Espeland, 2009) of such a coupling relationship

---

[5] An organizational field is defined as "a community of organizations that partakes of a common meaning system and whose participants interact more frequently and fatefully with one another than with actors outside of the field" (Scott, 1995, p. 56). Note that organizational fields are not limited to specific industries but are also expected to be formed across industries for specific issues such as pollution problems (Greenwood et al., 2015).

[6] According to DiMaggio and Powell (1983), coercive isomorphism refers to isomorphism by conforming to regulations or powerful stakeholder demands. Mimetic isomorphism is a phenomenon in which one organization imitates another organization that it perceives to be successful in an uncertain environment. In addition, normative isomorphism refers to the isomorphic change process by professional norms based on education and networks.

between formal structure and practice are worth analyzing in the context of CSR performance measurement practice.

The analytical framework is as follows. First, we classify CSR performance measurement practice into two stages based on the GRI (2016): (1) materiality assessment of CSR issues and (2) setting performance indicators in individual activities to show the extent of institutional isomorphism in each stage. Second, in the stage of setting performance indicators for individual activities, we address the coupling relationship between disclosure and performance measurement practices in CSR reports.

10.4 Research Method

We conducted a case study approach on the practices of Misawa, a home building firm.[7] Misawa have conducted environmental conservation activities, and engaged in industrywide environmental action planning as a member of the environment subcommittee of the Japan Prefabricated Construction Suppliers and Manufacturers Association (hereinafter, the JPA).[8] Therefore, its activities should be observed at the company and industry unit levels to address the research question.

The case data were obtained through interviews, internal documents, CSR reports, and collection of published materials by an industry association (the JPA). A total of four interviews were conducted. In the first and second interviews, questions were asked about the outline of CSR activities and the process of assessing the materiality of the CSR issues in the CSR report at Misawa; Sect. 10.5.2 discusses these interviews. Furthermore, in the third and fourth interviews, questions were asked about the outline of individual CSR activities and the use of performance indicators; these interviews are mentioned in Sect. 10.5.3. The interviews were semi-structured; Table 10.1 presents the outline of each interview.[9] All the interviews were recorded and then transcribed for reference.

We describe the process of assessing the materiality of CSR issues at Misawa based on the interview data and present the practices of individual CSR activities, including CSR activities for which goals have been set at the industry association level and CSR activities unique to the company. As an example of the first, we describe a waste reduction activity, and as an example of the second, we describe the case of an educational support program named "Antarctic class" offered at elementary schools by members of the Antarctic observation team.

[7]Misawa was listed in the First Section of the Tokyo Stock Exchange during the interviews (Table 10.1). It became a wholly owned subsidiary of Prime Life Technologies Corporation in January 2020.

[8]The Japan Prefabricated Construction Suppliers and Manufacturers Association (2019).

[9]We express our sincere gratitude to all those who kindly responded to our interviews. The job titles shown in Table 10.1 are those at the time of the interview conducted.

Table 10.1 Interview summary

Date and time	Interview format and questions	Respondents
Session 1 (90 min) June 14, 2017	Semi-structured interview (CSR report preparation process)	1 executive officer in charge of IR 3 CSR officers
Session 2 (90 min) January 23, 2019	Semi-structured interview (CSR report preparation process)	1 corporate adviser in charge of IR 2 CSR officers
Session 3 (90 min) February 28, 2019	Semi-structured interview (performance measurement of individual CSR activities)	1 person in charge of CSR 4 employees
Session 4 (90 min) April 15, 2019	Semi-structured interview (performance measurement of individual CSR activities)	1 person in charge of CSR 1 employee

10.5 A Case Study of CSR Performance Measurement at Misawa

10.5.1 An Overview of CSR Management

Misawa has a long history of environmental conservation activities and was the first in the Japanese homebuilding industry to obtain ISO 14001 certification for its environmental management system in 1997. In recent years, the company has also received external recognition, including the Eco Mark Award 2018 excellence prize from the Japan Environment Association and the "Health and Productivity Management Outstanding Organizations" certification by the Nippon Kenko Kaigi and the Ministry of Economy, Trade and Industry.

10.5.2 Assessing the Materiality of CSR Issues

Misawa issued the industry's first environmental report in 1999 and has been issuing CSR reports since 2007. Initially, the issuing department was the technological division. Since 2015, the corporate communications division, a subordinate organization of the corporate planning department, has been in charge of publishing the report.

The medium-term management plan is formulated on a three-year basis, and CSR-related issues have been positioned as a priority item since 2011. Furthermore, the 2011 CSR report includes a list of CSR performance indicators. However, as it is not easy to prioritize a wide range of CSR issues, Misawa assessed the materiality of CSR issues based on questionnaires collected from various stakeholders twice, in 2013 and in 2017.

10.5.2.1 The Introduction of the Materiality Assessment

There were two reasons underlying Misawa's introduction of the materiality assessment of CSR issues. The first was to link CSR issues with management indicators and to clarify the differences in perception between stakeholders and the company so as to persuade the management regarding proposed improvements. Therefore, the CSR department wanted to collect data on stakeholder needs and evaluations. The second, in line with the external adviser's suggestion regarding CSR reporting, was to improve Misawa's CSR report to be more consistent with the GRI guidelines and include more key performance indicators. During the process, the adviser noted the necessity of communication with stakeholders.

Regarding the method of communicating with stakeholders, Misawa had previously conducted a questionnaire targeting customers. Therefore, as a means of collecting stakeholder opinions, it adopted a questionnaire on CSR similar in format to the customer questionnaire. A questionnaire was deemed suitable owing to the adviser's emphasis on the need to prioritize several CSR indicators.

Misawa conducted a questionnaire on the materiality of selected CSR issues based on the core subjects of ISO 26000, targeting stakeholders such as financial analysts, business partners, employees, customers, and general consumers.[10] The results of the questionnaire were analyzed based on "importance to other companies and stakeholders" and "importance to Misawa Homes" in accordance with the mapping of materiality assessment presented by the GRI (2016) (Fig. 10.1). Here, as the axis in Fig. 10.1 shows, Misawa referred to the CSR reports of other companies in the same industry and reflected them in its materiality.[11]

Figure 10.1 shows that the questionnaire identified the following areas: financial (Issue 1), compliance (Issue 2), products and services (Issue 4), labor practices and training (Issue 5), community (Issue 7), and the environment (Issue 8) as important to either (or both) the stakeholders and Misawa's management, and management indicators were set for each item. The targets were set in conjunction with the medium-term management plan by considering not only Misawa's but also other companies' current performance and by coordinating with the relevant departments.

Thus, while the assessment of the materiality of CSR issues influenced the setting of CSR performance indicators at Misawa, some challenges were also discovered. The questionnaire responses showed no significant difference between the issues that stakeholders rated as important and those that Misawa rated as important, except for some items such as compliance. Therefore, the CSR department considered the first questionnaire insufficient to clarify the differences in perceptions between stakeholders and the company and to propose improvements. To solve this problem,

---

[10] Based on all the CSR reports published by Japanese homebuilding firms in 2013 that were examined by the author, no other company conducted a large-scale questionnaire survey of stakeholders when assessing materiality.

[11] For details, see Misawa Homes Co., Ltd. (2014, p. 16). Other companies also refer to the trends of their peers (e.g., Sekisui Chemical Co., Ltd., 2018, p. 14).

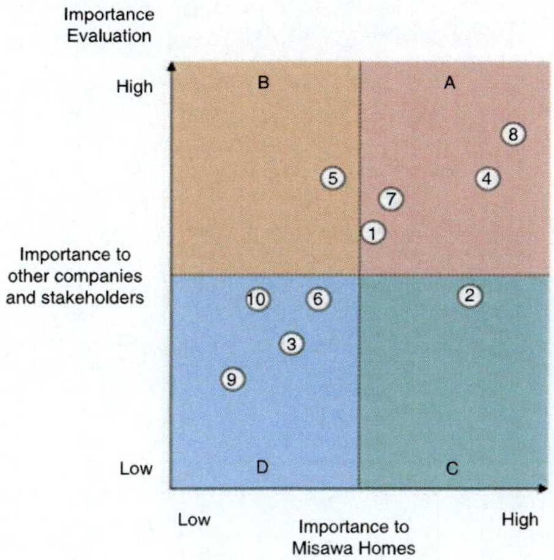

①	Financial	⑥	CSR procurement
②	Compliance	⑦	Community
③	Human rights prohibition of forced labor	⑧	Environment
④	Products and services	⑨	Global response
⑤	Labor practices and training	⑩	Local economy

Fig. 10.1 Materiality assessment of CSR issues in 2013. Source: adapted from Misawa Homes Co., Ltd. (2014, p. 16)

they felt the need to change the questionnaire analysis method to address the perspective of differences between stakeholder expectations and evaluations.

Moreover, in 2017, when the mid-term management plan was updated, there were changes in policies and social trends in Japan, such as the "Work Style Reform," compared to the first questionnaire survey conducted in 2013. Therefore, Misawa changed the questionnaire items and conducted the second questionnaire survey in 2017 to analyze the results from the perspective of stakeholder expectations and assessments.

10.5.2.2 Changes in the Assessment of the Materiality of CSR Issues

The process of assessing the materiality of CSR issues based on the second questionnaire in 2017 was performed in the following three stages. The first stage was the selection of CSR issues. Nine categories and 23 issues related to CSR initiatives were identified with reference to the GRI standards, ISO 26000, and the trends of other companies in the same industry (Fig. 10.2).

The second step was the establishment of "Key CSR Issues." At this stage, expectations and evaluations of 23 CSR issues were compiled through a questionnaire survey of 1880 stakeholders. The issues with the highest expectations or ratings were set as CSR material issues, and the results were disclosed in the 2018 CSR Report.

Based on the results of the questionnaire (Fig. 10.2), improvement of the core business, such as the environmental responsiveness of housing (Issues 1, 5, and 7), and compliance with laws and regulations (Issue 9) were identified as items whose achievement was both highly expected and highly evaluated by stakeholders. In

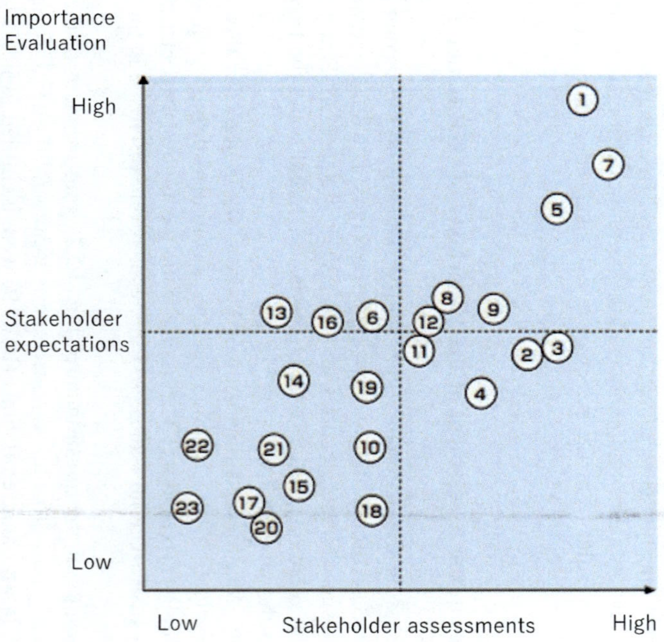

Environment	①	Developing ZEH, durable high-quality housing, and other Decarbonization, environmentally conscious housing
	②	Zero emissions activities at factories and construction sites
	③	Reducing VOCs (Volatile organic compounds) in components and materials, reducing harmful chemical usage
	④	Procuring certified wood according to wood procurement guidelines
Products services	⑤	Providing quality housing and services on the strength of excellent designs and technology
	⑥	Creating new value using IoT and other technological innovations
	⑦	Building safe, secure, disaster-resilient homes
	⑧	Customer services promotion activities for improving customer satisfaction
Compliance	⑨	Complying with laws and regulations, and maintaining ethical integrity in business activities
	⑩	Enhancing information security
Community	⑪	Community building through smart wellness, smart cities, and the like
	⑫	Assistance for medical care, elderly care, and child raising

Work style reform	⑬	Activities for improving employee satisfaction
	⑭	Utilizing diverse human resources, namely women and elderly people
	⑮	Enhancing training and making other efforts to develop human resources
Financial	⑯	Ensuring profitability through consistent, long-term growth
	⑰	Appropriate dividends to shareholders
	⑱	Timely disclosure of financial reports and other management information
Suppliers	⑲	Building fair relationships with suppliers
	⑳	Cooperating with suppliers toward social responsible actions
Cultural activities	㉑	Engaging in social contribution activities in art, culture, education and welfare
Global response	㉒	Contribution activities through overseas business expansion
	㉓	Efforts to combat poverty and resolve conflict around the world

Fig. 10.2 Materiality assessment of CSR issues in 2017. Source: adapted from Misawa Homes Co., Ltd (2018, p. 9)

addition, environmental responsiveness (Issues 2, 3, and 4) and smart cities (Issue 11) were identified as items that were highly evaluated by stakeholders. Moreover, technological innovations such as the Internet of Things (Issue 6), securing profits (Issue 16), and improving employee satisfaction (Issue 13) were identified as items whose accomplishment was not sufficiently evaluated despite high expectations from stakeholders.

The third step was the establishment of CSR indicators for key issues. The CSR indicators for these key issues were set, and the results were compiled each year.

As described above, the materiality of CSR issues was assessed from the perspective of stakeholder expectations and stakeholder assessment. To measure the materiality of CSR issues, the external adviser of CSR reporting preferred the GRI analysis method (GRI, 2016) similar to the first materiality assessment. However, in Misawa, for example, the gap between expectation and evaluation emerged in the item of employee satisfaction, and the second survey analysis was more satisfactory than the first.

10.5.3 Setting CSR Performance Indicators

As indicated, Misawa determines important CSR issues by assessing the materiality of CSR issues through stakeholder questionnaires. However, not all of the CSR issues that Misawa considers important are measured and evaluated in a unified manner; they vary according to the various CSR activities. This study presents two cases of important CSR activities[12] at Misawa, one in which performance is measured and the other in which it is not. The first case is a waste reduction activity measured based on a performance method established within the industry. The second case is one of Misawa's original activities, called "Antarctic class," in which Misawa employees who participated in the Antarctic observation team provide experience-based lessons at elementary schools.

10.5.3.1 Waste Reduction Activities

The reduction of waste at construction sites is one of Misawa's main issues. In the past, the company did not directly handle the waste generated at construction sites because it did not perform construction work at the sites. However, since 2009, Misawa has been collecting waste from construction sites and recycling it by obtaining certification under the wide-area certification system covering the Tokyo Metropolitan Area (one metropolitan area and seven prefectures). At construction sites, waste is sorted into 19 categories and recycled through the Resource Recycling

[12] The performance indicators related to the waste reduction activities and Antarctic class discussed here are disclosed in the CSR report (Misawa Homes Co., Ltd., 2014, 2018).

Center in Chiba Prefecture. The data on construction waste materials collected is used for resource-conscious design.

Waste performance is measured by the weight of waste per square meter of building standardized by the JPA. The JPA has published "Eco-Action 2020," an industrywide environmental management action plan which sets targets for waste reduction. At the end of a given year, member companies report their performance to the JPA's environmental subcommittee, which aggregates the actual values by industry and publishes the industry's waste reduction performance.

During the compilation of actual values, those related to each member company's waste are compared side by side. These industry averages for waste are reported to Misawa's management. Consequently, the management gives instructions on waste reduction to the personnel in charge of waste management based on which departmental policies are prepared.

In Misawa, the Management by Objectives (MBO) system is used to evaluate the performance of employees. In the MBO, the person in charge of the work fills in the target based on the departmental policy, and the employee target is decided by coordinating with the department head. At the end of the term, each employee submits their performance against the target that is evaluated by the manager and the section chief, considering the degree of achievement and difficulty for each item entered. The targets include both quantitative and qualitative ones for waste reduction efforts. Therefore, the actual values of waste at other companies in the same industry are referred to as one of the performance evaluation targets at the level of the person in charge through management instructions, and they also influence the employee performance evaluation through the MBO.

10.5.3.2 Educational Support Program on Antarctic Observation Activities

Misawa has been delivering building materials to the Showa Station in Antarctica for more than 50 years, and Misawa employees continuously participate in Antarctic observations as team members. Since 2011, Misawa has been conducting the "Antarctic class," in which employees who participated in the Antarctic research expedition serve as instructors and provide lessons based on their experiences in Antarctica, mainly at elementary and junior high schools. The Antarctic class was introduced as one of the programs to provide non-housing support in the process of reconstructing housing after the Great East Japan Earthquake.

As Antarctic observation is a government project, it is difficult for Misawa to conduct the Antarctic class independently. Therefore, with the local boards of education and the National Institute of Polar Research, Misawa has been cooperating in the dissemination and education of Antarctic observation activities; during the first year, it conducted 18 classes in six months and has since conducted more than 100 classes per year.

Although the significance of Antarctic class as a social contribution has been recognized within the company, and it has also received external awards such as the

Kids Design Award and the Good Design Award in Japan, the implementation of the project is not always easy. One of the reasons is that it is difficult for the local employees who support the Antarctic class to coordinate their existing work with the support work. However, the proponents of the Antarctic class have been reluctant to establish the number of Antarctic class activities as a performance indicator for evaluation. The concern is that linking it directly to performance evaluation may cause the loss of the internal recognition within the company if it fails to show short-term results. Therefore, despite their belief that the initiative would be beneficial to Misawa in the long term, the promoters of the Antarctic class have preferred to continue the activity without making it a performance indicator.

10.6 Discussion

10.6.1 Isomorphism in Materiality Assessment

In this section, we reflect on the cases of Misawa to discuss the institutional isomorphism (DiMaggio & Powell, 1983) of the materiality assessment of CSR issues and the performance measurement of individual CSR activities. We then address the coupling between CSR reporting and performance measurement practices for individual CSR activities.

First, we address the materiality assessment of CSR issues: as described in Sect. 10.5.1, in 2013, when the materiality assessment was introduced, Misawa aimed to collect stakeholders' opinions while maintaining consistency with the GRI guidelines in line with the external adviser's suggestions. Furthermore, in identifying CSR issues, Misawa referred to the CSR reports of other companies in the same industry and exchanged information through industry associations. Therefore, it may be inferred that normative factors based on the external adviser's knowledge and imitation of peer companies (DiMaggio & Powell, 1983) were at work in conducting the materiality assessment.

However, along with Misawa's implementation of materiality assessment, the other objective was to collect the opinions of numerous stakeholders and establish indicators that would influence the top management to suggest CSR improvements. Therefore, Misawa, like other companies, reported the results of the materiality assessment in its CSR report. However, unlike other companies, it used a questionnaire survey in its assessment method. In the second materiality assessment conducted in 2017, Misawa changed from the GRI assessment dimensions (GRI, 2016) to its own dimensions of stakeholder expectations and assessments to propose improvement indicators based on stakeholder needs. Therefore, the materiality assessment at Misawa is highly unique in that the disclosure format of the CSR report is only superficially similar to that of other companies' reports, and the specific assessment method and assessment dimensions are different from those of the GRI (2016). Therefore, it can be inferred that the materiality assessment method in Misawa decoupled from the GRI (2016) to pursue company-specific objectives, thereby enhancing its originality (Meyer & Rowan, 1977).[13]

10.6.2 Homogenization in Setting Individual CSR Performance Indicators

In setting individual CSR performance indicators, we described the waste management activities for which performance was measured and evaluated. Then, we addressed the CSR activity called Antarctic class, for which no performance indicators were set for evaluation. Although both of these activities are considered important for Misawa's CSR, they differ in terms of whether performance was measured.

There is an established method for calculating companies' performance in waste reduction activities through industry associations and available industry averages. Member companies have the opportunity to compare their waste reduction performance through the same calculation method. Consequently, as one of the performance indicators related to waste, the data on waste reduction in construction sites were compared and influenced the performance evaluation of the person in charge. Institutional isomorphism was particularly promoted in the way that performance indicators were set because it was possible to refer to the expertise within the industry and the trends of other companies in the same industry. Furthermore, performance indicators influenced the evaluation of individual managers through the MBO, which indicates a strong coupling between CSR reporting and performance measurement and evaluation.

Moreover, as the Antarctic class was one of Misawa's original initiatives, there were no similar practices for reference. The proponents of the Antarctic class focused on gaining legitimacy for their activities within the company by increasing the number of internal activities while improving the external recognition of their CSR activities through external awards. Accordingly, institutional isomorphism with other companies was not observed in the Antarctic class. Although the CSR report mentioned the number of activities implemented by the Antarctic class, the interviews revealed that there was no intention to relate the number of activities implemented to business performance. As such, the Antarctic class is conceived as a case in which the importance of the activity is recognized internally and published in the CSR report but is not combined with performance evaluation (Meyer & Rowan, 1977).

[13] Meyer and Rowan (1977) note that the decoupling of practices from isomorphic structures allows isomorphic institutions to play only a ritualistic role. However, as discussed in Sect. 10.2, in CSR performance measurement, the loose conformity of corporate practices to reporting standards such as the GRI (2016) may not immediately imply ignoring social responsibility.

10.7 Conclusion

The relationship between CSR performance and financial performance is not clear, and it is not easy to assess the performance indicators that should be set and managed to cover a wide range of CSR aspects.

When the institutional environment is highly uncertain, the neo-institutional theory notes that various organizations belonging to the same organizational field become isomorphic. This study presented a case of a homebuilding firm's practices, including the materiality assessment of its CSR issues and the setting of performance indicators for individual CSR activities. It aimed to address the degree of institutional isomorphism in CSR performance measurement practices and interpret the degree of coupling between CSR reporting, performance measurement, and evaluation.

As a result of the case analysis, for the materiality assessment of CSR issues at Misawa, institutional isomorphism was initially observed by referring to professional norms and the trends of other companies in the same industry; however, the practices of materiality assessment then diverged from the GRI (2016) owing to company-specific objectives. Furthermore, the degree of coupling between CSR reporting and performance measurement in individual CSR activities differed depending on the existence of referenceable norms within the industry.

Therefore, this study finds that the practice of CSR performance measurement can be interpreted, at least partially, in terms of institutional isomorphism. Concurrently, the study also finds that the isomorphism of CSR performance measurement does not proceed uniformly within the firm but varies depending on specific internal management objectives and the existence of industry-specific norms as a reference.

In qualitative management accounting research related to CSR performance measurement, studies that support institutional isomorphism include Wijethilake et al. (2017) and George et al. (2016). However, these studies do not focus on institutional isomorphism and decoupling for the materiality assessment of CSR performance measurement and indicator-setting practices in individual CSR activities. Our findings are expected to contribute to management accounting research. In addition, from a practical point of view, this study contributes a reference case of peer companies' CSR performance measurement practices.

However, this study presents only a partial analysis of complex CSR performance measurement practices, and more studies based on institutional perspectives are needed to better understand corporate practices in this area (Contrafatto & Burns, 2013). In particular, this study has the following limitations.

First, as this study focuses on only one company's case, the generalizability of the findings needs to be carefully examined. Second, the scope of analysis in this study is limited to only some of the practices within a wide range of CSR performance measurement practices. Third, although the case descriptions in this study are mainly based on textualized interview data, there are limitations on the rigor of the data analysis methods and procedures. Fourth, the descriptions of the cases in this study are limited in persuasiveness because it was not possible to quote the interview contents directly.

Therefore, there is a need for further research on CSR performance measurement that overcomes the above limitations based on an institutional perspective. The analysis of institutional isomorphism for the case of CSR performance measurement as presented in this study is expected to facilitate additional discourse in management accounting research on CSR.

References

Ando, T. (2015). The significance and prospects in studies of environmental management and control systems. *Journal of Cost Accounting Research, 39*(2), 44–54. (in Japanese).

Arjaliès, D.-L., & Mundy, J. (2013). The use of management control systems to manage CSR strategy: A levers of control perspective. *Management Accounting Research, 24*(4), 284–300.

Battaglia, M., Passetti, E., Bianchi, L., & Frey, M. (2016). Managing for integration: A longitudinal analysis of management control for sustainability. *Journal of Cleaner Production, 136*(A), 213–225.

Bebbington, J., & Larrinaga, C. (2014). Accounting and sustainable development: An exploration. *Accounting, Organizations and Society, 39*(6), 395–413.

Contrafatto, M., & Burns, J. (2013). Social and environmental accounting, organizational change, and management accounting: A processual view. *Management Accounting Research, 24*(4), 349–365.

de Villiers, C., Rouse, P., & Kerr, J. (2016). A new conceptual model of influences driving sustainability based on evidence of the integration of corporate sustainability management control and reporting. *Journal of Cleaner Production, 136*(A), 78–85.

DiMaggio, P. J., & Powell, W. W. (1983). The iron cage revisited: Institutional isomorphism and collective rationality in organizational fields. *American Sociological Review, 48*(2), 147–160.

George, R. A., Siti-Nabiha, A. K., Jalaludin, D., & Abdalla, Y. A. (2016). Barriers to and enablers of sustainability integration in the performance management systems of an oil and gas company. *Journal of Cleaner Production, 136*(A), 197–202.

Global Reporting Initiative. (2016). *GRI 101: Foundation*. GRI. https://www.globalreporting.org/standards/media/1036/gri-101-foundation-2016.pdf

Gond, J.-P., Grubnic, S., Herzig, C., & Moon, J. (2012). Configuring management control systems: Theorizing the integration of strategy and sustainability. *Management Accounting Research, 23*(3), 205–223.

Greenwood, R., Jennings, P. D., & Hinings, B. (2015). Sustainability and organizational change: An institutional perspective. In R. Henderson, R. Gulati, & M. Tushman (Eds.), *Leading sustainable change: An organizational perspective* (pp. 323–355). Oxford University Press.

Guenther, E., Endrikat, J., & Guenther, T. W. (2016). Environmental management control systems: A conceptualization and a review of the empirical evidence. *Journal of Cleaner Production, 136*(A), 147–171.

Hansen, E. G., & Schaltegger, S. (2016). The sustainability balanced scorecard: A systematic review of architectures. *Journal of Business Ethics, 133*(2), 193–221.

Henri, J.-F., & Journeault, M. (2010). Eco-control: The influence of management control systems on environmental and economic performance. *Accounting, Organizations and Society, 35*(1), 63–80.

International Organization for Standardization. (2021). *ISO 14031 Environmental Management - Environmental Performance Evaluation - Guidelines*. ISO.

Ito, K. (2014). *The strategy formulation and execution using the balanced scorecard: Cases of intangibles management and contributions of management accounting to integrated reporting*. Dobunkan. (in Japanese).

Ito, Y. (2016). The effects of integrated reporting on the research and practice of management accounting. *Waseda Commercial Review, 446*, 29–51. (in Japanese).

Japan Prefabricated Construction Suppliers and Manufacturers Association. (2019). *FY2018 Results under the Eco-Action 2020 Environmental Action Plan*. https://www.purekyo.or.jp/bukai/jyutaku/pdf/eco_191029.pdf

Jollands, S., Akroyd, C., & Sawabe, N. (2015). Core values as a management control in the construction of "sustainable development". *Qualitative Research in Accounting and Management, 12*(2), 127–152.

Jollands, S., Akroyd, C., & Sawabe, N. (2018). Management controls and pressure groups: The mediation of overflows. *Accounting, Auditing and Accountability Journal, 31*(6), 1644–1667.

Kajiwara, T. (2011). Environmental management accounting to support environmental performance measurement and evaluation. In K. Kokubu (Ed.), *Accounting systems supporting environmental management decisions* (pp. 117–143). Chuokeizai-sha. (in Japanese).

Kerr, J., Rouse, P., & de Villiers, C. (2015). Sustainability reporting integrated into management control systems. *Pacific Accounting Review, 27*(2), 189–207.

Lisi, I. E. (2015). Translating environmental motivations into performance: The role of environmental performance measurement systems. *Management Accounting Research, 29*, 27–44.

Meyer, J. W., & Rowan, B. (1977). Institutionalized organizations: Formal structure as myth and ceremony. *American Journal of Sociology, 83*(2), 340–363.

Misawa Homes Co., Ltd. (2014). *2014 Misawa CSR Report*. https://www.misawa.co.jp/corporate/sr/pdf/csr2014.pdf (in Japanese).

Misawa Homes Co., Ltd. (2018). *2018 Misawa CSR Report*. https://www.misawa.co.jp/corporate/sr/pdf/csr2018.pdf (in Japanese).

Oka, S. (2010). The role of environmental performance indicators in the environmental cost management: For constructing SBSC. *Journal of Cost Accounting Research, 34*(1), 91–101. (in Japanese).

Sauder, M., & Espeland, W. N. (2009). The discipline of rankings: Tight coupling and organizational change. *American Sociological Review, 74*(1), 63–82.

Scott, R. W. (1995). *Institutions and organizations*. Sage.

Sekisui Chemical Co., Ltd. (2018). *CSR Report 2018*. https://www.sekisui.co.jp/csr/pdf/backnumber_report/2018/csr_report2018.pdf (in Japanese).

Simons, R. (1995). *Levers of control: How managers use innovative control systems to drive strategic renewal*. Harvard Business School Press.

Suchman, M. C. (1995). Managing legitimacy: Strategic and institutional approaches. *Academy of Management Review, 20*(3), 571–610.

Wijethilake, C., Munir, R., & Appuhami, R. (2017). Strategic responses to institutional pressures for sustainability: The role of management control systems. *Accounting, Auditing and Accountability Journal, 30*(8), 1677–1710.